CW00829319

# Grammatical Variation in British English Dialects

Variation within the English language is a vast research area, of which dialectology, the study of geographic variation, is a significant part. This book explores grammatical differences between British English dialects, drawing on authentic speech data collected in over 30 counties. In doing so it presents a new approach known as "corpus-based dialectometry," which focuses on the joint quantitative measurement of dozens of grammatical features to gauge regional differences. These features include, for example, multiple negation (e.g. *don't you make no damn mistake*), non-standard verbal *-s* (e.g. *so I says, What have you to do?*), or non-standard weak past tense and past participle forms (e.g. *they knowed all about these things*). Utilizing state-of-the-art dialectometrical analysis and visualization techniques, the book is original both in terms of its fundamental research question ("What are the large-scale patterns of grammatical variability in British English dialects?") and in terms of its methodology.

BENEDIKT SZMRECSANYI is a Fellow at the Freiburg Institute for Advanced Studies, Germany.

STUDIES IN ENGLISH LANGUAGE

General Editor
Merja Kytö (Uppsala University)

Editorial Board
Bas Aarts (University College London), John Algeo (University of Georgia), Susan Fitzmaurice (University of Sheffield), Christian Mair (University of Freiburg), Charles F. Meyer (University of Massachusetts)

The aim of this series is to provide a framework for original studies of English, both present-day and past. All books are based securely on empirical research, and represent theoretical and descriptive contributions to our knowledge of national and international varieties of English, both written and spoken. The series covers a broad range of topics and approaches, including syntax, phonology, grammar, vocabulary, discourse, pragmatics and sociolinguistics, and is aimed at an international readership.

Already published in this series:

# Grammatical Variation in British English Dialects

## A Study in Corpus-Based Dialectometry

BENEDIKT SZMRECSANYI

*Freiburg Institute for Advanced Studies*

CAMBRIDGE
UNIVERSITY PRESS

CAMBRIDGE UNIVERSITY PRESS
Cambridge, New York, Melbourne, Madrid, Cape Town, Singapore,
São Paulo, Delhi, Mexico City

Cambridge University Press
The Edinburgh Building, Cambridge CB2 8RU, UK

Published in the United States of America by Cambridge University Press, New York

www.cambridge.org
Information on this title: www.cambridge.org/9781107003453

First published 2013

Printed and Bound in the United Kingdom by the MPG Books Group

*A catalogue record for this publication is available from the British Library*

*Library of Congress Cataloging-in-Publication Data*
Szmrecsanyi, Benedikt, 1976–
    Grammatical variation in British English dialects : a study in corpus-based
dialectometry/Benedikt Szmrecsanyi.
        p.   cm. – (Studies in English language)
    ISBN 978-1-107-00345-3 (Hardback)
    1. English language–Dialects–Great Britain.   2. English language–Variation–Great Britain.
    3. English language–Grammaticalization.   4. Great Britain–Languages.
    5. English language–Syntax.   I. Title.
    PE1736.S96 2012
    427′.941–dc23
    2012024323

ISBN 978-1-107-00345-3 Hardback

# Contents

# Figures

# Maps

# Tables

# Preface and acknowledgments

This book is a revised version of my Habilitation thesis, which I submitted to the University of Freiburg in 2011. Partial summaries of the research discussed in this book have appeared, or are appearing, as Szmrecsanyi (2008, 2011, forthcoming) and Szmrecsanyi and Wolk (2011). Generous support, intellectual and material, by the Freiburg Institute for Advanced Studies (FRIAS) is gratefully acknowledged.

For assistance in writing this book, I owe gratitude to many individuals, including the following: Bernd Kortmann, for discussion, feedback, and support; Peter Auer, Bernd Kortmann, and Christian Mair, who acted as official reviewers of my Habilitation thesis and provided me with eminently helpful and constructive reports; Hans Goebl, for inviting me to Salzburg in 2009 and teaching me Salzburg dialectometry, and for invaluable, open-minded comments and feedback before, during, and after this visit; Bernhard Castellazzi, Hans Goebl, and Pavel Smecka, for creating a number of Salzburg-style dialectometry maps (Maps C.3–C.6 and C.11–C.12); Jack Grieve, for calculating the global spatial autocorrelation (*Moran's I*) scores reported in Chapter 3; Wilbert Heeringa, for a number of excellent comments and suggestions, and for providing me with a convenient software tool to conduct the Mantel test; Paul Kerswill, for discussing some morphosyntactically ill-behaved dialects with me; Peter Kleiweg, for creating and maintaining the *RuG/L04* dialectometry software (without which this book would be a lot less colorful); Merja Kytö, the series editor, and two anonymous referees for encouraging and constructive feedback; John Nerbonne, Wilbert Heeringa, and Bart Alewijnse, for having me over in Groningen in 2007 and explaining Groningen dialectometry to me; Sigrid Saou, for a close reading, many helpful comments, and good questions; and Christoph Wolk, for help with some of the statistics in this book. I also wish to thank Elin Arbin, for meticulous proof-reading, and Katharina Ehret, for help in preparing the final typescript.

The usual disclaimers apply. Specifically, none of the above individuals necessarily agrees with any or all of my interpretations and conclusions, and all errors are solely mine.

This book is dedicated to my wife Sigrid and to my daughter Leonore.

# 1      Introduction

In short, this book explores how and to what extent morphosyntactic variability in traditional British English dialects is structured geographically. Taking an interest in the forests rather than in individual trees, the study is concerned with *aggregate* dialectal (that is, morphosyntactic) variability among the measuring points investigated. We address this variability by establishing text frequencies of dozens of morphosyntactic features in a major naturalistic dialect corpus that covers dialect speech in over thirty counties all over Great Britain. Utilizing state-of-the-art dialectometrical analysis methods and visualization techniques, the study is original both in terms of its fundamental research question ("What are large-scale patterns of grammatical variability in traditional British English dialects?") and in terms of its methodology (CORPUS-BASED DIALECTOMETRY).

## 1.1    Rationale, method, and objectives

The study proceeds from the fact that we know next to nothing about aggregate morphosyntactic variability in British English dialects. While it is known that "every corner of the country demonstrates a wide range of grammatically non-standard forms" (Britain 2010, 53), we note that the bulk of the literature on dialect grammar consists of atomistic single-feature studies, and the handful of studies that have taken an aggregate approach typically focus on lexis and, in particular, phonology, but *not* morphosyntax. In this connection, it should also be noted that there is an oft-implicit notion in large parts of the dialectological community that morphological and (particularly) syntactic variation is not really patterned geographically. For example, Lass (2004, 374) contends that "English regional phonology and lexis ... are generally more salient and defining than regional morphosyntax" (for similar views, see Wolfram and Schilling-Estes 1998, 161 and, in the realm of German dialectology, Löffler 2003, 116).

To address these gaps and prejudices, the study utilizes a methodology we take the liberty to dub CORPUS-BASED DIALECTOMETRY. As a branch of geolinguistics, DIALECTOMETRY proper is concerned with measuring, visualizing, and analyzing aggregate dialect similarities or distances as a function of properties of geographic space; for seminal work, see Séguy (1971) (the paper that sparked the dialectometry enterprise); Goebl (2006), Bauer (2009), and Goebl (2010) (the "Salzburg School of Dialectometry"); and Nerbonne et al. (1999), Heeringa (2004), and Nerbonne (2006) (the "Groningen School of Dialectometry"). Whereas practitioners of traditional DIALECTOLOGY are dedicated to the study of "interesting" – typically phonological or lexical – dialect phenomena, one feature at a time in a handful of dialects at most, dialectometrical inquiry endeavors to identify "general, seemingly hidden structures from a larger amount of features" (Goebl and Schiltz 1997, 13). This means that dialectometricians put a strong emphasis on quantification, cartographic visualization, and exploratory data analysis to infer patterns from feature aggregates. Empirically, the bulk of the dialectometrical literature draws on linguistic atlas material as its primary data source. For example, Goebl (1982) investigates joint variability in 696 linguistic features that are mapped in the *Sprach- und Sachatlas Italiens und der Südschweiz* (AIS), an atlas that covers Italy and southern Switzerland; Nerbonne et al. (1999) analyze aggregate pronunciational dialect distances between 104 Dutch and North Belgian dialects on the basis of 100 word transcriptions provided in the *Reeks Nederlands(ch)e Dialectatlassen* (RND). Some dialectometricians have also relied on dialect dictionaries (for example, Speelman and Geeraerts 2008). Against this backdrop, Leinonen (2008), Grieve (2009), Heeringa et al. (2009), and Auer et al. (forthcoming) are rare examples of dialectometrical-geolinguistic work which bases claims about aggregate accent differences on the analysis, auditory or acoustic, of actual speech samples. In any case, given that most dialect atlases – the *Survey of English Dialects* is a good example – and dictionaries focus on lexis and pronunciation at the expense of syntax and morphology, it should surprise nobody that much of the dialectometrical literature drawing on such material is biased towards lexis and pronunciation at the expense of morphological and, especially, syntactic variation (but see Spruit 2005, 2006; Spruit et al. 2009 for some recent atlas-based yet syntax-centered dialectometrical work).

In an attempt to overcome this bias, the present study seeks to marry the qualitative-philological jeweler's-eye perspective inherent in the analysis of naturalistic corpus data with the quantitative-aggregational bird's-eye perspective that is the hallmark of dialectometry. This synthesis is desirable for two principal reasons. First, *multidimensional objects, such as dialects, call for aggregate analysis techniques.* That rigorous dialectology requires aggregation (in dialectological parlance, *bundling*) is by no means a new insight. Back in 1933 already, Bloomfield argued that

a set of isoglosses running close together in much the same direction – a so-called *bundle* of isoglosses – evidences a larger historical process and offers a more suitable basis of classification than does a single isogloss that represents, perhaps, some unimportant feature. (Bloomfield [1933] 1984: 342)

The point is that so-called "single-feature-based studies" (Nerbonne 2009, 176), with their atomistic focus on typically just one feature, are fine when it is the features themselves that are of analytic interest. They are woefully inadequate, however, when it comes to characterizing multidimensional objects such as dialects or varieties (or relations between them). Outside linguistics, this sort of inadequacy is well known: Taxonomists, for instance, typically categorize species not on the basis of a single morphological or genetic criterion, but on the basis of many; economists assess the economic climate not on the basis of individual macroeconomic indicators (e.g. unemployment), but also consider inflation, GDP per capita, interest rates, and so on. The problem with single-feature-based studies – in linguistics as well as everywhere else – is that feature selection is ultimately arbitrary (see Viereck 1985, 94), and that the next feature down the road may or may not contradict the characterization suggested by the previous feature. Thus, there is no guarantee that different dialects will exhibit the same distributional behavior in regard to different features; isoglosses do not necessarily overlap (again, see Bloomfield [1933] 1984: 329). In addition, individual features may have fairly specific quirks to them that are irrelevant to the big picture. This is why "[s]ingle-feature studies risk being overwhelmed by noise, i.e., missing data, exceptions, and conflicting tendencies" (Nerbonne 2009, 193). For these reasons, the aggregate perspective – in Goebl's parlance, "the synthetic interpretation" of linguistic data (Goebl 2006, 415) – is called for when the analyst's attention is turned to the forest, not the trees. Aggregation mitigates the problem of feature-specific quirks, irrelevant statistical noise, and the problem of inherently subjective feature selection, and thus provides a more robust linguistic signal.

Second, *compared to linguistic atlas material, corpora yield a more realistic linguistic signal.* Atlas-based dialectometry typically aggregates observations such as "in the Yorkshire dialect, the lexeme *bus* is typically pronounced /bʊs/," while corpus-based (that is to say, frequency-based) approaches seek generalizations along the lines of "in Nottinghamshire English, multiple negation is twice as frequent (6 occurrences per ten thousand words) in actual speech than in Yorkshire English (3 occurrences per ten thousand words)." The atlas-based method has undeniable advantages: We emphasize, in particular, a fairly widespread availability of data sources and superb areal coverage. By contrast, dialect corpora are a rarer species, and their areal coverage is typically inferior to dialect atlases. Having said that, as a data source, corpora appear to have two major advantages over dialect atlases. First and foremost, the atlas signal is categorical, exhibits a high level of data reduction, and may hence be less accurate than the corpus signal, which can provide graded frequency information and which is hence a more suitable method to get a handle on continuous linguistic variation (Holman et al. 2007; Anderwald and Szmrecsanyi 2009; Grieve 2009; Wälchli 2009). This highlights the most crucial difference between atlas-based and corpus-based dialectometry: *corpus-based dialectometry is frequency-based dialectometry in its purest form.*[1] The point is that although the exact cognitive status of text frequencies is admittedly still unclear (for example, we do not know about the precise extent to which corpus frequencies correlate with psychological entrenchment; see Arppe et al. 2010; Blumenthal 2011), we do claim that text frequencies better match the perceptual reality of linguistic input than discrete atlas classifications; this is true even though some varieties of atlas-based dialectometry derive – with considerable computational effort – some form of commonness weighting, for instance at the phonetic segment level, from the atlas signal. Second, we note that the atlas signal is non-naturalistic, meta-linguistic, and competence-based in nature. It typically relies on elicitation and questionnaires, and is analytically twice removed, via fieldworkers *and* atlas compilers, from the analyst – a limitation that is particularly acute when the atlas-based analysis is based on so-called "interpretive maps" (as opposed to "display maps"; see Chambers and Trudgill 1998, 25). By contrast, text corpora provide more direct, performance-based access to language form and function, and may thus yield a more realistic and trustworthy picture (see Chafe 1992, 84; Leech et al. 1994, 58). The well-known major intrinsic drawback of the corpus-based method is that it is unable to deal with rare phenomena (see Penke and Rosenbach 2004, 489; Haspelmath 2009, 157–158), and syntactic phenomena are a good deal rarer than, for example, phonetic phenomena (Chambers and Trudgill 1991, 291), which is why more text is needed to study (morpho)syntax than pronunciation. But then again, it is arguable whether phenomena that are so infrequent that they cannot be described on the basis of a major text corpus should have a place in an aggregate analysis at all.

Adopting a corpus-cum-aggregation approach exactly along these lines, this study taps the *Freiburg Corpus of English Dialects* (FRED), a sizable dialect corpus that samples old-fashioned dialect speech all over Great Britain (though we would like to mention right at the outset that the study also draws on two smallish reference corpora sampling Standard British and American English for benchmarking purposes). FRED is by design heavily biased towards elderly speakers with a working-class background – so-called NORMs (*non-mobile old rural males*) (see Chambers and Trudgill 1998, 29). The majority of the interviews in the corpus were conducted in the 1970s and 1980s, and most of the speakers were born around the beginning of the twentieth century. Dialect speech and dialect variability mirrored in

---

[1] This is why the present study's methodology is somewhat similar to the pioneering, frequency-based dialectometry approach of Hoppenbrouwers and Hoppenbrouwers (1988, 2001); see Heeringa (2004, 16–20) for a discussion in English.

FRED therefore reflect an intermediate stage between the state of affairs represented in the *Survey of English Dialects* of the 1950s and 1960s and present-day dialect variability in Great Britain. In short, then, the present study is overwhelmingly concerned not with geographic variation in modern or mainstream or urban dialects, but with TRADITIONAL DIALECTS, which Peter Trudgill defines as follows:

Traditional Dialects are what most people think of when they hear the term dialect. They are spoken by a probably shrinking minority of the English-speaking population of the world, almost all of them in England, Scotland and Northern Ireland. They are most easily found, as far as England is concerned, in the more remote and peripheral rural areas of the country, although some urban areas of northern and western England still have many Traditional Dialect speakers. (Trudgill 1990, 5)

We hasten to add that the present study also investigates some vernacular varieties spoken in Wales and the Scottish Highlands, which are rather young and thus cannot count, strictly speaking, as "traditional" (cf. Trudgill 2004a, 15). Yet for the most part it is traditional dialects in Trudgill's sense that really take center stage in this book. That these traditional dialects are dying out fast should be an added incentive to document them as best we can.

How does the study proceed empirically? In keeping true to the spirit of dialectometrical analysis, the goal was to base the analysis of dialect variability on as many morphosyntactic features as possible. The study thus defines a fairly comprehensive catalogue of fifty-seven features. These are essentially the usual suspects in the dialectological, variationist, and corpus-linguistic literature. The catalogue spans eleven major grammatical domains: (i) pronouns and determiners (e.g. non-standard reflexives), (ii) the noun phrase (e.g. preposition stranding), (iii) primary verbs (e.g. text frequencies of the verb TO DO), (iv) tense and aspect (e.g. the present perfect with auxiliary BE), (v) modality (e.g. text frequencies of epistemic/deontic MUST), (vi) verb morphology (e.g. non-standard weak past tense and past participle forms, such as *goed*), (vii) negation (e.g. *never* as a preverbal past tense negator), (viii) agreement (e.g. non-standard WAS), (ix) relativization (e.g. the relative particle *what*), (x) complementation (e.g. unsplit *for to*), and (xi) word order and discourse phenomena (e.g. lack of auxiliaries in *yes/no* questions).

Crucially, the book is not concerned with basing its empirical investigation on the mere presence or absence of individual features in particular locations. Instead, we seek to exploit the corpus material to the fullest and take an interest in graded text frequencies, feature by feature, in the interview material sampled in FRED. So, on the basis of fifty-seven feature frequencies extracted from texts from thirty-four measuring points (which yields a total of $34 \times 57 = 1{,}938$ continuous feature frequencies as data points), the study pursues two analytical avenues. For one thing, we utilize the well-known

Euclidean distance metric to derive a measure of aggregate morphosyntactic distance between measuring points. The resulting distance matrix is then subjected to a range of state-of-the-art dialectometrical analysis techniques – various cartographic projections to geography (many of which heavily rely on color coding to capture the inherent dimensionality of morphosyntactic variability) as well as a number of correlative techniques. Second, we rely on Principal Component Analysis to embark on an analysis of feature inter-dependencies for the sake of exploring linguistic structure in the aggregate view and uncovering the layered nature of joint morphosyntactic variability in Great Britain.

On the interpretational plane, this book explores joint morphosyntactic variability in Great Britain as a function of geographic space. It is a time-honored axiom in dialectology and geolinguistics that geographic distance should predict linguistic distance (see Nerbonne and Kleiweg 2007, 154 and Chapter 5 for a discussion). Nonetheless, this axiom has not yet been put to a systematic test outside the realm of atlas-based dialectometry; additionally, the geolinguistic underpinnings of dialectal morphosyntactic variability are generally underresearched. Thus, the set of more specific research questions that guide the analysis in this book can be succinctly summarized as follows:

(i)   Does a frequency-derived measure of morphosyntactic variability in traditional British English dialects exhibit a geographic signal?
(ii)  If there is a geographic signal, exactly how are morphosyntactic distances and similarities distributed? Specifically: Are we rather dealing with a dialect continuum scenario or with a dialect area scenario?
(iii) Do feature subsets make a difference, and what is the extent to which individual features gang up to create areal (sub)patterns?

In a nutshell, this book will suggest that aggregate morphosyntactic variability in British English dialects is indeed geolinguistically significant. More precisely, the distribution of morphosyntactic distances is such that Great Britain's morphosyntactic dialect landscape is neither a flawless dialect continuum, nor is it perfectly organized along the lines of dialect areas. Instead, we are dealing with a hybrid type, and with significant differences between the dialect network in England and the dialect network in Scotland. Lastly, we shall see that there are a number of feature bundles which create layers of geolinguistically conditioned morphosyntactic variability. The most important of those is a bundle comprising a comparatively large number of well-known dialect features which creates a very substantial South–North continuum.

## 1.2   Previous big-picture accounts

Naturally, we would like to validate our findings against as much previous scholarship along the lines of ours as possible. Alas, big-picture accounts based on the study of feature bundles (as opposed to so-called single-feature studies) in English dialectology are rare, and such accounts as exist are typically not dedicated to morphosyntactic variability. Be that as it may, this section canvasses the literature for aggregate approaches to *structural variability* in British English dialects, be it phonetic/phonological or morphological in nature (we ignore research on lexical variability on account of the fact that lexis is arguably "the least structured and most fluctuating plane of language" [Viereck 1986a, 725]). As much of the relevant research is empirically based on the *Survey of English Dialects*, we begin by adding a few introductory remarks about this particular atlas project. In addition to this line of more traditional dialectological inquiry, we also review in this section an experiment that investigates the perceptual side of dialect variability in Great Britain (Inoue 1996).

### 1.2.1    *On the* Survey of English Dialects

A project headed by Harold Orton and Eugen Dieth, the *Survey of English Dialects* (henceforth: SED) (Orton and Dieth 1962) was conducted between 1948 and 1961, primarily in rural England. The target informants were NORMs in 313 localities all over England, interviewed by nine trained fieldworkers. The SED database principally consists of the so-called *Basic Material*, which details responses to the extensive SED questionnaire that comprises no less than 1,326 questions and is organized into nine "books" ("The Farm," "Animals," etc.). After the publication of the *Basic Material* in the 1960's, a number of linguistic atlases interpreting the SED material were published: *A Word Geography of England* (WGE) (Orton and Wright 1974), the *Linguistic Atlas of England* (LAE) (Orton et al. 1978), the *Atlas of English Sounds* (AES) (Kolb 1979), the *Structural Atlas of the English Dialects* (SAED) (Anderson 1987), and the *Computer Developed Linguistic Atlas of England* (CLAE) (Viereck et al. 1991). Though the LAE and the CLAE specifically cover lexical, pronunciational as well as morphological and syntactic variability, it seems fair to say that syntactic variability especially is generally given rather short shrift – not only in the interpretation atlases, but also in the SED questionnaire itself (on this point, cf. Shorrocks 2001, 1557). For contemporary evaluations of the SED endeavor, see Goebl and Schiltz (2006, 2356–2357), Sanderson and Widdowson (1985), and Viereck (1988, 267–268).

### 1.2.2    *Nineteenth-century accent differences: Alexander Ellis' survey of English dialects (1889)*

We begin this literature review with a precursor of sorts to the SED. In the nineteenth century, Alexander J. Ellis, a gentleman scholar of independent means, conducted a rather monumental survey of dialect pronunciations in England, Wales, and Scotland (see Shorrocks 1991; Francis 1992; Ihalainen 1994 for contemporary reviews). The resulting database – deriving from a translation task (a "comparative specimen"), a shorter "dialect test," and a "classified word list" – is documented in *The Existing Phonology of English Dialects*, the fifth volume of Ellis' series *On Early English Pronunciation* (Ellis 1889). Ellis gathered data on 1,454 locations, an endeavor which took more than twenty years (see Ellis 1889, xvii–xix) and left us with one of the first dialect surveys "based on rich, systematically collected evidence" (Ihalainen 1994, 232).

The appendix of Ellis (1889) features two synopsis maps to project group-ings of dialect features to geography – the first of their kind (Sanderson and Widdowson 1985, 36). The criteria used by Ellis to group dialects are pronunciational. Thus in the maps we find forty-two Districts, "in each of which a sensible similarity of pronunciation prevails" (Ellis 1889, 3), as well as six major dialect areas ("divisions," in Ellis' parlance): (1) South-ern dialects, (2) Western dialects, (3) Eastern dialects, (4) Midland dialects, (5) Northern dialects, and (6) Lowland (Scots) dialects. In addition, the maps detail what Ellis refers to as "varieties, or parts of Districts separately con-sidered" (Ellis 1889, 3), and "Ten Transverse Lines" (1889, 3), which map isoglosses of particular accent features (e.g. the pronunciation of words such as *some* or *house*).

*1.2.3   SED-based analyses I: Trudgill's (1990) division of traditional dialects*

Trudgill (1990) is one of the best-known contemporary dialectological accounts of dialect differences in Great Britain. To establish traditional dialect areas, Trudgill considers accent differences only. Specifically, he bases his classification on "eight major features of English Traditional Dialects which we can use to divide the country up into different dialect areas" (1990, 32): The vowels in *long* (/læŋ/ vs. /lɒŋ/), *night* (/niːt/ vs. /naɪt/), *blind* (/blɪnd/ vs. /blaɪnd/), *land* (/lænd/ vs. /lɒnd/), and *bat* (/bat/ vs. /bæt/); postvocalic /r/, as in *arm* (/aːrm/ vs. /aːm/); h-dropping, as in *hill* (/hɪl/ vs. /ɪl/); and voicing, as in *seven* (/sevn/ vs. /zevn/). On the basis of the regional distribution of these features according to the SED, Trudgill presents a composite map that defines thirteen tra-ditional dialect varieties (Northumberland, the Lower North, Lancashire, Staffordshire, South Yorkshire, Lincolnshire, Leicestershire, the Western Southwest, the Northern Southwest, the Eastern Southwest, the Southeast, the Central East, and the Eastern Counties) plus Scots. These thirteen vari-eties are grouped into six major dialect areas: (1) Scots, (2) Northern dialects, (3) Western Central (Midlands) dialects, (4) Eastern Central (Midlands) dialects, (5) Southwestern dialects, and (6) Southeastern dialects. As for higher-level groupings, Trudgill offers that "the major division of English dialects is into dialects of the North and dialects of the South, and that the boundary between them runs from the Lancashire coast down to the mouth of the River Humber" (1990, 35).

### 1.2.4  SED-based analyses II: The Salzburg School of Dialectometry

In the course of the past fifteen years, Hans Goebl and his collaborators have marshalled the full range of dialectometrical analysis techniques developed by the Salzburg School of Dialectometry (henceforth S-DM) to analyze the SED material, as available through the CLAE database (Viereck et al. 1991; see also next section). True to S-DM's spirit of generating a large number of colorful maps, Goebl and his collaborators' foray into dialect variability in England has left us with a sizable body of cartographic projections, mostly based on lexical and morphosyntactic SED material: similarity maps (Goebl 1997a, 2001, 2007), so-called parameter maps (Goebl and Schiltz 1997; Goebl 2001, 2007), dendrogrammatic cluster maps (Goebl 1997b, 2007), honeycomb maps (Goebl 2007), beam maps (Goebl 2007), and proximity profiles (for instance, Goebl 2007). In short, Goebl and his co-workers show that there is a fairly clear North–South split in the data in that, for instance, all Southern SED localities have their similarity minima in the North, and vice versa (Goebl 1997a). Second, beyond this very robust split, dialect area boundaries are, according to Goebl and Schiltz (1997) and also Goebl (1997b), largely in accordance with Peter Trudgill's dialect division (see Section 1.2.3). Third, as for dialect integration, the South of England is on the whole more integrated than the North. In terms of morphosyntax specifically, though, it appears that there are actually two fairly well-integrated areas: "One is located in the South and centred near Salisbury; the second area lies further northeast in Nottingham/Lincolnshire" (Goebl and Schiltz 1997, 18).

### 1.2.5  SED-based analyses III: Bamberg-type dialectometry

In the 1980s and 1990s, a Bamberg research team headed by dialectologist Wolfgang Viereck generated a number of basic dialectometrical accounts of dialectal variability in England, all drawing on the SED-based *Computer Developed Linguistic Atlas of England* (CLAE) (Viereck et al. 1991) compiled in Bamberg. Some of the principal findings of this research include the following. Viereck (1986b, 243) reports that, all in all, there is substantial agreement between the geography of lexical, phonological, and morphological variability in dialectal England. Viereck (1997) and Händler and Viereck (1997) utilize a so-called "gravity center approach" (an actually fairly simple method designed to detect the geographic center of particular linguistic variants) and find that there is "a rather clear linguistic divide between the southeast and the southwest of England" (Viereck 1997, 3). What is more, Händler and Viereck (1997, 34) offer that "[t]he North is . . . a

dialectal area that is more strongly shaped lexically" than morphosyntactically. Viereck (1986b), mentioned above, is also concerned with establishing
dialect divisions, relying on forty-five vocalic and consonantal features as
well as fifty-three morphological features. Viereck (1986b, 243) distinguishes
between the following five major dialect areas in England: (1) Northern
dialects, (2) Lincolnshire plus East Anglia, (3) the West Midlands, (4) the
Southeast of England, and (5) the Southwest of England.

### 1.2.6   SED-based analyses IV: Shackleton (2007)

In a paper entitled "Phonetic Variation in the Traditional English Dialects"
(Shackleton 2007), Robert G. Shackleton Jr. offers a detailed account of
aggregate phonetic variability in English English dialects whose "results
largely corroborate standard characterizations in the literature" (2007, 87).
The paper features cartographic visualizations in the spirit of the Groningen School of Dialectometry and an array of parametric and non-parametric
statistical analysis techniques (regression analysis, Multidimensional Scaling, Cluster Analysis, and Principal Component Analysis). Empirically,
Shackleton (2007) draws on the original SED database as well as on the
SED-derived *Structural Atlas of the English Dialects* (SAED) (Anderson
1987) to construct two different datasets. The feature-based dataset rests
on a set of fifty-five words (and their pronunciation) in English English
dialects, while his variant-based dataset "summarizes over 400 responses,
grouping them into 199 variants of thirty-nine phonemes or combinations
of phonemes" (2007, 36 and 38). We may summarize the insights afforded
by Shackleton (2007) as follows: To begin with, phonetic variation in traditional English English dialects is, on the whole, "not very systematic,
but instead tends to involve largely uncorrelated variations that, in some
areas, coalesce into patterns that appear more systematic" (2007, 42). Second, a small number of variants accounts for most usage, in accordance
with Kretzschmar and Tamasi's (2002) *A-curve* principle (2007, 40). Third,
correlating as-the-crow-flies distances with phonetic distances, Shackleton
finds that both feature-based linguistic distances and variant-based distances
correlate quite robustly with geographic distances ($r \geq .7$) (2007, 47–48).
Shackleton's more sophisticated subsequent regression analysis shows that
geographic distance and dialect area membership explain circa 77 percent
of the variability in linguistic distances (depending on the dataset used) –
and in regression analysis, geographic distance alone accounts for more than
half of the variability (2007, 61). Thus, for explaining phonetic distances
it is apparently geographic separation between the dialect locations that
counts – rather than dialect area affiliation (2007, 64). This comparatively
weak explanatory potency of dialect area membership notwithstanding,
Shackleton applies multiple cluster analyses to partition the SED locations
into the following seven major regions (2007, 52–53 and 88–89): (1) the Far

North, (2) the Upper North, (3) the Lower North, (4) the Central Midlands, (5) the Upper Southwest, (6) the Southeast, and (7) the Lower Southwest. As for the relative importance of dialect divisions, Shackleton points out that "the most important boundary separates the South and Midlands, and the second most important separates the Southeast from the Southwest and West Midlands" (2007, 58). Needless to say, this analysis largely corresponds to Peter Trudgill's dialect division (see Section 1.2.3).

### 1.2.7   The network perspective: McMahon et al. (2007)

In their (2007) paper ("The Sound Patterns of Englishes: Representing Phonetic Similarity"), McMahon et al. use a measure of aggregate phonetic similarity to calculate phonetic similarities between varieties of Germanic. Subsequently, the authors use originally biometric tree and network diagrams to visually depict their results. Empirically, the authors define a list of sixty Germanic cognates (including words for, e.g., "beech," "blood," and "bloom," and so on), on the basis of which they compare "fairly close" (2007, 123) phonetic transcriptions in twenty varieties of Germanic, among them eleven dialects in Great Britain: Standard Scots, Glasgow English (Scottish Lowlands), Buckie English (Scottish Lowlands), Berwick English (North of England), conservative Tyneside English (North of England), Middlesbrough English (North of England), Liverpool English (English Midlands), Derby English (English Midlands), Sheffield English (English Midlands), RP, and Wisbech English (Southeast of England) (the dialect area labels given here orient on Trudgill 1990, map 9).

Methodically, McMahon et al. utilize an algorithm to establish phonetic similarities; the technicalities need not concern us here. The result is a $20 \times 20$ similarity matrix, which the authors then process utilizing the well-known *SplitsTree4* package (Huson and Bryant 2006), which was originally developed to address evolutionary biology issues. In the realm of linguistics, *SplitsTree4* and similar packages have recently been advanced to explore genetic relationships and aggregate similarities between languages (for instance, Dunn et al. 2005). It is important to stress, however, that McMahon et al.'s perspective in the paper under review is "synchronic and variety-based" (2007, 115) (i.e. phonetic), rather than historical and language (or even language family) based.

The analysis in McMahon et al. (2007) brings to the fore two major facts about British English dialects. First, there is a fairly coherent cluster of Scottish Lowlands dialects (Buckie, Glasgow, and Standard Scottish). This cluster is distinct from the cluster of English English varieties. Second, there appears to be a good deal of dialect contact and mixing. For the purposes of the present study, we conclude that McMahon et al.'s analysis testifies to a clear split between Scottish Lowland dialects and English English dialects.

*1.2.8   The perceptual dialectology perspective: Inoue (1996)*

In the realm of perceptual dialectology, which abstracts away from individual dialect features and thus counts as an "aggregate" approach to dialect variability, Inoue (1996) reports an experiment to study the subjective dialect division in Great Britain. Seventy-seven students at several universities in Great Britain were asked, among other things, to draw lines on a blank map "according to the accents or dialects they perceived" (1996, 146), based on their past "personal experience" (1996, 158), which may arguably be a blend of pronunciational, morphological, syntactic, and lexical experiences. The key divisions that emerge from Inoue's experiment may be summarized as follows. First, dialects of English in Wales and Scotland are perceived as being fairly different from English English dialects (1996, 153). Second, within England, there is a tripartite division such that the North is differentiated from the Midlands, and the Midlands are differentiated from the South (1996, 153). Third, in the South of England, subjects differentiate between Southwestern and Southeastern English English dialects (1996, 153). Note that this division is quite compatible with Trudgill's (1990) classification, except that in Inoue's (1996) experiment, Lancashire is part of the North, not of the western Midlands, and the Northern Southwest (essentially, Shropshire and Herøfordshire) groups with Midland dialects, not Southwestern dialects.   ¢

*1.2.9   Synopsis*

In this section, we have reviewed seven major accounts that are concerned with aggregate linguistic variability in British English dialects. The following key points may be extrapolated from this literature. First and foremost, the plethora of studies – six of the seven studies subject to review – posit a Midlands dialect area in England: Ellis (1889), Viereck (1986b), Inoue (1996), Trudgill (1990), Goebl (2007), and Shackleton (2007). Likewise, five of the seven studies (Viereck 1986b; Inoue 1996; Trudgill 1990; Goebl 2007; Shackleton 2007) diagnose a split between Southwestern and Southeastern English English dialects. Third, four of the seven studies considered in this chapter also include varieties of English spoken in Scotland, and crucially, three of these four studies (namely, Ellis 1889; Inoue 1996; McMahon et al. 2007) find a robust opposition between Scottish varieties of English and English English varieties of English – as a matter of fact, only Trudgill (1990) groups Scots with Northern English English dialects (though he notes that within this grouping, there *is* a contrast between Scots and Northern varieties of English). Fourth, as for English English dialects, two of the seven studies (Trudgill 1990; Goebl 2007) explicitly stress an important contrast between Southern English English dialects and Northern English English dialects (observe, however, that this contrast is actually implicit in virtually all of the analyses reviewed except for McMahon et al. 2007). We note, finally, that two of the seven studies at least partially also draw on morphological and syntactic features (Viereck 1986b and Goebl 2007). Yet against the backdrop of the other studies reviewed in this chapter, this does not seem to have a major impact on the dialect divisions reported.

## 1.3    Structure

The remainder of the book is structured as follows:

**Chapter 2** ("Data and methods") introduces the *Freiburg Corpus of English Dialects* (FRED), with particular emphasis on its sampling principles and its areal coverage; the chapter also presents the study's two Standard English reference corpora. The remainder of the chapter is dedicated to explaining the technicalities behind the study's empirical approach. We elaborate on the creation of a so-called "frequency matrix," and the aggregation process via Euclidean distances that yields a so-called "distance matrix." We moreover provide a blueprint of the major approaches to visualizing, analyzing, and interpreting the aggregate dataset.

**Chapter 3** ("The feature catalogue") details the 57-feature catalogue that serves as the basis for the study's analysis of morphosyntax aggregates, and discusses in detail the criteria guiding the feature selection process. The chapter also includes very concise literature reviews for each of the features considered, sketches the technicalities of the extraction process as well as coding guidelines, offers frequency overviews, and presents some summary statistics elucidating the variability captured by the feature catalogue as a whole.

**Chapter 4** ("Surveying the forest: on aggregate morphosyntactic distances and similarities") is descriptive in nature and surveys aggregate morphosyntactic distances between British English dialects, drawing heavily on cartographic projections to geography. We are also concerned here with aggregate morphosyntactic distances between traditional British English dialects and spoken Standard English, British and American.

**Chapter 5** ("Is morphosyntactic variability gradient? Exploring dialect continua") probes the assumption shared by many dialectologists and geolinguists that dialectal similarity is directly proportional to geographic proximity. Cartographically, we draw on Multidimensional Scaling to create maps depicting the extent to which dialect transitions are smooth, as opposed to abrupt. Quantitatively, the chapter tests a number of language-external distance measures – such as as-the-crow-flies distance, least-cost travel time, and linguistic gravity – for their explanatory power.

Chapter **6** ("Classification: the dialect area scenario") investigates an alternative scenario according to which dialect landscapes may be organized not so much in terms of gradient dialect continua but rather along the lines of geographically coherent and linguistically homogeneous dialect areas. We start out by proceeding deductively, testing a number of dialect divisions for their explanatory power in terms of the present study's dataset. Subsequently, we take an inductive approach and utilize Hierarchical Agglomerative Cluster analyses to derive dialect groupings from the FRED dataset.

Chapter **7** ("Back to the features") takes a step back from the aggregate perspective and revisits the actual features on which the study is based. For one thing, we will be interested in the extent to which the behavior of a number of renegade measuring points in the FRED network (for instance, Warwickshire and Middlesex) can be blamed on abnormal frequencies of individual morphosyntactic features. Second, the chapter marshals Principal Component Analysis to identify, via frequency interdependencies, feature bundles which create layers of aggregate morphosyntactic variability.

Chapter **8** ("Summary and discussion") pulls together the study's major findings, highlighting its principal insight that morphosyntactic variability in British English dialects is demonstrably structured geographically. The chapter specifically considers the intricacies of the geographical signal uncovered in the book's empirical part against the backdrop of a wider analytical and theoretical context.

Chapter **9** ("Outlook and concluding remarks") sketches directions for future research, and offers some concluding remarks.

# 2     Data and methods

This chapter provides an overview of the data sources tapped, and methods used in the book. Thus Section 2.1 is dedicated to introducing the *Freiburg Corpus of English Dialects*, as well as two smallish reference corpora sampling Standard British and American English for benchmarking purposes. Section 2.2 sketches the technicalities behind the study's empirical approach in generic terms (more detailed introductions to particular techniques are reserved for those chapters where those techniques are actually utilized).

## 2.1   Data

This study draws on three naturalistic text corpora: First and foremost, the *Freiburg Corpus of English Dialects* (Section 2.1.1), and second, two compact reference corpora sampled from the British component of the *International Corpus of English* and the *Corpus of Spoken American English* for benchmarking purposes (Section 2.1.2).

### 2.1.1   The *Freiburg Corpus of English Dialects*

The *Freiburg Corpus of English Dialects* (henceforth: FRED) (see Kortmann and Wagner 2005; Hernández 2006; Anderwald and Wagner 2007; Szmrecsanyi and Hernández 2007) is a major dialect corpus that samples traditional dialect speech all over Great Britain. The version used here (we removed some localities with comparatively thin textual coverage from the full corpus[1]) contains 368 individual texts (that is, interviews) and spans 2,437,000 words of running text, interviewer utterances excluded.

FRED makes second-hand use of so-called "oral history" interviews, sometimes with more than one informant at once (note that some informants also star in more than one interview, and that some interviews have more than

---

[1] Specifically, we removed texts coming from counties that would have been represented by a single interview spanning less than 5,000 words of running text. This concerned the counties of Kinross-shire (text KRS001), Inverness-shire (text INV001), Fife (text FIF001), and Lanarkshire (text LKS001).

one interviewer). The corpus manual describes the data collection process as follows:

> Tape and mini-disc copies were made of pre-selected original tape recordings made available by various fieldworkers, historians, local museums, libraries and archives from different locations in England, Scotland, Wales, the Hebrides and the Isle of Man. Back at Freiburg University, the tapes were digitised for protection . . . and stored on DVD. The interviews deemed most suitable for our purposes were then transcribed (either from scratch or revised) by English native speakers and linguistically trained staff. (Hernández 2006, 2)

"Most suitable for our purposes" is another way of saying that the material was screened, and only rather dialectal material was retained for inclusion in the corpus. Most of the oral history interviews that eventually ended up in the corpus were recorded in the 1970s and 1980s. Typically, a fieldworker interviewed an informant about life, work, etc. in former days (we reiterate that fieldworker utterances are excluded from analysis). The 427 informants (that is, interviewees) sampled in the corpus are usually elderly people with a working-class background – so-called NORMs (see Chambers and Trudgill 1998, 29). We know about the exact age of 280 informants in the corpus, and these have a mean age of 71 years and were typically born around the beginning of the twentieth century. Representative occupations – or former occupations (most informants are actually retired at the time of the interview) – include basket maker, blacksmith, cleaner, cloth miller, farm hand, fitter, forester, gamekeeper, gardener, mender, pipe worker, relief warden, shipwright, stoker, weaver, and so on. To illustrate, (1) is the beginning of an interview conducted in 1978 in St. Ives, Cornwall (FRED text CON003). The informant is an 86-year-old male ("CAVA_PV"), who is interviewed by two interviewers ("IntRS" and "Inf"). Interviewer utterances are enclosed in curly brackets (to reiterate, interviewer utterances are excluded from analysis in the present study).

(1)   {<u IntRS>        Well you're a St. Ives man. Where were you born?}

      <u CAVA_PV>        Born Belyars Lane, eighteen ninety-two. Eighteenth of December. Worn sovereign in the cupper. Born sovereign. The poor times then, you know (gap "indistinct") boiling potatoes and t – inkle mosses.

      {<u IntRS>        Did you, did you, how long did you live there?}

      <u CAVA_PV>        Oh we lived there about, oh about twelve years, I suppose. Then we went up to a

Rosewall Terrace. Hmm. So everything's
altered now to what er was then, I mean.

{<u IntRS>        Mhm.}
{<u Inf>          And you live on Baronon Hill?}
<u CAVA_PV>       On Baronon Hill, for a few years, uhuh. And
                  I was only thinking here this afternoon about
                  when we live in them Baronon Hill, you
                  know. 'Course the back of the, the back of
                  the castles, (gap "mumbling") – I don't know
                  whether you could in there or no, I don't
                  much, but uh, (v "laughter") I can remem-
                  ber, course she was . . . put to bed. We used
                  to live right opposite [. . .]

[CON003][2]

FRED's coverage of traditional dialects in the British Isles is currently unparalleled, yet needless to say the corpus also has some weaknesses. Chiefly among these we mention that textual coverage of dialect locations is not entirely evenly balanced, such that some locations are only represented by one or two interviews while others are covered by dozens of interviews (see the following section for more detail). While this issue is no doubt a challenge to quantitative analysis, we provide evidence in Section 2.2.2 below that the degree of unbalanced coverage to be found in FRED is not a fatal problem.

*Areal coverage*

The interviews analyzed in this book were conducted in 158 different locations – that is, villages and towns – in thirty-four different pre-1974 counties in Great Britain plus the Isle of Man and the Hebrides (note that this count considers the Hebridean Islands as one super-county, which is historically speaking not accurate). For reasons of statistical robustness, observations for individual locations will as a rule be aggregated to the county level, so that the basic geographical units in this book are counties in Great Britain. The only exception is the Principal Components Analysis afforded in Chapter 7, which operates on the level of individual FRED locations.

At yet a lower level of granularity, FRED comes with a ninefold a-priori regionalization which, as far as England and Lowland Scotland are concerned, roughly follows Trudgill's (1990) seminal dialect division on pronunciational grounds (see Section 1.2.3): England's (1) Southwest, (2) Southeast, (3) Midlands, and (4) North; Scotland is divided into the

---

[2] Unless indicated otherwise, corpus examples in this book are drawn from the FRED corpus and are referenced by FRED corpus text identifiers, which consist of a three character Chapman county code followed by a running text number.

(5) Scottish Lowlands and (6) Scottish Highlands; (7) Wales; (8) the Isle of Man; and (9) the Hebridean Isles.

As for annotation, FRED is currently neither syntax parsed nor part-of-speech (POS) annotated. The version of FRED used here provides, however, longitude/latitude information for each of the locations sampled. Because the level of areal granularity in this book is the county level, we use this annotation to derive county coordinates (mean longitude and latitude) by computing the arithmetic mean of all the location coordinates associated with a particular county.

What follows is a list of the thirty-four measuring points (counties) considered in the present study. Except for the measuring points "Hebrides" and "Yorkshire," these coincide with pre-1974 counties in Great Britain, before administrative borders in England, Scotland and Wales were reorganized. Table 2.1 gives a quick overview, and Map 2.1 depicts the areal distribution of FRED measuring points.

> **Angus** (ANS); FRED regionalization: Scottish Lowlands; 4 interviews, 20,000 words of running text, 3 locations (Arbroath, Forfar, Kirkton), 6 speakers (mean age: 79 years).
> **Banffshire** (BAN); FRED regionalization: Scottish Lowlands; 1 interview, 6,000 words of running text, 1 location (Keith), 1 speaker (age: 76 years).
> **Cornwall** (CON); FRED regionalization: Southwest of England; 12 interviews, 107,000 words of running text, 11 locations (Carnelloe, Churchtown, Gulval, Gurnard's Head, Heamoor, Ludgvan, Nancledra, Pendeen, Sennen, St. Ives, St. Just), 14 speakers (mean age: 70 years).
> **Denbighshire** (DEN); FRED regionalization: Wales; 4 interviews, 6,000 words of running text, 1 location (Conwy), 6 speakers (mean age: 87 years).
> **Devon** (DEV): FRED regionalization: Southwest of England; 11 interviews, 97,000 words of running text, 6 locations (Blackawton, Brixham, Buckfast, Dartmouth, Galmpton, Totnes), 16 speakers (mean age: 83 years).
> **Dumfriesshire** (DFS); FRED regionalization: Scottish Lowlands; 1 interview, 10,000 words of running text, 1 location (Mickle Kirkland), 2 speakers (mean age: 72 years).
> **Durham** (DUR); FRED regionalization: North of England; 3 interviews, 28,000 words of running text, 2 locations (Birtley, Hartlepool), 3 speakers (mean age: 77 years).
> **East Lothian** (ELN); FRED regionalization: Scottish Lowlands; 15 interviews, 40,000 words of running text, 1 location (Tranent), 16 speakers (mean age: 17 years). The FRED material documenting East Lothian English derives from the *Edinburgh Corpus of Spoken Scottish English* (ECOSSE), and the informants are typically pupils and thus

Table 2.1. *FRED counties considered in the present study. Map labels (for L04 maps), polygon numbers (for VDM maps) (see Section 2.2.5), FRED a-priori regionalization, mean longitude, mean latitude.*

| map label | polygon number | county | a-priori regionalization | mean longitude | mean latitude |
|---|---|---|---|---|---|
| ANS | 6  | Angus | Scottish Lowlands | −2.627 | 56.659 |
| BAN | 4  | Banffshire | Scottish Lowlands | −2.949 | 57.543 |
| CON | 26 | Cornwall | Southwest of England | −5.502 | 50.175 |
| DEN | 24 | Denbighshire | Wales | −3.743 | 53.146 |
| DEV | 27 | Devon | Southwest of England | −3.681 | 50.378 |
| DFS | 13 | Dumfriesshire | Scottish Lowlands | −3.839 | 55.003 |
| DUR | 15 | Durham | North of England | −1.703 | 54.890 |
| ELN | 11 | East Lothian | Scottish Lowlands | −2.954 | 55.945 |
| GLA | 25 | Glamorganshire | Wales | −3.634 | 51.641 |
| HEB | 1  | Hebrides | Hebrides | −7.038 | 57.502 |
| KCD | 5  | Kincardineshire | Scottish Lowlands | −2.465 | 56.974 |
| KEN | 34 | Kent | Southeast of England | 0.835 | 51.246 |
| LAN | 18 | Lancashire | North of England | −2.730 | 53.653 |
| LEI | 21 | Leicestershire | English Midlands | −1.623 | 52.752 |
| LND | 32 | London | Southeast of England | −0.068 | 51.504 |
| MAN | 17 | Isle of Man | Isle of Man | −4.446 | 54.257 |
| MDX | 31 | Middlesex | Southeast of England | −0.382 | 51.594 |
| MLN | 10 | Midlothian | Scottish Lowlands | −3.265 | 55.918 |
| NBL | 14 | Northumberland | North of England | −1.680 | 55.302 |
| NTT | 20 | Nottinghamshire | English Midlands | −1.055 | 53.011 |
| OXF | 30 | Oxfordshire | Southwest of England | −1.598 | 51.787 |
| PEE | 9  | Peebleshire | Scottish Lowlands | −3.377 | 55.721 |
| PER | 7  | Perthshire | Scottish Lowlands | −3.530 | 56.368 |
| ROC | 3  | Ross and Cromarty | Scottish Highlands | −4.776 | 57.808 |
| SAL | 23 | Shropshire | English Midlands | −2.471 | 52.653 |
| SEL | 12 | Selkirkshire | Scottish Lowlands | −3.002 | 55.502 |
| SFK | 33 | Suffolk | Southeast of England | 1.699 | 52.555 |
| SOM | 28 | Somerset | Southwest of England | −2.792 | 51.112 |
| SUT | 2  | Sutherland | Scottish Highlands | −4.676 | 58.144 |
| WAR | 22 | Warwickshire | English Midlands | −1.968 | 52.574 |
| WES | 16 | Westmorland | North of England | −2.962 | 54.428 |
| WIL | 29 | Wiltshire | Southwest of England | −2.031 | 51.259 |
| WLN | 8  | West Lothian | Scottish Lowlands | −3.784 | 56.001 |
| YKS | 19 | Yorkshire | North of England | −1.174 | 54.424 |

very young. Nonetheless, compared to other FRED measuring points with more typical NORM profiles, the measuring point East Lothian is geolinguistically well-behaved (as the subsequent analyses will demonstrate), which is why we opted to retain the material.

**Glamorganshire** (GLA); FRED regionalization: Wales; 7 interviews, 53,000 words of running text, 7 locations (Bedlinog, Bishopston, Cwmfelin, Plasmarl, Pontardulais, Swansea, Townhill), 7 speakers (mean age: 82 years).

Map 2.1. FRED counties considered in the present study.

**Hebrides** (HEB); FRED regionalization: Hebrides. HEB is the only measuring point in the sample that does not correspond to a pre-1974 county. Instead, it comprises all interviews from the Hebrides even though some of the isles "form part of administrative counties on the Scottish 'mainland' (e.g. the islands North Uist, South Uist and Skye would belong to Invernessshire according to the Chapman codes)" (Hernández 2006, 15). 41 interviews, 73,000 words of running text, 19 locations (Balmaquien, Bornaskitaig, Clachan, Claddach, Hacklett, Howbeg, Innes, Iochdar, Loch Carnan, Locheport, Maliger, North Duntulm, Portree, Portree Kingsburgh, Portree Staffin, Staffin, Staffin Clachan, Stenscholl, Struan), 53 speakers (mean age: 40 years).

**Isle of Man** (MAN); FRED regionalization: Isle of Man; 2 interviews, 11,000 words of running text, 2 locations (Laxey, Ramsey), 2 speakers (mean age: 81 years).

**Kent** (KEN); FRED regionalization: Southeast of England; 11 interviews, 177,000 words of running text, 6 locations (Faversham, Lydd, Sheerness, Sittingbourne, Tenterden, Whitstable), 10 speakers (mean age: 85 years).

**Kincardineshire** (KCD); FRED regionalization: Scottish Lowlands; 1 interview, 8,000 words of running text, 1 location (Gourdon), 2 speakers (mean age: 71 years).

**Lancashire** (LAN); FRED regionalization: North of England; 23 interviews, 205,000 words of running text, 6 locations (Barrow, Crompton, Huyton, Prescott, Preston, Wigan), 26 speakers (mean age: 67 years).

**Leicestershire** (LEI); FRED regionalization: English Midlands; 2 interviews, 6,000 words of running text, 1 location (Caldwell), 3 speakers (age unknown).

**London** (LND); FRED regionalization: Southeast of England; 7 interviews, 111,000 words of running text, 2 locations (London North, Poplar), 37 speakers (mean age: 65 years).

**Middlesex** (MDX); FRED regionalization: Southeast of England; 2 interviews, 32,000 words of running text, 1 location (Pinner), 2 speakers (mean age: 75 years).

**Midlothian** (MLN); FRED regionalization: Scottish Lowlands; 7 interviews, 32,000 words of running text, 1 location (Edinburgh), 10 speakers (age unknown).

**Northumberland** (NBL); FRED regionalization: North of England; 5 interviews, 31,000 words of running text, 4 locations (Cammerse, Choppington, Fenwick Steads, Swarland), 6 speakers (mean age: 82 years).

**Nottinghamshire** (NTT); FRED regionalization: English Midlands; 16 interviews, 151,000 words of running text, 3 locations (Lambley, Nottingham, Southwell), 17 speakers (mean age: 80 years).

**Oxfordshire** (OXF); FRED regionalization: Southwest of England; 2 interviews, 15,000 words of running text, 1 location (Leafield), 4 speakers (mean age: 85 years).

**Peebleshire** (PEE); FRED regionalization: Scottish Lowlands; 2 interviews, 14,975 words of running text, 2 locations (West Linton, Netherurd), 2 speakers (mean age: 56 years).

**Perthshire** (PER); FRED regionalization: Scottish Lowlands; 5 interviews, 21,000 words of running text, 3 locations (Abernethy, Crieff, Perth), 6 speakers (mean age: 79 years).

**Ross and Cromarty** (ROC); FRED regionalization: Scottish Highlands; 2 interviews, 10,000 words of running text, 2 locations (Aultbea, Hill of Fearn), 2 speakers (mean age: 80 years).

**Selkirkshire** (SEL); FRED regionalization: Scottish Lowlands; 3 interviews, 9,000 words of running text, 3 locations (Ettrick, Selkirk, Yarrow), 3 speakers (mean age: 71 years).

**Shropshire** (SAL); FRED regionalization: English Midlands; 39 interviews, 169,000 words of running text, 14 locations (Broseley, Coalbrookdale, Coalport, Craigside, Dawley, Farley, Ironbridge, Ketley, Lawley, Madeley, Oakengates, Shifnal, Telford, Wellington), 38 speakers (mean age: 81 years).

**Somerset** (SOM); FRED regionalization: Southwest of England; 36 interviews, 208,000 words of running text, 30 locations (Ashwick, Babcary, Baltonsborough, Barton St. David, Bridgwater, Buckleigh, Butleigh, Churchingfold Beaminster, Coley, Compton Dundon, Evercreech, Fivehead, Galhampton, Glastonbury, Hatch Beauchamp, Henley, Horton, Kingston Seymour, Moorwood Oakhill, North Bridgwater, North Burrowbridge, North Curry, North Petherton, Petherton, Stoke St. Gregory, Street, Sunnyside, Wedmore, West Stoughton, Yeovil), 41 speakers (mean age: 80 years).

**Suffolk** (SFK); FRED regionalization: Southeast of England; 39 interviews, 313,000 words of running text, 2 locations (Lowestoft, Yarmouth), 32 speakers (mean age: 74 years).

**Sutherland** (SUT); FRED regionalization: Scottish Highlands; 4 interviews, 11,000 words of running text, 4 locations (Assynt, Boulstoer, Durness, Terryside), 4 speakers (mean age: 67 years).

**Warwickshire** (WAR); FRED regionalization: English Midlands; 1 interview, 8,000 words of running text, 1 location (Walsall), 1 speaker (age unknown).

**West Lothian** (WLN); FRED regionalization: Scottish Lowlands; 6 interviews, 18,000 words of running text, 1 location (Falkirk), 4 speakers (mean age: 67 years).

**Westmorland** (WES); FRED regionalization: North of England; 19 interviews, 158,000 words of running text, 1 location (Ambleside), 23 speakers (mean age: 80 years).

**Wiltshire** (WIL); FRED regionalization: Southwest of England; 24 interviews, 186,000 words of running text, 7 locations (Donhead St. Andrew, Edington, Enford, Melksham. Trowbridge, Urchfont, Westbury), 37 speakers (mean age: 76 years).

Yorkshire (YKS); FRED regionalization: North of England. In this study, the label "Yorkshire" is shorthand for the pre-1974 county "Yorkshire: North Riding" ("East Riding" and "West Riding" are not covered in FRED). 11 interviews, 91,000 words of running text, 6 locations (Guisborough, Hebden Bridge, Hinderwell, Loftus, Middlesbrough, Redcar), 15 speakers (mean age: 83 years).

## 2.1.2 Standard English text corpora

This study is also going to be interested in the linguistic distances between the dialects sampled in FRED and the two major national Standard varieties, British English and American English. This is why we also created two small reference corpora containing extracts from the British component of the *International Corpus of English*, and from the *Santa Barbara Corpus of Spoken American English*.

**The British component of the *International Corpus of English (ICE-GB)***
The *International Corpus of English* is an ongoing project to compile a huge corpus database representing varieties of English worldwide (see Greenbaum 1996 and http://ice-corpora.net/ice/). We tapped the British component of ICE (ICE-GB) (Nelson et al. 2002) – the project's flagship subcorpus – to create a data point representing colloquial, non-dialectal, Standard British English. To this end, we selected the first twelve S1A ("spoken : dialogue : private : direct conversations") texts (S1A-001 through S1A-012) for inclusion in the reference corpus. The conversations transcribed in these files total 25,000 words of running text and were recorded in Middlesex and London in the 1990s.

**The *Santa Barbara Corpus of Spoken American English (CSAE)***
The *Santa Barbara Corpus of Spoken American English* (CSAE) samples colloquial, not heavily dialectal American English from all over the United States (note that the CSAE will furnish the spontaneous spoken section of the forthcoming American component of the *International Corpus of English*). Thus, to create a reference corpus representing colloquial Standard American English, we selected the first five transcripts (SBC001 *Actual Blacksmithing*, SBC002 *Lambada*, SBC003 *Conceptual Pesticides*, SBC004 *Raging Bureaucracy*, and SBC005 *A Book about Death*) from Part I of the corpus (see Du Bois et al. 2000 and www.linguistics.ucsb.edu/research/sbcorpus.html). The interactions, which were recorded in the 1990s, are all casually conversational in nature and were recorded in Hardin, Montana; San Francisco, California; an undisclosed location in Southern California;

Santa Fe, New Mexico; and Santa Barbara, California. The five transcripts total 27,200 words of running text.

## 2.2   Method: corpus-based dialectometry

This section offers a cooking recipe for conducting CORPUS-BASED DIALECTOMETRY (CBDM). We describe the different steps necessary to obtain an appropriate corpus-based dataset – defining a feature catalogue, extracting feature frequencies and creating a frequency matrix, and calculating a distance matrix. We shall also discuss some of the technicalities behind the cartographic projections to geography presented in this book, and add a word on suitable software tools.

### 2.2.1   The empirical foundation: defining the feature catalogue

The first step in CBDM defines the FEATURE CATALOGUE as the empirical basis for the corpus-cum-aggregation endeavor. In keeping true to the spirit of dialectometrical analysis, the goal is to base the analysis on as many features as possible. The study reported in this book is based on a feature catalogue spanning fifty-seven features. These and the feature selection process are discussed in more detail in Chapter 3.

### 2.2.2   Data mining: extracting feature frequencies and creating a frequency matrix

The second step in CBDM consists in extracting feature frequencies and creating a FREQUENCY MATRIX. Once feature frequencies are extracted (once again, see Chapter 3 for details in regard to the present study's feature catalogue), the analyst will normalize text frequencies – for example, to frequency per ten thousand words (*pttw*) – if, as is the case with most relevant corpora, textual coverage of individual dialects varies.

A potential problem is that normalization carries with it the danger of inflating the effect of freak occurrences due to poor sampling, especially if the corpus is not entirely balanced and textual coverage for some measuring point is comparatively thin. Fortunately, this does not seem, by and large, to be a major problem in the current dataset. Correlating aggregate pairwise morphosyntactic distances (see below, Section 2.2.3) with pairwise differences in textual coverage (for instance, Cornwall has a textual coverage of 107,000 words of running text and Devon 97,000 words, so the pairwise differential is about 10,000 words) yields an insignificant ($p = .143$) and exceedingly weak Pearson correlation coefficient of $r = .05$.[3] In other

---

[3] Here as well as in Chapters 5 and 8, we use the Mantel test (Mantel 1967; Heeringa 2004, 74–75) to assess the significance of correlations between distance matrices.

words, in our dataset large sample size differentials do not generally have an effect on this study's morphosyntax measurements, because sample size differentials do not predict inflated dialectal distances. This general statement notwithstanding, we will conclude in Chapter 7 that two measuring points in our dataset, Banffshire and Denbighshire, turn out as outliers probably because of poor sampling.

At this stage, we also recommend a *log*-transformation as a customary method to de-emphasize large frequency differentials and to alleviate the effect of frequency outliers, thus increasing reliability of the frequency matrix. An additional argument for *log*-transformation is that "small differences have a relatively greater perceptual distance and should be given greater weight relative to larger ones" (Shackleton 2007, 43). A *log*-transformation thus amounts to an implicit frequency weighting such that rarer features receive relatively more weight than more frequent features, an idea that also underlies the Salzburg School's GIW (*Gewichteter Identitätswert*) similarity measure (see, e.g., Goebl 1983, 12–17).

Let us illustrate the procedure outlined so far. In FRED, the county of Cornwall has a textual coverage of 12 interviews totalling about 107,000 words of running text. In this material, feature [34] (negative contraction, e.g. *they* won't *do anything*) occurs 326 times, which translates into a normalized text frequency of $326 \times {}_{10,000}/_{107,000} \approx 30$ occurrences per ten thousand words. A *log*-transformation[4] of this frequency yields a value of $log_{10}(30) \approx 1.5$. This is the figure that characterizes this specific measuring point (Cornwall) in regard to feature [34].

The next step calls for creating an $N \times p$ FREQUENCY MATRIX in which the $N$ objects of interest (in our case, dialects) may be arranged in rows and the $p$ features to characterize each of the objects may be arranged in columns, such that each cell in the matrix specifies a particular (normalized and *log*-transformed) feature frequency. Our case study thus yields a $34 \times 57$ frequency matrix: $N = 34$ British English dialects, each characterized by a vector of $p = 57$ text frequencies. We add for the sake of completeness that the $N \times p$ notation used here was pioneered, in the field of dialectology, by Hans Goebl (see, e.g., Goebl 1982, 9).

Either way, at this point the analyst must assess the RELIABILITY of the frequency matrix: Are the features included in the catalogue a heterogeneous, mixed bag (for which an aggregate analysis would be meaningless), or is there a sufficient degree of consistency? Calculating a statistic known as Cronbach's $\alpha$ (see Cronbach 1951; Nunnally 1978) can address this issue. Cronbach's $\alpha$ is, technically speaking, a coefficient measuring the

---

[4] Text frequencies of 0 (for instance, feature [4] [archaic *ye*, as in ye'*d dancing every week*] does not occur in material from Cornwall) were rendered as 0.1, which yields a *log*-transformed value of $log_{10}(0.1) = -1$.

average inter-item (in our case, inter-feature) correlation, and is defined as follows:

$$\alpha = \frac{p}{p-1}\left(1 - \frac{\sum s_i^2}{s_T^2}\right) \tag{2.1}$$

where $p$ is the number of features, $s_i^2$ is the variance of the $i^{\text{th}}$ feature, and $s_T^2$ is the variance obtained when summing up all features. Cronbach's $\alpha$ can take values between negative infinity and 1. An $\alpha$ value of 0 indicates that the features under consideration are not at all related, and a value of 1 means that all the features are perfectly correlated. Higher $\alpha$ values thus indicate a higher reliability of the frequency matrix. By convention – in dialectometry (see Heeringa 2004, 173) and elsewhere (see, e.g., Bland and Altman 1997) – researchers aim for Cronbach's $\alpha$ values of .7 or higher. If a given frequency matrix yields a Cronbach's $\alpha$ value smaller than .7, there is a problem that should be addressed by expanding or altering the composition of the feature catalogue. The present study's full $34 \times 57$ frequency matrix yields a Cronbach's $\alpha$ value of .77, a score that comfortably passes the conventional threshold.[5]

A point that should be emphasized here is that the frequency matrix used in this chapter specifies *absolute* feature frequencies. The alternative is a more compact and more genuinely variationist (in the Labovian sense; see Labov 1966) *relative* frequency matrix that would not encompass, for example, two separate and absolute frequency vectors each for the *of*-genitive (feature [8]) and the *s*-genitive (feature [9]), but only one relative frequency vector, or a variant rate vector, specifying the percentage of the *s*-genitive among all genitive occurrences (*s*-genitives and *of*-genitives) for each sampling point under study. We base the analysis on absolute feature frequencies for three main reasons. First, a relative frequency matrix – by virtue of containing percentages, not frequencies – could not straightforwardly weigh variables according to their absolute frequency of use, which is somewhat reductionist and thus undesirable. Second, while many features in the catalogue (such as *of*- versus *s*-genitives) could be easily organized into Labov-style variables, some features in the catalogue do not have easily definable (or codable) variant forms. Take feature [21] (progressive verb forms): setting this feature up in terms of a variable would be extremely difficult because the alternative to a progressive verb form is strictly speaking a simple verb form, and annotating all simple verb forms in the corpus is not feasible. Third, we actually experimented with both designs and found that

---

[5]   There is an alternative way to calculate the Cronbach's $\alpha$ statistic, which we report here for the sake of completeness. To calculate $\alpha$, we draw not on an $N \times p$ frequency matrix but on an $N \times (N-1)/2 \times p$ table where cases are not absolute frequency observations but frequency *differentials* between all possible dialect location pairings. When calculated in this way, we obtain a marginally acceptable Cronbach's $\alpha$ value of .68.

Map 2.2. Distance measures matter. Clustering morphosyntactic dialect distances (cluster algorithm: Ward; displayed: 2-cluster solution; black: first dialect area, white: second dialect area). Left: Euclidean distance measure. Middle: Manhattan distance measure. Right: Chi-square measure.

absolute frequency matrices tend to yield a clearer and more interpretable geographic signal.

A frequency matrix along the lines described here will serve as direct input to the Principal Component Analysis conducted in Chapter 7.

### 2.2.3   Aggregation: obtaining a distance matrix

Most of the empirical analyses presented in this book (specifically, those in Chapters 4, 5, and 6) operate on the basis of a measure of *aggregate* morphosyntactic distance between the measuring points studied. To obtain this measure, the CBDM analyst converts the $N \times p$ frequency matrix into an $N \times N$ DISTANCE MATRIX. This transformation is an AGGREGATION step, in that the resulting distance matrix abstracts away from individual feature frequencies and specifies pairwise distances between the objects considered, similar to distance tables to be found in, for example, road atlases. How do we calculate aggregate distances between dialects? Standard software packages offer a bewildering array of distance measures, and choice of distance measure definitely matters. To highlight this point, the projections in Map 2.2, which aim to partition Great Britain into two dialect areas, are all based on the present study's $34 \times 57$ frequency matrix. They depict the outcome of three fairly simple cluster analysis runs, each based on a distance matrix calculated using a different distance measure. While it is easy to see that the result – some sort of division between Northern British dialects and Southern British dialects – is not radically dissimilar, the three distance measures do yield divisions that differ in detail, although we reiterate that the input is the exact same frequency matrix.

Against this backdrop, we advocate usage of the well-known and fairly straightforward EUCLIDEAN DISTANCE MEASURE (see, e.g., Aldenderfer and Blashfield 1984, 25) unless there is a good reason not to use it. Drawing on the Pythagorean theorem (see Nishisato 2007, 77), the Euclidean distance measure defines the distance between two objects $a$ and $b$ as the square root of the sum of all $p$ squared frequency differentials:

$$d(a,b) = \sqrt{(a_1 - b_1)^2 + (a_2 - b_2)^2 + \cdots + (a_p - b_p)^2}$$

$$= \sqrt{\sum_{i=1}^{p}(a_i - b_i)^2} \tag{2.2}$$

where $p$ is the number of features, $a_1$ is the frequency of feature 1 in object $a$, $b_1$ is the frequency of feature 1 in object $b$, $a_2$ is the frequency of feature 2 in object $a$, and so on. The Euclidean distance measure is, for one thing, interpretationally convenient – in two-dimensional space, it yields the distance between two points that one would measure with a ruler, which is why the measure is also sometimes referred to as "ruler distance" (Giles 2002, 139). Furthermore, the Euclidean distance measure is theory-neutral in that all features receive the same weight in the distance calculation (this holds true in spite of the fact that the input values may be *log*-transformed; see Section 2.2.2). Having said that, we stress that bigger frequency *differentials* receive proportionally more weight than smaller frequency differentials, which must appear as a desirable property to all those who believe that corpus frequencies mirror some sort of psychological and perceptual reality.

The chart in Figure 2.1 illustrates the aggregation process. In step 1, we start out with a fictional 3 × 2 frequency matrix, which has six cells specifying frequencies of two features in three dialects. In step 2, we calculate three distances: the distance between dialects $a$ and $b$ (which we define as identical to the distance between dialects $b$ and $a$), the distance between dialects $a$ and $c$, and the distance between dialects $b$ and $c$. In step 3, we enter these distances into a 3 × 3 distance matrix, which has $3 \times \frac{3-1}{2} = 3$ unique cells, i.e. dialect/dialect pairings. The other cells are redundant in that the distance between a given dialect and itself is by definition always zero, and the distances in the upper right half of the matrix would mirror the distances in the lower left half of the matrix.

*2.2.4   Cartographic projections to geography*

CBDM datasets can be analyzed in a myriad ways. To analyze the data against the backdrop of the set of research questions outlined in Chapter 1, the present study will draw on a number of statistical analysis methods:

| | | text frequencies feature 1 | text frequencies feature 2 |
|---|---|---|---|
| 1  the frequency matrix | dialect *a* | 11 | 8 |
| | dialect *b* | 5 | 2 |
| | dialect *c* | 1 | 7 |

$$\downarrow$$

2  aggregation via the Euclidean distance measure

$$d\,(a,b) = \sqrt{(11-5)^2 + (8-2)^2} = 8.5$$

$$d\,(a,c) = \sqrt{(11-1)^2 + (8-7)^2} = 10.0$$

$$d\,(b,c) = \sqrt{(5-1)^2 + (2-7)^2} = 6.4$$

$$\downarrow$$

3  the distance matrix

| | dialect *a* | dialect *b* | dialect *c* |
|---|---|---|---|
| dialect *a* | | | |
| dialect *b* | 8.5 | | |
| dialect *c* | 10.0 | 6.4 | |

Figure 2.1. Converting a fictional $3 \times 2$ frequency matrix into a $3 \times 3$ distance matrix utilizing Euclidean distance as an aggregation measure.

descriptive statistics, statistical graphics, correlation tests, exploratory techniques (such as Multidimensional Scaling, Cluster Analysis, and Principal Component Analysis), and regression analysis.

Needless to say, we will also utilize a range of cartographic mapping techniques to project aggregate linguistic relationships to geography. Particular techniques will be introduced in more detail in those chapters where they are actually applied. Here, we would like to dwell on general aspects of dialect cartography.

The plethora of map types utilized in this book (specifically: similarity maps, skewness maps, kernel maps, continuum maps, cluster maps, and component score maps) rely on a partition of map space that gives each sampling site a colorable polygon. Technically, this is achieved by utilizing customary Voronoi tesselation (Voronoi 1907; Heeringa 2004, 161–162) to assign each sampling point on the map a convex polygon such that each point within the polygon is closer to the generating sampling point than to any other dialect site, a method that is more verbosely known as the Haag/Thiessen/Delaunay–Voronoi principle (see Goebl 2005, 509). To illustrate, the left projection in Map 2.3 exhaustively tessellates map space

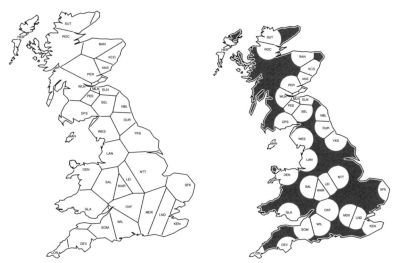

Map 2.3. A Voronoi tesselation of Great Britain's map space. Left: exhaustive tesselation. Right: polygons have a radius of 50km or less.

in Great Britain into Voronoi polygons. A tesselation such as this is most sensible when areal coverage of the linguistic datasource is very fine-grained (as is usually the case in dialect atlases). However, subject to FRED's limits we shall cover Great Britain with $N = 34$ sampling points, which is why we will often prefer to limit the radius of the Voronoi polygons to approximately 50km in order to do visual justice to the areal coverage of the dialect corpus used. The resulting non-exhaustive tesselation is shown in the right projection in Map 2.3, which will serve as the basis for many of the colorful cartographic projections to geography presented in this book. Blank – in this specific case, grey – areas in this map depict linguistic landscapes not covered by the dialect corpus.

### 2.2.5   Software tools

Many of the cartographic projections and most of the non-trivial statistical analyses (such as Multidimensional Scaling and Cluster Analysis) presented in this book were created and conducted using the Groningen linguist Peter Kleiweg's *RuG/L04* dialectometry software package (available online at www.let.rug.nl/~kleiweg/L04/). L04 maps typically come with map labels as indicated in the first column of Table 2.1 (p. 19). When map space is Voronoi-tesselated, L04 maps reported in this book draw on a non-exhaustive tesselation (see the right map in Map 2.3).

The beam maps, honeycomb maps, similarity maps, skewness maps, and kernel maps discussed in Chapter 4 were created using the *Visual DialectoMetry* (VDM) package, a free software developed in Salzburg (Haimerl 2006). VDM maps exhaustively tesselate map space (see the left map in Map 2.3) and typically use numbers – as indicated in the second column in Table 2.1 – instead of map labels to identify dialect sites. Note further that whereas the Groningen School of Dialectometry operates, much as this book does in general, with distance matrices as the primary input to dialectometrical analysis, the Salzburg School of Dialectometry draws on *similarity* matrices. This difference is methodologically and statistically trivial but necessitates the following transformation:

$$ES(a, b) = 100 - 10 \times d(a, b) \qquad (2.3)$$

where *ES* is the Euclidean similarity between two dialects $a$ and $b$, and $d$ is the Euclidean distance (calculated as shown in Section 2.2.3) between two dialects $a$ and $b$; to illustrate: a Euclidean distance of 5 translates into an *ES* value of $100 - 10 \times 5 = 50$. All VDM maps, map legends, and accompanying diagrams in the maps, are based on *ES* values.

# 3      The feature catalogue

This chapter details the 57-feature catalogue that serves as the basis for the study's analysis of morphosyntax aggregates. We sketch the feature selection criteria (Section 3.2) and the technicalities of the extraction process (Section 3.3). We also present concise literature reviews for each of the features considered (Section 3.4). Section 3.5 is a chapter summary that discusses some of the frequency variability thus uncovered against the backdrop of the literature.

## 3.1    The feature catalogue: an overview

What follows is a list of features in the catalogue, annotated with linguistic examples. The features fall into eleven major domains of English morphosyntax: pronouns and determiners, the noun phrase, primary verbs, tense and aspect, modality, verb morphology, negation, agreement, relativization, complementation, and word order and discourse phenomena.

A.   Pronouns and determiners

     [1]    non-standard reflexives (e.g. *they didn't go* theirself)
     [2]    standard reflexives (e.g. *they didn't go* themselves)
     [3]    archaic *thee/thou/thy* (e.g. *I tell* thee *a bit more*)
     [4]    archaic *ye* (e.g. ye*'d dancing every week*)
     [5]    *us* (e.g. us *couldn't get back, there was no train*)
     [6]    *them* (e.g. *I wonder if they'd do any of* them things *today*)

B.   The noun phrase

     [7]    synthetic adjective comparison (e.g. *he was always* keener *on farming*)
     [8]    the *of*-genitive (e.g. *the presence* of *my father*)
     [9]    the *s*-genitive (e.g. *my father's presence*)
     [10]   preposition stranding (e.g. *the very house* which *it was* in)
     [11]   cardinal number + *years* (e.g. *I was there about* three years)
     [12]   cardinal number + *year-Ø* (e.g. *she were* three year old)

C.  Primary verbs

[13]  the primary verb TO DO (e.g. *why* did *you not wait?*)
[14]  the primary verb TO BE (e.g. *I* was *took straight into this pitting job*)
[15]  the primary verb TO HAVE (e.g. *we thought somebody* had *brought them*)
[16]  marking of possession – HAVE GOT (e.g. *I* have got *the photographs*)

D.  Tense and aspect

[17]  the future marker BE GOING TO (e.g. *I*'m going to *let you into a secret*)
[18]  the future markers WILL/SHALL (e.g. *I* will *let you into a secret*)
[19]  WOULD as marker of habitual past (e.g. *he* would *go around killing pigs*)
[20]  *used to* as marker of habitual past (e.g. *he* used to *go around killing pigs*)
[21]  progressive verb forms (e.g. *the rest* are going *to Portree School*)
[22]  the present perfect with auxiliary BE (e.g. *I*'m come *down to pay the rent*)
[23]  the present perfect with auxiliary HAVE (e.g. *they*'ve killed *the skipper*)

E.  Modality

[24]  marking of epistemic and deontic modality: MUST (e.g. *I* must *pick up the book*)
[25]  marking of epistemic and deontic modality: HAVE TO (e.g. *I* have to *pick up the book*)
[26]  marking of epistemic and deontic modality: GOT TO (e.g. *I* gotta *pick up the book*)

F.  Verb morphology

[27]  *a*-prefixing on *-ing* forms (e.g. *he was* a-waiting)
[28]  non-standard weak past tense and past participle forms (e.g. *they* knowed *all about these things*)
[29]  non-standard past tense *done* (e.g. *you came home and* done *the fishing*)
[30]  non-standard past tense *come* (e.g. *he* come *down the road one day*)

G.  Negation

[31]  the negative suffix *-nae* (e.g. *I* cannae *do it*)
[32]  the negator *ain't* (e.g. *people* ain't *got no money*)
[33]  multiple negation (e.g. *don't you make* no *damn mistake*)

[34]   negative contraction (e.g. *they* won't *do anything*)

[35]   auxiliary contraction (e.g. *they*'ll not *do anything*)

[36]   *never* as past tense negator (e.g. *and they* never *moved no more*)

[37]   WASN'T (e.g. *they* wasn't *hungry*)

[38]   WEREN'T (e.g. *they* weren't *hungry*)

H.   Agreement

[39]   non-standard verbal -*s* (e.g. *so* I says, *What have you to do?*)

[40]   *don't* with 3rd person singular subjects (e.g. *if this man* don't *come up to it*)

[41]   standard *doesn't* with 3rd person singular subjects (e.g. *if this man* doesn't *come up to it*)

[42]   existential/presentational *there is/was* with plural subjects (e.g. there was children *involved*)

[43]   absence of auxiliary BE in progressive constructions (e.g. *I said, How* Ø *you doing?*)

[44]   non-standard WAS (e.g. *three of them* was *killed*)

[45]   non-standard WERE (e.g. *he* were *a young lad*)

I.   Relativization

[46]   *wh*-relativization (e.g. *the man* who *read the book*)

[47]   the relative particle *what* (e.g. *the man* what *read the book*)

[48]   the relative particle *that* (e.g. *the man* that *read the book*)

J.   Complementation

[49]   *as what* or *than what* in comparative clauses (e.g. *we done no more* than what *other kids used to do*)

[50]   unsplit *for to* (e.g. *it was ready* for to *go away with the order*)

[51]   infinitival complementation after BEGIN, START, CONTINUE, HATE, and LOVE (e.g. *I* began to take *an interest*)

[52]   gerundial complementation after BEGIN, START, CONTINUE, HATE, and LOVE (e.g. *I* began taking *an interest*)

[53]   zero complementation after THINK, SAY, and KNOW (e.g. *they just thought [Ø it isn't for girls]*)

[54]   *that* complementation after THINK, SAY, and KNOW (e.g. *they just thought [that it isn't for girls]*)

K.   Word order and discourse phenomena

[55]   lack of inversion and/or of auxiliaries in *wh*-questions and in main clause *yes/no*-questions (e.g. *where* Ø *you put the shovel?*)

[56]   the prepositional dative after the verb GIVE (e.g. *she gave [a job] [to my brother]*)

[57]   double object structures after the verb GIVE (e.g. *she gave [my brother] [a job]*)

Appendix A provides some instructive summary statistics elucidating the variability captured by the feature catalogue.

## 3.2   Feature selection

In keeping true to the spirit of dialectometrical analysis, the overarching aim was to include all available data (Nerbonne forthcoming b; see also Goebl 1982, 1984). This means that we sought to include in the catalogue as many linguistic features as possible, an endeavor that resulted in the above list of $p = 57$ features. Would our results be substantially different had we chosen fifty-seven different features? Naturally, this question is difficult to answer and ultimately an empirical one, but recall (see Section 2.2.2) that our frequency portfolio yields a Cronbach's $\alpha$ value of .77, which indicates sufficient consistency and reliability; the odds are that the present study's results can be generalized to other feature portfolios. Having said that, we concede right at the outset that a certain degree of subjectivity in feature selection is inevitable – but we maintain that this problem is no worse in corpus-based dialectometry than in atlas-based dialectometry (see our discussion in Section 8.2).

Where do the fifty-seven features in our feature catalogue come from? Essentially, we canvassed the *dialectological* literature (e.g. Ihalainen 1976; Klemola 1996; Britain 2007, whence feature [13]: the primary verb TO DO), the *variationist* literature (e.g. Tagliamonte 2003, whence feature [16]: marking of possession – HAVE GOT), and the *corpus-linguistic* literature (e.g. Mair 2004, whence feature [17]: the future marker BE GOING TO) to identify suitable phenomena. Particular attention was paid to comparative sources, such as the comparative morphosyntax survey reported in Kortmann and Szmrecsanyi (2004) (e.g. feature [28]: non-standard weak verb forms) and the battery of morphosyntactic features covered in the SED (see Orton et al. 1978; Viereck et al. 1991) (e.g. feature [12]: cardinal number + *year*-Ø).

We emphasize that for a feature to be included in the catalogue, it did not matter if the feature had previously been reported geographically distributed or not. For instance, feature [31] (the negative suffix -*nae*) (see Section 3.4.7) has a well-known regional distribution, but feature [10] (preposition stranding) has not been reported as a regionalism (and indeed, the feature does not have a regional distribution in FRED either). The idea behind keeping such features in the catalogue nonetheless is that, first, geographically distributed or not, such features are part of the linguistic reality and should thus be considered. Second, features that are individually not regionally distributed may still gang up and help to create an aggregate regional pattern.

Also note that the catalogue contains fairly categorical and thus somewhat salient non-standard features, which tend to be either present or absent – feature [31] (the negative suffix -*nae*) is again a good example – but also features whose variation is more statistical in nature, and thus arguably less salient. Features [8] and [9] on gradient genitive variation are good examples of the latter feature type.

In a similar vein, the features included in the catalogue also differ in terms of their "standardness" – feature [2] (standard reflexives) (cf. Section 3.4.1), for instance, is examined with respect to the text frequency of perfect standard forms, while feature [28] (non-standard weak verb forms) is not really acceptable in Standard English. The present study's take on the issue of standardness, then, is that an adequate and comprehensive description of the morphosyntax of British English dialects can and should also include features that happen to be popular in both Standard English and (some) British English dialects; the mere fact that some feature is used in the standard variety was not considered a knock-out criterion for inclusion in the feature catalogue. The rationale is the well-known fact that in interactional discourse, dialect speakers do tend to switch back and forth (to varying extents, depending on the speech of other interactional parties, and so on) between dialect forms and standard variants. So including standard phenomena in the feature catalogue is likely to yield a more realistic picture.

In short, the feature catalogue seeks to span as many features as possible, regardless of their geographic distribution, the scope of their variability, and their standardness. The rationale is that non-geographic or random variability will cancel out in the aggregate view, and that a "large number of variables, even though they will contain a great deal of variation irrelevant to questions of geographic or social conditioning, will nonetheless provide the most accurate picture of the relations among the varieties examined" (Nerbonne 2006, 464; see also Goebl and Schiltz 1997, 13). This is why for most of this study, we will study the 57-feature catalogue in aggregate, although we note here that Chapter 7 is dedicated to revisiting and addressing some of the aforesaid heterogeneity in the feature catalogue.

Yet despite this study's the-more-the-merrier spirit, two criteria had to be met for a candidate feature to be included in the catalogue, one having to do with a feature's frequency (an empirical issue), and the other relating to the ease with which the feature can be extracted from corpus data (a feasibility issue). We estimate that with a dialect corpus ten times as big as FRED and given unlimited manual coding resources, the catalogue in its current design (which – quite philologically – centers on features, and not, e.g., on $n$-grams) could have been expanded to twice as many features.

### 3.2.1   Frequency

The number of observations the corpus analyst makes is directly proportional to the reliability and generalizability of the results he or she will generate. In Chapter 1 we thus alerted the reader in passing that quantitative corpus-based approaches are ill suited to analyze rare phenomena

(Penke and Rosenbach 2004, 489; Haspelmath 2009, 157–158) and, in particular, to deal with null observations. To ensure a minimum statistical robustness of the text frequencies that fed into the aggregate analysis, a candidate feature for inclusion in the feature catalogue had to be relatively frequent. Specifically, a feature had to have a raw frequency of at least 100 hits in FRED, which corresponds to a normalized frequency of .4 *pttw*. This (admittedly somewhat arbitrary) criterion ruled out a number of interesting and much-discussed but textually demonstrably infrequent phenomena which include the following:

- *mun* for *must* (e.g. Viereck et al. 1991, map S21 [CLAE1]), which attests 5 hits in FRED;
- forms such as *yun't*, *bain't*, or *ben't* for *(she) isn't* (e.g. Orton et al. 1978, map M10 [LAE]), which have a combined raw frequency of ten hits in FRED;
- *was sat* or *was stood* with progressive meaning (e.g. Kortmann and Szmrecsanyi 2004, feature [32]) (no more than twenty hits in FRED);
- resumptive relative pronouns (e.g. Kortmann and Szmrecsanyi 2004, feature [67]), which attest only a few dozen times in FRED;
- double modals (e.g. Brown 1991), of which there are not more than a handful of certain cases in FRED;
- so-called "Bybee verbs," i.e. verbs with a mid-central vowel in the past tense, such as *spin-spun* (Anderwald 2009) (ninety-three hits in FRED);
- the relativizers *at* and *as* (see Herrmann 2003);
- *need* and *dare* with bare infinitives (see Duffley 1994).

Inclusion of such features would have added frequency vectors with many null observations in them. For instance, the "Bybee verbs" feature yields a vector with twenty-seven null frequencies and only seven non-null frequencies. While processing such vectors is technically not a problem, it is unclear (to say the least) whether those null cells really boil down to evidence of absence – the interpretation that the statistical analysis would adopt – or absence of evidence due to insufficient corpus size. Dialect *a* may not attest Bybee verbs because this particular dialect does not have Bybee verbs, but we may not find Bybee verbs in dialect *b* simply because we do not have enough textual material. To avoid this vexed issue, we opted to err on the conservative side and excluded infrequent phenomena, although we acknowledge explicitly that low-frequency features, despite their absence in speech corpora, may be structurally interesting and perceptually in fact salient (see Glaser forthcoming for a discussion).

### 3.2.2    *Feasibility*

A candidate feature also had to be extractable – subject to a reasonable input of labor resources – by a human coder. This can turn out to be a

daunting task given that the version of FRED used here is neither POS annotated nor syntax parsed. The feasibility criterion thus knocked out a number
of extremely hard-to-retrieve null phenomena (such as zero relativization;
see Herrmann 2003), which is why features where semantics plays a crucial
role (such as gendered pronouns; see Wagner 2004), or features where heavy
contextual disambiguation is necessary (such as the Northern Subject Rule;
Pietsch 2005) are not considered.

## 3.3   Feature extraction

This section describes, in general terms, how the features were extracted
from the primary datasource (FRED) as well as from the two smaller reference corpora (the CSAE and ICE-GB). As far as the technicalities of
the extraction process are concerned, the items in the feature catalogue fall
into two broad groups: features that could be extracted fully automatically,
as opposed to features which required manual coding prior to the actual
extraction procedure.

### 3.3.1   Fully automatic extraction

Thirty-one features are sufficiently "surfacy" to be extractable without
human intervention. For instance, feature [32] (*ain't*) can be reliably identified by computer software. In such cases, a retrieval script written in
the programming language *Perl* identified occurrences of the target phenomenon in the dataset and established the relevant text frequencies per
FRED county.

### 3.3.2   Semi-automatic extraction

Twenty-six features in the catalogue required manual disambiguation prior
to the actual extraction procedure, and in all the dataset as a whole is based
on well over 85,000 manual coding decisions. For instance, feature [48] (the
relative particle *that*) (see Section 3.4.9) cannot be automatically extracted
by software, since untagged, non-parsed corpus material as in FRED does
not permit reliable automatic disambiguation between relativizer *that* and
other uses of *that* (such as demonstrative *that* or complementizer *that*). In
cases like this, we typically relied, first, on screening scripts written in *Perl*
to considerably narrow down the number of phenomena which had to be
inspected manually. For example, in the case of relativizer *that*, a screening
script discarded the sequence *when that*, in which *that* can never function
as a relativizer. After the pre-screening process, the remaining corpus hits
were inspected manually and annotated if they constituted instantiations of
the target phenomenon. In a last step, retrieval scripts relied on the manual

annotation to automatically establish the relevant text frequencies per FRED county and location.

Szmrecsanyi (2010) discusses in detail the technicalities behind the coding and extraction process on a feature-by-feature basis, and provides the coding protocols underpinning it (the document also encompasses cartographic projections of feature frequency distributions to geography). We exemplify the procedure by reporting how feature [21] (the progressive) was extracted (Szmrecsanyi 2010, 23–25; example numbering the present study's):

A screening script flagged all *-ing* forms in the dataset, ignoring

- all obviously non-verbal *-ing* forms (e.g. *something*, *shilling*, *nothing*, and some 14 other frequent non-verbal forms);
- *-ing* forms that could not possibly be part of a progressive construction (e.g. tokens preceded by *the* and *a*, among some 24 other knock-out collocates).

This procedure yielded more than 4,500 tokens in the dataset where the *-ing* ending was potentially a progressive morpheme. These tokens were inspected manually/qualitatively and – following the criteria detailed in Hundt (2004, 56) – tagged if the *-ing* ending indeed coded a progressive form (be it a present progressive [as in (1a)], a past progressive [as in (1b)], a present perfect progressive [as in (1c)], a past perfect progressive [as in (1d)], or a progressive infinitive [as in (1e)]):

(1)    a.    . . . the rest *are going* to Portree School now . . . [HEB001]
       b.    . . . and my father *was leaving* the farm he was on . . . [ANS001]
       c.    Yes, you would *have been looking* down on, on Dherue [SUT001]
       d.    War *had been going* on for at least two or three years . . . [YKS010]
       e.    He likes to *be joking*, Desmond [HEB001]

Tokens were not tagged if the *-ing* ending was indicative of, e.g., a gerund, as in (2a), a form of BE GOING TO used to express futurity, as in (2b), a construction with an adjectival participle, as in (2c), or an appositional participle, as in (2d):

(2)    a.    we did no *trawling* then . . . [KEN008]
       b.    They wouldn't go, not to, not if they *were going to* do any damage [KEN001]
       c.    That *is interesting* [ELN009]
       d.    I used to go in the passing shop, *inspecting* shop with Joe Grant . . . [WIL007]

Finally, a retrieval script identified and registered all *-ing* forms where the *-ing* suffix marked progressive aspect, as identified by the manual inspection procedure.

Note that as a rule, the manual coding process usually involved the full FRED dataset. However, in the case of nine features ([19], [20], [21], [23], [44], [45], [46], [47], and [48]) with fairly high text frequencies, we economized by manually inspecting not the full dataset, but an abridged version spanning 510,000 words of running text. It contains the same texts (interviews) as the full FRED dataset, the difference being that in case of texts longer than 1,500 words of running text, only the first 1,500 words were sampled into the abridged dataset (all other texts are represented in full length). For example, feature [19] (WOULD as a marker of habitual past) is known to be a rather frequent feature (especially in oral history interviews), yet its identification also involves a good deal of manual coding. Thus, we manually inspected FRED_{abridged}, where the phenomenon has 2,119 occurrences, which corresponds to a mean normalized text frequency of 42 *pttw* across FRED (see Table A.1, Appendix A, p. 167).

## 3.4   The feature catalogue in detail

This section discusses the features in the catalogue in more detail. We present concise literature reviews and additionally report two measures to assess the geographic distribution of the feature:

A FREQUENCY–DISTANCE CORRELATION COEFFICIENT   (henceforth: FDCC), which evaluates the extent to which text frequency differentials are proportional to geographic distance between measuring points. To calculate the FDCC statistic, the analyst applies the Euclidean distance measure (see Section 2.2.3) to a frequency matrix that encompasses one and only one frequency vector (that is to say, frequencies of the feature in question). This yields a single-feature-based distance matrix that specifies pairwise distances that are equivalent to simple frequency differentials between the measuring points. The analyst next calculates the Pearson product-moment correlation coefficient between this single-feature-based distance matrix and a distance matrix specifying geographic as-the-crow-flies distances. A significant positive correlation coefficient indicates that the feature in question has a continuum-like relationship with geography.

GLOBAL SPATIAL AUTOCORRELATION (henceforth: *Moran's I*), which is a diagnostic of the overall clustering of the data (see Cliff and Ord 1973 and Grieve 2009, 159–161 for the technicalities). *Moran's I*, which is widely used in Geographic Information Science but not in dialectology, has a lower ceiling of −1 and an upper ceiling of +1; a significant positive *Moran's I* value indicates that neighboring measuring points tend to have similarly high or low frequencies of the feature in question, which points to clustering effects. We used a binary weighting function which only considers the scores of features for measuring points within 250 km of each other.

Whenever a feature turns out to be geographically distributed in a significant way according to a fairly strict Bonferroni-corrected (see Abdi 2007) $\alpha$ level of $p = 0.05/57 \approx .001$ (either in terms of the FDCC statistic, or in terms of the *Moran's I* statistic, or in terms of both), we shall additionally present:

- a boxplot that depicts frequency variability by a-priori dialect area (roughly following Trudgill's dialect division on pronunciational grounds [Trudgill 1990, map 9]), on the basis of frequency variance across the $N = 156$ locations sampled in the corpus;
- a projection to geography that depicts relative text frequency variability.

(Notice here that Szmrecsanyi 2010 has boxplots and projections to geography for *all* of the features listed below.) A few technical comments are necessary here, though. In the boxplots, the boxes depict the interquartile frequency range comprising the middle 50 percent of all frequency observations, with the thick line in the boxes indicating the median. The whiskers to the left and right of the boxes (where applicable) extend to data points that score no more than 1.5 times the interquartile range. As for the projections to geography, the observable frequency range was divided into ten percentile groups such that each group contained roughly the same number of observations. Each county's 10-tile rank was then mapped on the black–white color continuum, assigning a perfect deep black hue to the highest 10-tile group, a perfect white hue to the lowest 10-tile group, and gradient gray hues to the 10-tile bins in between. Subsequently, the county polygons in a Voronoi-tesselated map (see Section 2.2.4) were shaded accordingly. Thus in the maps, the blacker the tone, the relatively higher the text frequency whereas the whiter the tone the relatively lower the text frequency.

### 3.4.1   *Pronouns and determiners*

*Reflexive pronouns: feature [1] (non-standard reflexives) and feature [2] (standard reflexives)*
The formation of reflexive pronouns in Standard English is irregular in that some reflexive pronouns are based on possessive determiners (e.g. *yourself*) while others are based on object pronouns (e.g. *himself*). Many dialects have a more regular system (e.g. Trudgill 1999; Stenström et al. 2002; Britain 2007) or exhibit variation; see (3).

(3)   a.   they make *theirselves* fast to a stone or shell or that. (standard reflexive) [SFK030]
      b.   they didn't go *theirself*, but they made sure you went … (non-standard reflexive) [LAN003]

According to Kortmann (2004b, 1097), "regularized reflexives paradigms … are attested everywhere in the British Isles except for WelE as well as Orkney

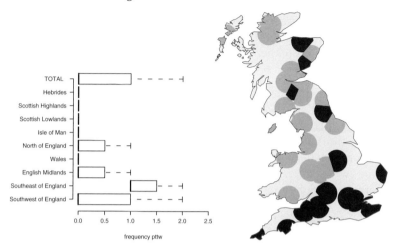

Map 3.1. Feature [1] (non-standard reflexives). Left: Boxplot (variance by dialect area). Right: Projection of frequencies to
geography (blacker shades indicate higher frequencies).

and Shetland," and in the survey in Kortmann and Szmrecsanyi (2004,
1163–1164) the phenomenon is among the top twenty non-standard features in the British Isles. Evidence from the SED (Orton et al. 1978, map
M80 [LAE]) likewise suggests that some regularized reflexives (i.e. *hisself*,
*hissell*, *hissen*) are pervasive in English English dialects. For an in-depth analysis of pronouns in British English dialects based on FRED, see Hernández
(2010).

   In FRED, feature [1] (non-standard reflexives) has a significant geographic distribution according to the FDCC statistic ($r = .257$, $p < .000$);
*Moran's I* yields a marginally significant positive value ($I = .115$, $p = .013$).
Non-standard reflexives are particularly frequent in the South of England
(see Map 3.1). Feature [2] (standard reflexives) does not have a significant
geographic distribution in FRED.

*2nd person singular pronouns: feature [3] (archaic* thee/thou/*and* thy*) and*
*feature [4] (archaic* ye*)*
There is an extensive literature on historical variation between THOU/THEE
and YE/YOU as well as between derived possessive determiners (for
an overview, see Busse 2002). What is important in the context of the
present study is that these archaic pronouns and determiners are still
in existence – if rare – in some traditional British English dialects (see
Sanderson and Widdowson 1985, 35; Beal 2004, 118; Penhallurick 2004a,

105; Johnston 2007, 118) – as "echoes of earlier ... grammar," as Kortmann and Upton (2004, 28) succinctly put it. Consider (4) and (5):

(4)    a.    I asked, does *thou* wash *thy* hands after *thou* use that stuff? [SAL008]
       b.    I tell *thee* a bit more yet [SOM028]

(5)    aye, *ye*'d dancing every week at that time [ANS001]

The SED evidence (cf. Orton et al. 1978, map M67 [LAE]) suggests that *thee* and *thou* are particularly widespread in the Southwest and North of England, while *ye* occurs in some Northern English counties. Notice that the form *thine* only attests one occurrence in FRED, and was thus not considered.

Feature [3] does not have a significant geographic distribution in FRED. Feature [4] has a marginally significant geographic distribution in FRED according to the *Moran's I* statistic ($I = .100$, $p = .020$) such that archaic *ye* tends to be particularly frequent in Scotland.

*1st person plural pronouns and determiners: feature [5] (*us*)*
According to the survey in Kortmann and Szmrecsanyi (2004), non-standard usage of *us* (see (6)) is attested for Scots (see also Johnston 2007, 118), dialects in the North of England, and the English Southwest/Southeast.

(6)    *Us* couldn't get back, there was no train [DEV007]

The SED record suggests that *us* as a subject pronoun replacing standard *me* (Orton et al. 1978, map M74 [LAE]) is widespread in English English dialects except in some areas in the Southwest; *us* as a possessive determiner replacing standard *our* (Orton et al. 1978, map M75 [LAE]) appears to be considerably rarer. Note also that the feature is part of a more general phenomenon known as "pronoun exchange," which according to Ihalainen (1994, 231) is "interesting in that it is one of the few features that divide the country up in an east-west direction." On a technical note, feature [5] measures overall text frequencies of *us*, which includes standard *and* non-standard usages. The rationale is that dialects exhibiting non-standard *us* will tend to exhibit higher overall text frequencies of *us*, all other things being equal.

Feature [5] does not have a significant geographic distribution in FRED.

*Demonstrative determiners: feature [6] (*them*)*
The survey in Kortmann and Szmrecsanyi (2004) indicates that usage of *them* instead of demonstrative *those*, as in (7), is attested in all surveyed dialects in the British Isles except Orkney/Shetland. Likewise, Britain (2010) lists demonstrative *them* as belonging to a "common core" of

non-regional non-standard forms (see also Cheshire 1982; Edwards 1993; Hughes and Trudgill 1996).

(7)    I wonder if they'd do any of *them things* today? [SAL017]

According to the SED as well, *them* for *those* is pervasive in English English dialects, with the possible exception of dialects spoken in the Southwest and in the eastern Midlands (Orton et al. 1978, map M83 [LAE]). On a technical note, feature [6] measures overall text frequencies of *them*, which includes standard *and* non-standard usages. The rationale is that dialects exhibiting non-standard *them* will tend to exhibit higher overall text frequencies of *them*, all other things being equal.

Feature [6] does not have a significant geographic distribution in FRED.


*3.4.2   The noun phrase*

*Synthetic adjective comparison: feature [7]*
This feature is about occurrences of synthetic adjective comparison that are, in principle, interchangeable with analytic adjective comparison.[1] Consider (8):

(8)    He was always *keener* on farming than I was. (∼ he was always *more keen*) [CON008]

The alternation between synthetic comparison and analytic comparison with *more* is comparatively well researched (see Szmrecsanyi 2006, 63–67 for a literature review). In summary, *more*-comparison is an innovation not attested prior to the thirteenth century (see Mitchell 1985, 84-85). By the beginning of the sixteenth century, though, it was about as frequent as it is today (Pound 1901); Kytö and Romaine (1997) detail the rivalry between the two strategies after Late Modern English. What is important in the context of the present study is that the historical rivalry between the two marking strategies may have a synchronic echo in geographic variability in English dialects.

Feature [7] has a marginally significant geographic distribution in FRED according to the FDCC statistic ($r = .117$, $p = .002$) such that synthetic adjective comparison tends to be somewhat more popular in the Southwest of England, in South Wales, and in pockets in the North of England and in Scotland.

---

[1] Note that due to comparatively low token frequencies, analytic adjective comparison is not part of the feature catalogue.

*Genitives: feature [8] (the* of-*genitive) and feature [9] (the* s-*genitive)*
This feature pair is concerned with interchangeable genitives, as in (9):

(9)  a.  somehow the presence *of* my father seems to make me a bit
         more embarrassed. (the *of*-genitive; ~ my father*'s* presence)
         [HEB009]
     b.  I kept mi mother*'s* house clean for twenty five year ... (the
         *s*-genitive; ~ the house *of* mi mother) [DUR003]

Of the two genitives in English, the *of*-genitive is the incoming form,
which appeared during the ninth century. During the wholesale reorganization of the Old English case system, the *of*-genitive expanded substantially
(Jucker 1993, 121). Intriguingly, the *s*-genitive recovered during the Modern English period and is argued to be spreading right now (e.g. Potter
1969, 105–106; Dahl 1971, 141; Raab-Fischer 1995; Rosenbach 2003, 394–
395; Hinrichs and Szmrecsanyi 2007). Szmrecsanyi (2006, 98) submits
that different dialect areas in Britain exhibit significantly different relative
frequencies of each genitive type. Note also that while this study categorizes genitive variation as a noun phrase phenomenon, the alternation
is at the same time positional-syntactic in nature, as the analyses in (10)
illustrate.

(10)  a.
      b.

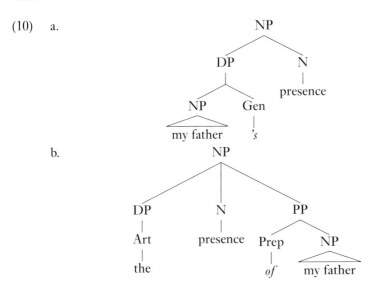

Feature [8] does not have a significant geographic distribution in
FRED. Feature [9] has a significant ($I = .115$, $p = .001$) geographic distribution according to the *Moran's I* statistic: the *s*-genitive is particularly

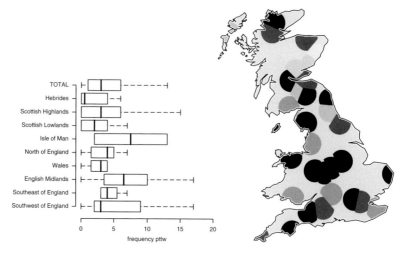

Map 3.2.  Feature [9] (the *s*-genitive). Left: Boxplot (variance by dialect
area). Right: Projection of frequencies to geography (blacker
shades indicate higher frequencies).

frequent in the English Midlands, in North Wales, and on the Isle of Man
(see Map 3.2).

*Preposition stranding: feature [10]*
Since Late Middle English, preposition stranding with *wh*-relatives, as in *the
house which I looked at* has been in existence as a syntactic word-order alternative (consider the syntactic analysis in (11)) to the so-called pied piping
construction (see Ross 1986, 121).

(11)   a.

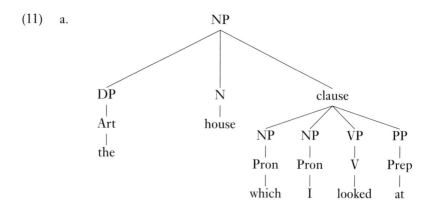

b.

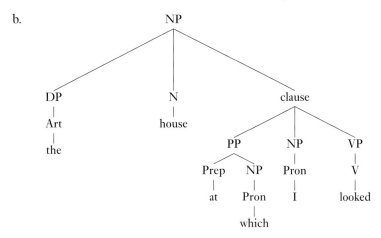

While it is clear that the frequency of preposition stranding is sensitive, at least to some extent, to text type (see Johansson and Geisler 1998; Biber et al. 1999, 106; Bergh and Seppänen 2000, 310), much less is known about dialectal differences. Shorrocks (1992, 308) notes that pied piping is virtually absent in his Lancashire data, and Herrmann (2003, 124) similarly reports that "while pied piping is typical of (written) Standard English, dialects obviously prefer preposition stranding." As a matter of fact, however, while preposition stranding is, of course, attested in FRED (consider (12) for some representative examples), with a mean frequency of 3.5 hits *pttw* it is relatively infrequent.

(12)  a.  my father was leaving the farm [he was *on*] [ANS001]
      b.  This is [what you sat *on*] [ANS001]
      c.  he dare not ask them [where the money went *to*] [GLA001]

Feature [10] has a marginally significant geographic distribution in FRED according to the *Moran's I* statistic ($I = .084$, $p = .038$): preposition stranding tends to be particularly frequent in Scotland and in Northern England.

*Plural marking: feature [11] (cardinal number + years) and feature [12] (cardinal number + year-Ø)*
Plural marking after measure nouns is optional in many Scottish (see Johnston 2007, 118) and English (see Britain 2007, 95) varieties of English. In fact, according to the morphosyntax survey in Kortmann and Szmrecsanyi (2004), absence of plural marking after measure nouns is attested in all surveyed British English dialects. Consider (13):

(13)  a.  I was there about *three years* I think. (explicit plural marker present) [WES014]

      b.    She were *three year* old when I got home. (explicit plural marker absent) [NTT004]

We are interested here in zero or explicit plural marking on the noun *year*, as in *two years ago* vs. *two year ago*). SED-based evidence (see Viereck et al. 1991, map M3 [CLAE1]) suggests that the zero option occurs all over England; the explicit option is somewhat restricted to the English Midlands and to the Southeast of England.

    Features [11] and [12] do not have a significant geographic distribution in FRED.


### 3.4.3   Primary verbs

*Primary verbs: feature [13] (*TO DO*), feature [14] (*TO BE*), and feature [15] (*TO HAVE*)*

Of the three primary verbs (i.e. verbs that can serve both as lexical and as auxiliary verbs) in English, TO DO is the most versatile one, especially as a tense and aspect marker (see Kortmann 2004a). In British English dialects, it occurs as a marker of habituality, and as a tense and aspect marker (see Sanderson and Widdowson 1985, 35; Kortmann and Szmrecsanyi 2004, survey features 23 and 27). Most notable is its use as an unstressed periphrastic tense carrier, widely reported for dialects in the Southwest of England, especially Somerset (see, e.g., Ellis 1889; Ihalainen 1976, 1994; Klemola 1996; Jones and Tagliamonte 2004), and for Welsh English (Penhallurick 2007, 166). Global text frequencies of TO BE – which likewise occurs as a habitual marker in some dialects, for instance in Welsh English (Penhallurick 2007, 167) – and TO HAVE are included in this section for the sake of completeness (note that more specific usages of these verbs – for instance, as perfect markers – are dealt with separately). We are concerned here with global text frequencies of forms of TO DO, TO BE, and TO HAVE (as in (14) to (16)), and this means that no distinction is made between auxiliary usage (as in the (a) examples below) and full verb usage (as in the (b) examples below). The assumption is that non-standard usages (e.g. TO DO as an unstressed periphrastic tense carrier) in particular dialects will result in higher text frequencies vis-à-vis dialects that do not attest such usages.

(14)    a.    Why *did* you not wait till about ten or eight o'clock? [HEB018][2]
          b.    We *did* no trawling then [KEN008]

(15)    a.    I *was* took straight into this pitting job [LEI002]
          b.    and eh he worked there till he *was* sixty-five [LEI002]

---

[2] Note here that in an oral history corpus such as FRED, the frequency of questions (on the part of informants) tends to be rather low, which will depress the frequency of DO periphrasis.

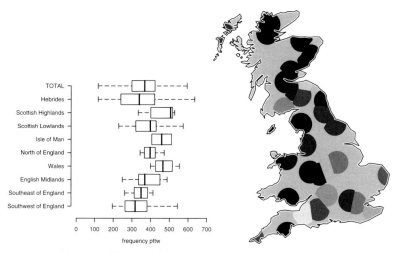

Map 3.3. Feature [14] (TO BE). Left: Boxplot (variance by dialect area). Right: Projection of frequencies to geography (blacker shades indicate higher frequencies).

(16)    a.    we thought somebody *had* brought them you know [NTT005]
        b.    they never *had* no annual holiday at all [NTT005]

Feature [13] (TO DO) does not have a significant geographic distribution in FRED. Feature [14] (TO BE) has a significant ($r = .129$, $p = .001$) geographic distribution according to the FDCC statistic in that TO BE is particularly frequent in Scotland and becomes increasingly less frequent as one moves south (see Map 3.3). Feature [15] (TO HAVE) has a marginally significant geographic distribution in FRED according to the FDCC statistic ($r = .098$, $p = .009$) such that TO HAVE tends to be particularly frequent in the North of England.

*Marking of possession: feature [16]* (HAVE GOT)
Gronemeyer (1999, 25) dates the emergence of the HAVE GOT + object construction indicating possession, as in (17), to the early seventeenth century.

(17)    Yes, I *have got* the photographs [LAN023]

In a number of contemporary varieties of English, there is variability such that HAVE GOT + object can serve as a substitute for HAVE + object to indicate possessive meaning (see e.g., Tagliamonte 2003). According to SED evidence (see Viereck et al. 1991, map S19 [CLAE1]), the HAVE GOT option is frequent in the English Midlands and in the eastern Southeast of England (see also Schulz 2010).

Feature [16] does not have a significant geographic distribution in FRED.

### 3.4.4   Tense, mood, and aspect

*Future markers: feature [17] (*BE GOING TO*) and feature [18]* (*WILL/SHALL*)
Modern English has two overt marker families for indicating futurity: the periphrastic construction BE GOING TO + verb, as in (18a), and the modals WILL/SHALL, as in (18b).

(18)   a.   I'*m going to* let you into a secret [WES010]
      b.   I *won't* run after him [SOM032]

Danchev and Kytö (1994) have shown that BE GOING TO had developed into a future marker prior to the middle of the seventeenth century, though Mair (2004, 128) reports that "a marked rise in frequency did not occur until the end of the 19th century." What is important here is that there is demonstrably a good deal of regional variability, for instance between American English and British English (see e.g. Tottie 2002; Szmrecsanyi 2003). Features [17] and [18] probe variability in British English dialects.

Features [17] and [18] do not have a significant geographic distribution in FRED.

*Habitual past: feature [19] (*WOULD*) and feature [20] (*used to*)*
English has two overt markers to indicate habitual past as an aspectual category, WOULD + verb (see (19a)) and *used to* + verb (see (19b)).

(19)   a.   <u Heb18> But things was – well money was very very scarce at that time, and things was cheap too.
          <u HebMMcl> Money *would* go farther then [HEB001]
      b.   he *used to* go around killing pigs [NTT008]

WOULD is the older form, in existence since Old English times, while *used to* is younger and a loan from Old French (Tagliamonte and Lawrence 2000, 328). Schulz (2010) presents evidence that there is significant dialectal variability in the frequency of use of WOULD and *used to* as markers of habitual past.

Feature [19] (WOULD) does not have a significant geographic distribution in FRED. Feature [20] (*used to*) has a significant geographic distribution according to both the FDCC statistic ($r = .442$, $p < .001$) and the *Moran's I* statistic ($I = .363$, $p < .001$): *used to* is particularly frequent in the Southeast of England and in the English Midlands and becomes increasingly less frequent as one moves north (see Map 3.4).

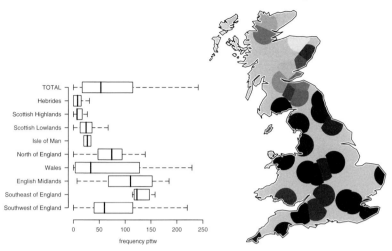

Map 3.4. Feature [20] (*used to*). Left: Boxplot (variance by dialect area). Right: Projection of frequencies to geography (blacker shades indicate higher frequencies).

*The progressive: feature [21]*

The progressive form, as in (20), dates back to the Middle English period, yet "the rules for the use of this aspectual form as we know them today only emerge in the course of the seventeenth century" (Hundt 2004, 47).

(20)    War *had been going* on for at least two or three years [YKS010]

In addition to historical variability, usage of the progressive is also subject to regional variability. According to the survey in Kortmann and Szmrecs- anyi (2004), a number of British varieties of English (specifically, Orkney and Shetland English, Scots, and dialects spoken in the North of England) permit a wider range of uses of the progressive – for instance, Johnston (2007, 129) reports the use of the progressive with stative verbs (e.g. "*Where are you staying in Edinburgh?*") for varieties of English spoken in Scotland, and Hamer (2007, 174) suggests that on the Isle of Man, BE + *-ing* forms can be used to indicate habitual aspect. On a technical note, this feature is concerned with overall frequencies of progressive verb forms, standard or non-standard.

Feature [21] has a marginally significant geographic distribution in FRED according to the FDCC statistic ($r = .079$, $p = .036$): progressive verb forms tend to be particularly frequent in Scotland.

*The present perfect: feature [22] (auxiliary* BE*) and feature [23] (auxiliary* HAVE*)*

The present perfect as a grammatical category became established during the Middle English period (see Denison 1993, 352). Initially, HAVE and BE competed as perfect auxiliaries; eventually, HAVE prevailed over BE in standard English varieties (Denison 1993, 344). Crucially, though, the historical competition between HAVE and BE as perfect auxiliaries has demonstrably left a robust synchronic echo of variability in regional varieties of English (see Tagliamonte 2000, 330–331). Consider (21):

(21)   a.   I'm *come* down to pay the rent (auxiliary BE) [CON009]
       b.   And that *has helped*, really. (auxiliary HAVE) [CON011]

Britain's (2010) literature review suggests that the BE-perfect is still alive in the eastern Midlands and western parts of East Anglia. According to the morphosyntax survey in Kortmann and Szmrecsanyi (2004), BE as a perfect auxiliary is attested in Orkney and Shetland English, Scots, and in the traditional dialects spoken in the North and Southwest of England. In addition, Kortmann and Szmrecsanyi's survey shows that a number of British varieties of English (Scots, Welsh English, and dialects in the North and Southwest of England) level the functional difference between the present perfect and the preterite, which should induce additional text frequency variability especially in feature [23]. We coded the feature by manually screening all forms of the verbs TO HAVE and TO BE in the dataset for present perfect usages.

Features [22] and [23] do not have a significant geographic distribution in FRED.

### 3.4.5   *Modality*

*Marking of epistemic and deontic modality: feature [24] (*MUST*), feature [25] (*HAVE TO*) and feature [26] (*GOT TO*)*
Variability between the modal verb MUST (the oldest variant, as in (22a)) and its younger periphrastic alternatives HAVE TO (as in (22b)) and (HAVE) GOT TO (as in (22c)) is comparatively well researched (see, e.g., Krug 2000, chapter 3; Jankowski 2004; Tagliamonte 2004; Schulz 2010).

(22)   a.   And I *must* say that, you know, we were never home [WIL024]
       b.   Not very often did we *hafta* stop fishing [SFK020]
       c.   I said, You *gotta* give somebody a chance somewhere [LND001]

As for dialectal variability specifically, SED-based research (see Viereck et al. 1991, map S21 [CLAE1]) indicates that HAVE TO is particularly widespread in the northern Midlands and in the North of England, while GOT TO occurs predominantly in Southern English dialects and on the Isle of Man. According to the corpus evidence in Schulz (2010), we are dealing with pervasive geographic variability especially in the domain of past tense modality (*had to* vs. *had got to*).

Feature [25] (HAVE TO) does not have a significant geographic distribution in FRED. Feature [24] has a marginally significant geographic

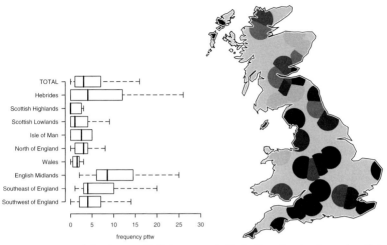

Map 3.5. Feature [26] (GOT TO). Left: Boxplot (variance by dialect area). Right: Projection of frequencies to geography (blacker shades indicate higher frequencies).

distribution in FRED according to the *Moran's I* statistic ($I = .096$, $p = .011$) indicating that MUST tends to be particularly frequent in the Scottish Lowlands. Feature [26] has a statistically significant geographic distribution in FRED according to the *Moran's I* statistic ($I = .157$, $p < .001$), and a marginally significant geographic distribution according to the FDCC statistic ($r = .088$, $p = .020$) such that GOT TO is particularly popular in the South of England and in the English Midlands. The construction becomes increasingly rarer as one moves north (see Map 3.5).

### 3.4.6    Verb morphology

*A-prefixing on* -ing *forms: feature [27]*
*A*-prefixing on *-ing* forms, as in (23), is an echo of an earlier construction going back to the Old English period and is reported for a number of non-standard varieties of English, particularly in the United States (see e.g. Wolfram 1976).

(23)    And he was *a*-wait*ing* there [KEN003]

Crucially, the phenomenon is also attested in a number of British dialects: According to Kortmann and Szmrecsanyi (2004), *a*-prefixing of *-ing* forms is attested in Welsh English as well as for the dialects spoken in East Anglia, the English Southeast, and the English Southwest (see also Viereck et al. 1991, maps M41, M42, and S11 [CLAE2]).
    Feature [27] does not have a significant geographic distribution in FRED.

*Conjugation regularization: feature [28] (non-standard weak past tense and past participle forms)*
Since Old English times, a great number of originally strong verbs (e.g. *sing – sang – sung*) have become weak verbs (e.g. *help – helped – helped*). Synchronically, we observe variability such that a number of verbs that are strong in Standard English have weak paradigms in non-standard varieties of English (see Anderwald 2009 for a comprehensive, corpus-based overview). Consider (24)–(31):

(24)  They *knowed* all about these things [NTT013]

(25)  Course we all *runned* away from school [WIL003]

(26)  so he run and he *catched* me [WES004]

(27)  I never *drawed* the curtains [SAL024]

(28)  Ah, there was a fellow *telled* me that [PEE002]

(29)  Now then, we *selled* manure, four-and-six a load [YKS003]

(30)  No, he just *growed* oats for his horses, see [KEN002]

(31)  He *throwed* un in the fire [SOM028]

The survey in Kortmann and Szmrecsanyi (2004) suggests that the phenomenon can be observed in all surveyed British dialects except Scots. The SED record (Orton et al. 1978, maps M52 and M53 [LAE]) likewise suggests that forms such as *catched* (instead of *caught*) and *growed* (instead of *grew*) are widespread in English English dialects. Given the phenomenon's pervasiveness, Chambers (e.g. 2004, 129) considers the kind of conjugation regularization at issue here a "vernacular universal."
    Feature [28] does not have a significant geographic distribution in FRED.

*Non-standard past tense* done*: feature [29]*
In a number of dialects of English, the standard three-way paradigm of the verb TO DO (*do – did – done*) is leveled and differentiated functionally: *do – did* is the paradigm for auxiliary DO, and *do – done – done* is the paradigm for main verb DO (Anderwald 2009). Consider (32):

(32)  'cause he *done* all his painting inside. ( ~ he *did* all his painting) [CON004]

    The corpus analysis in Anderwald (2009) strongly suggests that past tense *done* is particularly frequent in the South of England, and particularly infrequent in Scots and Northern English English dialects.
    In FRED, feature [29] has a significant ($r = .258$, $p < .001$) geographic distribution according to the FDCC statistic, and a marginally significant ($I = .127$, $p = .007$) geographic distribution according to the *Moran's I*

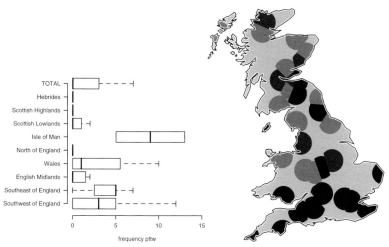

Map 3.6. Feature [29] (non-standard past tense *done*). Left: Boxplot (variance by dialect area). Right: Projection of frequencies to geography (blacker shades indicate higher frequencies).

statistic: non-standard past tense *done* is relatively frequent in the South of England and becomes less frequent as one moves north (see Map 3.6).

*Non-standard past tense* come: *feature [30]*
This feature is about what has come to be known as *come/came* variation, as in (33):

(33)    And he *come* down the road one day (∼ he *came* down the road) [CON005]

According to Tagliamonte (2001, 42), "[o]ne of the most familiar features of English dialects is the alternation between *come* and *came* in past-reference contexts." Chambers (1995, 240–241) actually considers the phenomenon a vernacular universal. SED evidence (Orton et al. 1978, map M51 [LAE]) suggests that past tense *come* is indeed widespread, and the corpus analysis in Anderwald (2009) likewise demonstrates that the phenomenon is fairly pervasive in British English dialects. At the same time, though, Anderwald detects a regional distribution such that past tense *come* is more frequent in Southern dialects than in Northern dialects.

In FRED feature [30] has a significant ($r = .201$, $p < .001$) geographic distribution according to the FDCC statistic. Non-standard past tense *come* is relatively frequent in the South of England and in the Scottish Lowlands, but relatively rare in the North of England and in the Scottish Highlands (see Map 3.7).

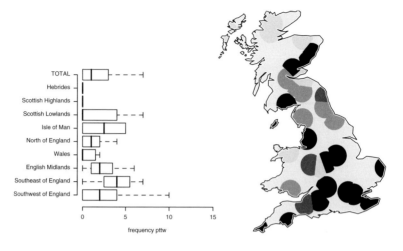

Map 3.7. Feature [30] (non-standard past tense *come*). Left: Boxplot (variance by dialect area). Right: Projection of frequencies to geography (blacker shades indicate higher frequencies).

### 3.4.7   Negation

*Negative suffixes: feature [31] (-*nae*)*
In Scots, the suffix -*nae*, as in (34), can be used to negate modal verbs and the auxiliary DO (see e.g. Miller 2004, 50; Johnston 2007, 119).

(34)   a.   I *cannae* remember the name. (~ I *cannot* remember) [NBL003]
       b.   He *doesnae* take an interest in anybody else except they two.
            (~ he *doesn't* take) [ELN012]

The marker is also reported as occurring in the North of England and in the English Midlands (see, for instance, Händler and Viereck 1997, 35; Pust 1998).

In FRED, feature [31] has a significant geographic distribution both according to the FDCC statistic ($r = .161$, $p < .001$) and to the *Moran's I* statistic ($I = .372$, $p < .001$). Not surprisingly, -*nae* is restricted to the Scottish Lowlands and to Northumberland (see Map 3.8).

*Ain't: feature [32]*
The etymology of *ain't* – which can serve as the negated form of BE and HAVE (and, in some varieties, even DO) – is somewhat unclear: Jespersen (1940, 431) derives the form from contracted *have not*, the *Oxford English Dictionary* from contracted *are not*. Be that as it may, while the form is often considered a "vulgarism" (Jespersen 1940, 431) – probably,

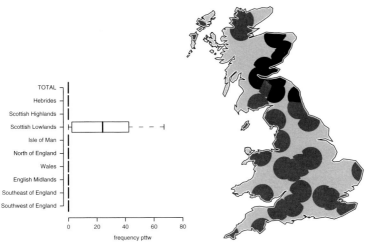

Map 3.8.  Feature [31] (the negative suffix -*nae*). Left: Boxplot (variance by dialect area). Right: Projection of frequencies to
geography (blacker shades indicate higher frequencies).

according to many Britons, of American provenance – *ain't* does occur in
British English dialects (see (35)):

(35)    Hm, I mean people, people *ain't* got no money you see (∼ people
        *haven't* got no money) [NTT013]

According to the survey in Kortmann and Szmrecsanyi (2004), *ain't* as the
negated form of BE is attested in Welsh English, East Anglian English, and
in dialects in the Southeast and Southwest of England. Except for Welsh
English, these varieties are also classified as having *ain't* as the negated form
of HAVE. In a similar vein, SED evidence (cf. Orton et al. 1978, maps M9–
M15, M26–M27 [LAE]) indicates that *ain't* is used in a number of English
English dialects (particularly in the Southeast), and Anderwald (2003a, 149)
concludes, on the basis of corpus evidence drawn from the *British National
Corpus*, that "*ain't* is present throughout England."

    In FRED, feature [32] has a significant geographic distribution according
to the FDCC statistic ($r = .358$, $p < .001$) and the *Moran's I* statistic ($I = .230$,
$p < .001$): *ain't* is relatively frequent in the South of England and becomes
less frequent as one moves north (see Map 3.9).

*Multiple negation: feature [33]*
This feature deals with another shibboleth in modern Standard English –
multiple negation (also known as "negative concord"), as in (36):

(36)    'cause you dare *not* say *no*thing [LND001]

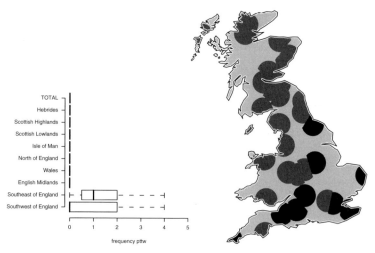

Map 3.9. Feature [32] (*ain't*). Left: Boxplot (variance by dialect area). Right: Projection of frequencies to geography (blacker shades indicate higher frequencies).

Multiple negation was perfectly acceptable in Old English but became stigmatized later. It subsequently disappeared from standard English, partly thanks to the influence of prescriptive grammarians (see Tieken-Boon van Ostade et al. 1999, 1; Beal and Corrigan 2006, 145). In non-standard varieties of English, however, multiple negation is alive and kicking. For example, all British varieties surveyed in Kortmann and Szmrecsanyi (2004) except for Orkney/Shetland attest it. In fact, the feature is so pervasive in many varieties of English around the world that Chambers (e.g. 2004: 129) considers multiple negation another candidate for vernacular universalhood. Note, however, that despite its overall pervasiveness the phenomenon seems to have an interesting geographic distribution in Great Britain: Anderwald (2005) draws on FRED to demonstrate that there is a robust North–South continuum in the data such that the text frequency of multiple negation increases the further south in Britain one goes (see also Cheshire et al. 1989, 205).

In FRED, feature [33] has a significant geographic distribution according to both the FDCC statistic ($r = .352$, $p < .001$) and the *Moran's I* statistic ($I = .170$, $p < .001$). Multiple negation is relatively frequent in the South of England and becomes less frequent as one moves north (see Map 3.10).

*Contraction: feature [34] (negative contraction) and feature [35] (auxiliary contraction)*
The alternation between negative contraction (see (37a)) and auxiliary contraction (see (37b)) is comparatively well researched (see Tagliamonte and Smith 2002 and Britain 2007, 2010 for literature reviews).

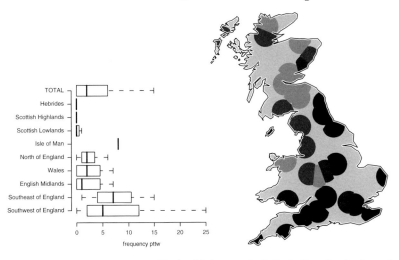

Map 3.10.  Feature [33] (multiple negation). Left: Boxplot (variance by
dialect area). Right: Projection of frequencies to geography
(blacker shades indicate higher frequencies).

(37)   a.   They *won't* do anything [WES011]
       b.   She*'ll not* know where Jerusalem Terrace is [ANS004]

The majority view in the literature is that negative contraction is more fre-
quent, relative to auxiliary contraction, in Southern British dialects than in
Northern British dialects (e.g. Swan 1980, 159; Trudgill 1978, 13). Auxil-
iary contraction, by contrast, is supposed to be more dominant in the North
(Hughes and Trudgill 1996).
   Features [34] and [35] do not have a significant geographic distribution in
FRED.

*Never as past tense negator: feature [36]*
Kortmann (2004b, 1093), on the basis of the survey in Kortmann and Szmrecsanyi (2004), lists *never* as an unstressed preverbal past tense negator (see
(38)) as one of "[t]he two by far most pervasive negation features in the
British Isles, attested everywhere except for the Orkney and Shetland Isles"
(see Cheshire et al. 1993; Britain 2010 for similar statements).

(38)   she'd been divorced then, she was home, see. 'cause I can't mind her
       married, but I can mind going down to the farm when I was a little
       boy, where she was still. And she was drunk. And I don't know come
       Uncle Den, I couldn't tell you that, you know, 'cause I wasn't more
       than, just like that. I was – the other put- Aunt Joan sat down there,
       and Kira there, and they *never moved* no more, neither one of them,
       *never tried* to. (~ they *didn't* move, they *didn't* try to) [CON005]

Interestingly, the SED (see Orton et al. 1978, map S9 [LAE]) suggests that the phenomenon is significantly less widespread and more regional.

Feature [36] does not have a significant geographic distribution in FRED.

*The* was–weren't *split: feature [37] (*WASN'T*) and feature [38] (*WEREN'T*)

In a number of varieties of English (see Britain 2002, 19 for an overview), *was/were* variability is differentiated functionally such that affirmative past tense BE is coded by the form *was* while negative past tense BE is coded by the form *weren't*: *you was hungry, weren't you?* and *he was thirsty, weren't he?* (Britain 2002, 19; Chambers 2004, 131). According to Kortmann and Szmrecsanyi's (2004) survey data, the *was–weren't* split is attested in dialects in the North of England, in East Anglia, and the Southeast of England; Britain (2010) offers that the *was–weren't* split is dominant in southern Great Britain. This study seeks to approach this phenomenon by establishing the text frequencies of WASN'T forms (as in (39a)) and WEREN'T forms (as in (39b)) separately.

(39)   a.   It *wasn't* very dead, no it were just busy [LAN015]
       b.   If Miss Skinner *weren't* there there was another girl used to do it [WIL023]

Features [37] and [38] do not have a significant geographic distribution in FRED.

### 3.4.8   Agreement

*Non-standard verbal* -s: *feature [39]*

In many varieties of English, we find verbal -*s* with non-3rd person singular subjects. Consider (40):

(40)   So I say*s*, What have you to do? [LAN001]

The body of literature on this topic is sizable (see Godfrey and Tagliamonte 1999; Britain 2010 for literature reviews). According to the survey in Kortmann and Szmrecsanyi (2004), the phenomenon is attested in Northern English dialects, in Welsh English, and in dialects in the Southwest and Southeast of England.

Feature [39] does not have a significant geographic distribution in FRED.

Don't–doesn't *variability: feature [40] (don't with 3rd person singular subjects) and feature [41] (doesn't)*

In a number of varieties of English, the form of negated auxiliary DO in the 3rd person singular is *don't*, not *doesn't* (Cheshire et al. 1989; Stenström et al. 2002; Anderwald 2003b). The survey data discussed in Kortmann and Szmrecsanyi (2004) suggest that invariant *don't* for all persons in the present tense is attested in dialects in East Anglia, the Southeast and Southwest, and

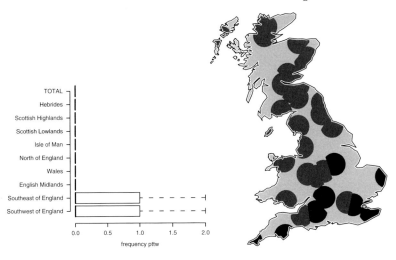

Map 3.11.  Feature [40] (*don't* with 3rd person singular subjects). Left: Boxplot (variance by dialect area). Right: Projection of frequencies to geography (blacker shades indicate higher frequencies).

for Welsh English. Orton et al.'s (1978: map M37 [LAE]) SED evidence suggests that invariant *don't* is widespread in Southern English English dialects. The present study's approach to this variation consists of (i) determining the text frequency of *don't* forms with 3rd person singular subjects, as in (41a), and (ii) determining the global text frequency of *doesn't* forms, as in (41b):

(41)  a.   and then I'll send thee a letter, if *this man don't* come up to it (~ if this man *doesn't* come up to it) [SOM032]
      b.   Charcoal that's right, he *doesn't* know how to burn a barrel ... [SOM001]

In FRED, feature [40] has a significant geographic distribution according to both the FDCC statistic ($r = .434$, $p < .001$) and the *Moran's I* statistic ($I = .285$, $p < .001$). *Don't* with 3rd person singular subjects is observable in the Southwest and Southeast of England, but tends to be rare elsewhere (see Map 3.11). Feature [41] has a marginally significant geographic distribution ($r = .091$, $p < .015$) according to the FDCC statistic in that *doesn't* tends to be relatively frequent in Scotland but not elsewhere.

*Existential/presentational* there is/was *with plural subjects: feature [42]*
*There is/was* with plural subjects – as in (42) – is, among British varieties, the most widely attested non-standard phenomenon in Kortmann and Szmrecsanyi's (2004) survey, and Britain (2010) classes the feature as belonging to a "common core" of non-regional non-standard forms in Great Britain.

(42)    *there was thirty-seven children* involved [LAN018]

We are dealing here, at base, with a variety of subject-verb non-concord; thus the feature's pervasiveness should not be surprising given that subject-verb non-concord has been labeled a "vernacular universal" (for instance, Chambers 2004).

Feature [42] does not have a significant geographic distribution in FRED as a whole. However, if attention is restricted to measuring points in England the FDCC statistic yields a statistically significant correlation ($r = .348$, $p < .001$): *there is/was* with plural subjects is comparatively more popular in the North of England and becomes increasingly less frequent as one moves south.

*Copula/auxiliary absence: feature [43] (absence of auxiliary* BE *in progressive constructions)*
There is a sizable body of literature on copula absence, or "copula deletion" (as in (43)), particularly in regard to African American Vernacular English (see Labov 1969).

(43)    I said, How Ø you doing? [CON006]

According to Chambers, the feature is a vernacular universal (though it should be noted that Chambers does not appear to differentiate between copula absence and auxiliary absence; see Chambers 2004, 129). For the purposes of the present study, we will be interested in text frequencies of auxiliary absence in progressive constructions.

Feature [43] has a marginally significant geographic distribution ($r = .100$, $p < .008$) according to the FDCC statistic, indicating that absence of auxiliary BE in progressive constructions tends to have its frequency epicenter in the Southeast of England.

*Was/were variation: feature [44] (non-standard* WAS)
The feature is the first installment of the present study's take on what is known as "*was/were* variation" (feature [45] is the second installment). Adger and Smith (2005, 155) argue that non-standard WAS with plural subjects – also known as "*was*-generalization" or "*s*-generalization" (see, e.g., Trudgill 2008) – is a very frequent feature in varieties of English worldwide (see Britain 2002, 19 and Tagliamonte 2009 for an overview), so it will come as no surprise that the phenomenon ranks among the top twenty non-standard features in the British Isles according to Kortmann and Szmrecsanyi's (2004) survey. Similarly, Britain (2010) includes non-standard WAS in his catalogue of non-standard yet supra-regional forms. For an example of non-standard WAS from FRED, consider (44):

(44)    three of them came back. Three of them *was* killed. (~ three of them *were* killed) [WLN004]

Chambers (2004, 131) goes so far as to consider the feature a vernacular universal. At the same time, though, Tagliamonte (1998, 153) and Anderwald (2001, 1), among others, point out that the phenomenon is subject to "endemic" variation, which makes it an ideal feature for dialectometrical inquiry (see also Orton et al. 1978, maps M20–M25 [LAE]).

Feature [44] does not have a significant geographic distribution in FRED.

*Was/were variation: feature [45] (non-standard* WERE*)*
Non-standard WERE with 1st or 3rd person singular subjects – also known as "*were*-generalization," "*were*-leveling," or "*r*-generalization" (see e.g., Trudgill 2008) – is attested in a number of British dialects (see Orton et al. 1978, maps M20–M25 [LAE]; Kortmann and Szmrecsanyi 2004; Klemola 2006; Trudgill 2008). Consider (45):

(45)   He run away from home when he *were* a young lad. (∼ when he *was* a young lad) [LAN005]

Feature [45] does not have a significant geographic distribution in FRED.

### 3.4.9   Relativization

*Relativizer choice: feature [46] (*wh*-relativization), feature [47] (the relative particle* what*), and feature [48] (the relative particle* that*)*
Features [46] through [48] deal with three overt markers that introduce relative clauses: *wh*-relativization (see (46a)), the relative particle *what* (see (46b)), and the relative particle *that* (see (46c)).

(46)   a.   and it was the poor people *who* poached usually [SOM019]
       b.   He never had any of the money *what* he earnt [KEN010]
       c.   The highest number *that* I can remember, I think, was fifty-two [CON007]

Historically, relative *that* and *what* are comparatively old forms while *wh*-relativization – especially *who* – is a relatively recent addition to the system (Herrmann 2003, chapter 4; Tagliamonte et al. 2005, 77–78). Today, regional variation in Great Britain is pervasive (see Britain 2010 and the references therein). The survey conducted by Kortmann and Szmrecsanyi (2004) suggests that the relative particle *what* occurs in the North of England, in East Anglia, in the Southwest and Southeast of England, and in Wales. According to the SED record (see Orton et al. 1978, map S5 [LAE]), (i) *wh*-relativization is a southern English feature, (ii) the relative particle *what* is the dominant relativization strategy in some pockets in the Southeast and the eastern Midlands, and (iii) the relative particle *that* is dominant only in some northern pockets. For an in-depth analysis of relative clauses in British English dialects based on FRED, see Herrmann (2003, 2005).

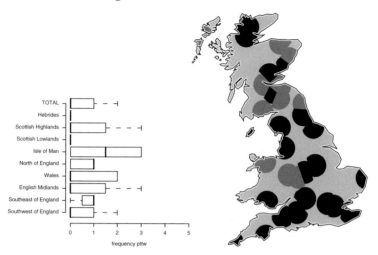

Map 3.12. Feature [49] (*as what/than what* in comparative clauses). Left: Boxplot (variance by dialect area). Right: Projection of frequencies to geography (blacker shades indicate higher frequencies).

Features [46] (*wh*-relativization) and [48] (the relative particle *that*) do not have a significant geographic distribution in FRED. Feature [47] has a marginally significant geographic distribution ($r = .095$, $p < .011$) according to the FDCC statistic such that the relative particle *what* tends to be particularly frequent in the Southwest and Southeast of England.

### 3.4.10    Complementation

As what *or* than what *in comparative clauses: feature [49]*
According to the survey results presented in Kortmann and Szmrecsanyi (2004), *as what* or *than what* in comparative clauses, as in (47), is attested in all surveyed British dialects except Orkney and Shetland English; along these lines, the phenomenon is classified as being "pervasive" in the North of England, in East Anglia, and in Welsh English.

(47)    a.    And it, I saw it as many times *as what* the operators did [YKS001]

       b.    well we we done no more *than what* other kids used to do [LEI002]

Feature [49] has a significant ($r = .159$, $p < .001$) geographic distribution according to the FDCC statistic – *as what* or *than what* in comparative clauses is particularly frequent in some parts of the English Midlands, the Isle of Man, and in the Scottish Highlands (see Map 3.12).

*Unsplit* for to: *feature [50]*
In a number of regional non-standard varieties, the infinitive marker *to* is sometimes preceded by *for*. Consider (48):

(48)  a.   It was ready *for to* go away with the order, or whatever [SAL016]
      b.   and one *for to* look after the bundles as them come out the other end [CON007]
      c.   And *for to* launch him they used to take him over and go down the slipway [SOM036]

Unsplit *for to* is "widespread throughout the country" (Wakelin 1972) and recurs in many regional varieties of British English. According to Kortmann and Szmrecsanyi's (2004) survey, unsplit *for to* in infinitival purpose clauses is attested in all British dialects except East Anglian English. SED data (see Orton et al. 1978, map S3 [LAE]), however, suggest that *for to* (as in *he came for to see*) is the *dominant* strategy only in some northern and southeastern areas in England. At any rate, unsplit *for to* is often argued to be in decline (see, e.g., Harris 1993, 167; Miller 2004, 64; Millar 2007, 76).

Feature [50] does not have a significant geographic distribution in FRED as a whole. However, if attention is restricted to measuring points in England the FDCC statistic yields a marginally significant correlation ($r = .178$, $p = .027$). Unsplit *for to* appears to be comparatively more popular in the South of England and in the Northeast of England.

*Verbal complementation after* BEGIN, START, CONTINUE, HATE, *and* LOVE: *feature [51] (infinitival complementation) and feature [52] (gerundial complementation)*
The alternation, after some lexical verbs, between infinitival complementation (as in (49a)) and gerundial complementation (as in (49b)) in English has generated a good deal of research.

(49)  a.   And then I *began to* take an interest in it [DFS001]
      b.   as things were getting worse they *began* call*ing* up the younger agricultural workers [CON008]

According to Quirk (1974, 66–67), "[t]here ought to be a big award for anyone who can describe exactly what makes him say 'I started to work' on one occasion and 'I started working' on another." In a similar spirit, Mair (2003, 329) argues that "this particular fragment of English grammar is in a state of flux diachronically, with *-ing* forms gradually encroaching on the infinitive," which "bedevils any attempt at an 'exact' synchronic description." As for regional differences, the findings in Szmrecsanyi (2006, 166) appear to suggest that gerundial complementation is particularly frequent in the North of England, while infinitival complementation is particularly frequent in the English Midlands.

Features [51] and [52] do not have a significant geographic distribution in FRED.

*Clausal complementation after* THINK, SAY, *and* KNOW: *feature [53] (zero complementation) and feature [54] (that complementation)*
In contemporary English, the clausal complementizer *that* is optional. Consider (50):

(50)   a.   But he *said* [Ø it was never the same] [KEN004]
       b.   No, they just *said* [*that* you were there] [HEB012]

In terms of text frequency, zero complementation is – by stark contrast to earlier stages of English – vastly more frequent than explicit *that* complementation in contemporary British dialects (and in spoken language in general). This is why the history of *that*/zero variability has been called "an astonishing trajectory of change" (Tagliamonte and Smith 2005, 291, citing Rissanen 1991, 279–282 and Warner 1982). The overall predominance of zero complementation in modern spoken English notwithstanding, note that we do observe regional variability: Kolbe (2008, chapter 3), in a corpus study based on FRED, shows that zero complementation is comparatively frequent in the North and Southeast of England, while *that* complementation is comparatively frequent in Scotland and Wales.

Features [53] and [54] do not have a significant geographic distribution in FRED as a whole. However, if attention is restricted to measuring points in England, feature [54] turns out to have a statistically significant ($r = .314$, $p < .001$) geographic distribution according to the FDCC statistic: *that* complementation is comparatively popular in the Southeast of England and tends to become less frequent as one moves west and north.

*3.4.11   Word order and discourse phenomena*

*Lack of inversion and/or of auxiliaries in* wh-*questions and in main clause* yes/no-*questions: feature [55]*
Lack of inversion or lack of auxiliaries in *wh*-questions (as in (51)) and lack of inversion in main clause *yes/no* questions (as in (52)) are among the most frequently occurring non-standard features in varieties of English worldwide (see Kortmann and Szmrecsanyi 2004, table 3).

(51)   a.   She says, *how long you've been out?* [NTT002]
       b.   but, *where you put the shovel?* [CON005]

(52)   a.   He says I'm going to let you home, there's no sign of the stone anyway, he says. *And you're feeling allright?* Yes says I, I'm feeling fine. [HEB018]

   b.   *you know that song?* [DEV008]

As for variability in British English dialects, note that Kortmann and Szm-recsanyi (2004) classify the features as attested in the following British English dialects: Scots, dialects in the North of England (pervasively), dialects in East Anglia, and Welsh English.

   Feature [55] does not have a significant geographic distribution in FRED.

*The dative alternation after* GIVE: *feature [56] (prepositional datives) and feature [57] (double object structures)*
Features [56] and [57] fall into the domain of the so-called "dative alterna-tion" – that is, the word order choice speakers of English have between the prepositional dative and the ditransitive dative construction. Consider (53) for corpus examples, and (54) for syntactic analyses:

(53)   a.   And, uh, he had a scheme there, the headmaster, where he used to *give three penny piece to the class* that was hundred percent all the week. (the prepositional dative construction) [LND004]

   b.   and eh I got a job and then she *gave me a job* in the warehouse. (the ditransitive dative construction) [WIL007]

(54)   a.

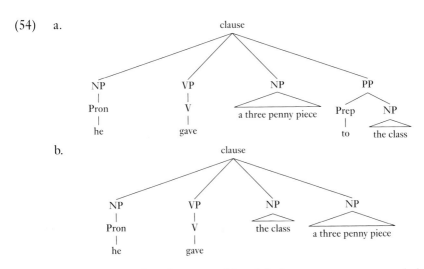

   b.

Note in this connection that prepositional dative structures were coded even if a corresponding double object structure would have been ungram-matical in Standard English due to a pronominal direct object, as in (55a). In

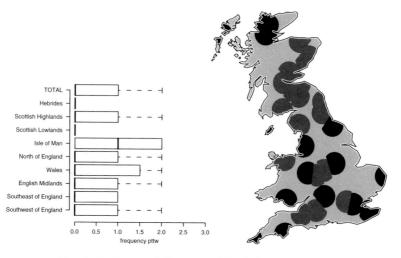

Map 3.13. Feature [56] (prepositional datives). Left: Boxplot (variance by dialect area). Right: Projection of frequencies to geography (blacker shades indicate higher frequencies).

a similar vein, some double object structures that would be ungrammatical in Standard English, as in (55b), were included in the tally:

(55)    a.    Oh nono, he says, don't *give it to him* ... [HEB018]
        b.    ... but he was on leave and he *give me it* ... [LAN010]

It is fair to say that the dative alternation is one of the most extensively studied alternations in the grammar of English or any other language (e.g. Bock 1986; Gropen et al. 1989; Gries 2005; Bresnan et al. 2007, and so on), yet not much is known about regional variability (see however, Bresnan and Hay 2008 for probabilistic differences between New Zealand English and American English). As for variability in British English dialects, the SED material (see Orton et al. 1978, map S1 [LAE], and Kirk 1985, 135 for a discussion) indicates that the prepositional dative construction is dominant in the English Southwest and in some pockets in the English Southeast and in East Anglia. Elsewhere in England – and particularly in the North and East Anglia – the double object construction is preferred.

In FRED, feature [56] has a significant geographic distribution according to the FDCC statistic ($r = .206$, $p < .001$), and a marginally significant geographic distribution according to the *Moran's I* statistic ($I = .134$, $p = .005$): prepositional datives are extremely unpopular in the Scottish Lowlands and in the far north of England (see Map 3.13). Feature [57] has a statistically significant geographic distribution according to the *Moran's I* statistic ($I = .208$, $p < .001$), and a marginally significant geographic distribution according to

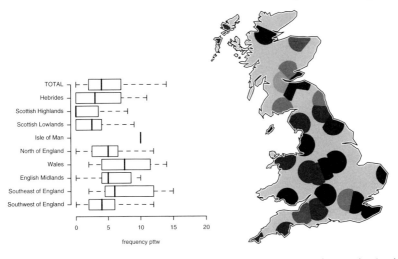

Map 3.14.  Feature [57] (double object structures). Left: Boxplot (variance by dialect area). Right: Projection of frequencies to geography (blacker shades indicate higher frequencies).

the FDCC statistic ($r = .112$, $p = .003$) – double object structures are particularly popular in the Southeast of England, in the English Midlands, and in Wales (see Map 3.14).

## 3.5   Chapter summary

By way of a chapter summary, let us explore a little bit the extent to which the frequency distributions presented in this chapter have news value, taking the survey in Britain (2010) ("Grammatical variation in the contemporary spoken English of England") as our point of departure. Britain lists the following features as non-standard *supra-regional* forms:[3]

- regularized reflexive pronouns
  (corresponding to feature [1] in the present study)
- *them* as a demonstrative
  (roughly corresponding to feature [6])
- absence of plural marking on nouns of measurement
  (roughly corresponding to feature [12])
- *ain't / in't*
  (as for *ain't*, see feature [32])

---

[3] Britain (2010) also characterizes as supra-regional present participles using the preterite rather than continuous forms and adverbs without -*ly*, two features not covered in the present study's feature catalogue.

- *never* as a past tense negator
  (feature [36])
- *there's/there was* with notional plural subjects
  (feature [42])
- non-standard WAS
  (feature [44]).

Now, given our frequency analyses we fully concur with Britain (2010) that feature [6] (*them*), feature [12] (cardinal number + *year-Ø*), feature [36] (*never* as past tense negator), and feature [44] (non-standard WAS) are relatively frequent and not regionally restricted – according to the metrics marshaled in this chapter, these features do not have a significant regional distribution and can thus be considered supra-regional. That said, we note – contra Britain (2010) – that the following three features actually do have a significant regional distribution in FRED, and are hence not regionally unrestricted. Feature [1] (non-standard reflexives) appears to be particularly popular in the South of England (see Section 3.4.1). Feature [32] (the negator *ain't*) likewise turns out to be relatively frequent in the South of England but becomes less frequent as one moves north. Lastly, feature [42] (existential/presentational *there is/was* with plural subjects) is comparatively popular in the North of England and becomes increasingly less frequent as one moves south.

We would, however, like to emphasize at this time that although individual features, when analyzed in isolation, may not have a regionally significant frequency distribution, they may still be implicated in regionally distinctive feature bundling, an issue that Chapter 7 will be concerned with. Along these lines, we shall see, for instance, that *them*, non-standard WAS, and *never* as past tense negator – although seemingly supra-regional when analyzed one-by-one – all load on geographically more or less focused principal components of morphosyntactic variability.

# 4      Surveying the forest: on aggregate morphosyntactic distances and similarities

This chapter is descriptive in nature, aiming to set the scene for more sophisticated analyses to be presented in subsequent chapters. We will canvass aggregate morphosyntactic distances and similarities in the dataset, both among British English dialects as well as between British English dialects and Standard English varieties. In addition to reporting summary statistics, the discussion will draw on a range of exploratory cartographic visualization techniques: (reverse) network maps, beam maps, honeycomb maps, similarity maps, skewness maps, and kernel maps. Thus, Section 4.1 considers the total set of measuring points sampled in FRED. Section 4.2 takes a closer, regionally restricted look at dialects spoken in England, and at dialects spoken in Scotland and the Hebrides. Section 4.3 explores linguistic compromise and exchange areas, and seeks to identify "dialect kernels" in the dataset. Section 4.4 probes aggregate morphosyntactic distances between FRED measuring points and Standard English, British and American. Section 4.5 summarizes this chapter's major findings.

## 4.1    Aggregate distances and similarities: the big picture

This section explores aggregate morphosyntactic relationships among the total set of measuring points sampled in FRED. Chapter 2 explained how the present study draws on the Euclidean distance measure to calculate pairwise morphosyntactic distances between measuring points ("dialects"); thus recall that the present study defines pairwise dialectal distances as the square root of the sum of all fifty-seven feature frequency differentials (given that our feature catalogue spans fifty-seven morphosyntactic features).

How are these distances distributed? To address this question, Table 4.1 reports a number of instructive summary statistics. The sample spanning $N = 34$ FRED measuring points yields $34 \times 33/2 = 561$ pairwise distances, i.e. measuring point pairings, each characterized by a specific Euclidean morphosyntactic distance. The MEAN Euclidean morphosyntactic distance is 5.41 distance points (to illustrate, this distance roughly corresponds to the distance between two hypothetical varieties A and B where variety

| | |
|---|---|
| measuring point pairings | 561 |
| mean | 5.41 |
| standard deviation | 1.11 |
| minimum | 2.32 |
| median | 5.40 |
| maximum | 8.14 |
| skewness | −.06 |
| kurtosis | −.37 |

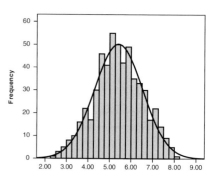

Table 4.1. *Aggregate morphosyntactic distances: summary statistics, all measuring points in dataset.*

Figure 4.1. Aggregate morphosyntactic distances: histogram, all measuring points in dataset.

A attests a normalized text frequency of 2 hits *pttw* for every one of the fifty-seven features under consideration, while variety B attests a normalized text frequency of approximately 10 hits *pttw* for every one of the fifty-seven features considered). As for the dataset-internal dispersion around the mean, we are dealing with a STANDARD DEVIATION of 1.11. Given that the distances are, as we shall see shortly, normally distributed, this is another way of saying that roughly two-thirds of the 561 measuring point pairings score a distance within 1.11 points of the mean, and that 95 percent of all pairwise distances do not deviate more than 2.22 points from the mean. The MINIMUM observable distance in the dataset is 2.32 distance points. This happens to be the distance between the county of Somerset and the county of Wiltshire, two neighboring counties located in the Southwest of England. The MEDIAN distance is 5.40. This is the distance that separates the higher half of the distance sample from the lower half. The MAXIMUM observable distance in the dataset is 8.14 distance points, which is the morphosyntactic distance between the county of Denbighshire in Wales and the county of Kincardineshire in the Scottish Lowlands.

Are pairwise morphosyntactic distances in the dataset normally distributed? In other words: is the distribution symmetric about the mean distance of 5.41? The HISTOGRAM in Figure 4.1, which plots the frequency of a number of distance brackets, suggests that they roughly are. Numerically speaking, the SKEWNESS value of −.06 suggests that there is only a very slight negative skew, which is another way of saying that there is a slightly greater number of larger distances than smaller distances. As for "peakedness," the KURTOSIS value of −.37 indicates that the distribution of distances is a bit flatter than it would be in a perfectly normal distribution. Having said that, skewness and kurtosis values of ±1.0 are by convention (Meyers et al. 2006, 90) taken to be indicative of a normal – albeit not perfectly normal – distribution.

*4.1.1   On the network nature of morphosyntax relationships*

Having paid due attention to the numerical preliminaries, we now move on to projecting aggregate distances and similarities to geography. The maps in Maps C.1 and C.2 are Groningen-style NETWORK MAPS (Nerbonne and Heeringa 1997), a comparatively simple map type designed to indiscriminately project dialect similarities or distances to geography without further statistical ado.[1]

Map C.1 (Appendix C, p. 173) is about dialectal *similarities*. The map (which, as an L04 map, is based on Euclidean distances; see Section 2.2.5 [p. 30]) links measuring points that are similar morphosyntactically through darker, more blueish lines, and morphosyntactically less similar measuring points through lighter, more yellowish lines. Visual inspection of Map C.1 reveals that we are dealing with a network of comparatively strong and coherent morphosyntactic links in England, and with a somewhat looser network structure in Scotland. Within England, we observe particularly strong link bundles in the South (encompassing Cornwall, Devon, Somerset, Wiltshire, and London) and in the North (Lancashire, Westmorland, Yorkshire). Northumberland seems to link well to some Scottish measuring points, and turning back to the literature we note that both Ellis (1889) and Trudgill (1990) actually consider the traditional dialect spoken in northern Northumberland a Scots variety. The Hebrides have strong morphosyntactic ties to measuring points all over Great Britain; notice in this connection that as a Scottish Highlands variety, Hebridean English is a relatively young dialect which Trudgill, for example, does not in fact categorize as a traditional dialect on account of the fact that it has "become English-speaking only relatively recently" (1990, 5). It is therefore not particularly surprising that Hebridean English lacks a clear-cut morphosyntactic profile of its own and bears similarities to dialects all over the place. The two measuring points in Wales (Denbighshire and Glamorganshire) are not particularly well connected to other measuring points in the dataset, and this holds even more true for Banffshire and Kincardineshire, two measuring points located in the Eastern Scottish Lowlands.

As a mirror image of sorts to Map C.1, Map C.2 (Appendix C, p. 173) – A REVERSE NETWORK MAP – highlights morphosyntactic *dissimilarities* in the dataset. This particular map omits links between dialects that are more than 250 km apart, which mainly serves presentational purposes by enhancing readability without swamping the reader with an abundance of dissimilarity links. In Map C.1 we observe, first, the striking tangle of dissimilarities covering much of the North of England and Scotland. In this connection (and in accordance with what was said in the foregoing discussion) Banffshire and Kincardineshire especially radiate strong beams of

---

[1] These and the network maps to follow were generated using the following contrast parameters: $c = 1$, $C = -.5$.

dissimilarity to other measuring points. The Isle of Man, too, is markedly dissimilar to a number of measuring points, particularly in Scotland. In England, there is a web of modest dissimilarities involving measuring points in the Midlands (Shropshire, Warwickshire, Leicestershire, and Nottinghamshire). Warwickshire is additionally dissimilar to a number of sites in the Southwest of England (Somerset, Wiltshire, and Oxfordshire). As for Wales, observe the strong signal of dissimilarity emanating from the county of Denbighshire in North Wales; by contrast, Glamorganshire in South Wales is fairly inconspicuous. This difference between the two measuring points in Wales is not exceedingly surprising. We know that there are robust lexical, phonological, and grammatical differences between dialects in North and South Wales (Penhallurick 1993), many of which can be traced back to an influx of Southwestern English speakers to South Wales beginning as early as the end of the eleventh century AD (Penhallurick 2004b, 98). By comparison, Denbighshire English in North Wales is a younger dialect with less well-established historical links to English English dialects.

### 4.1.2   Interpoint relationships

Rather than considering the full set of dialect relationships spawned by a given distance matrix all at once (which is the idea behind network maps), it is often instructive to selectively focus on so-called "interpoint" relationships (see Goebl 1982, 51; Lalanne 1953). In this spirit, we now turn to Map C.3 (Appendix C, p. 174), which features a Salzburg-style BEAM MAP (see Goebl 1993, 53).[2] Unlike network maps where each measuring point can potentially link up to any other measuring point on the map, beam maps restrict attention to interpoint relationships. In other words, only neighboring measuring points can connect, which is a way of distilling the essentials of what distance matrices have to tell us. In Salzburg-style beam maps, the color coding is such that "the colour *blue* symbolizes conflict ('the *cold* shoulder'), whereas the colour *red* illustrates contact ('*warm* friendship')" (Goebl 2007, 143; emphases original). So, morphosyntactically dissimilar neighbors are connected by cold (blueish) and thin beams; neighbors that are close morphosyntactically are connected by warm (reddish) and heavy beams. Visual inspection of Map C.3 points to four hotbeds of neighborly similarity in Great Britain. These highlight a very crucial dialect division, identified in virtually all of the big-picture studies discussed in Section 1.2, between dialects spoken in (i) the Southwest of England, (ii) the Southeast of England, (iii) the North of England, and (iv) Scotland:

---

[2] Note that as a VDM map, Map C.3 is based on Euclidean similarities (*ES* values; see Section 2.2.5 [p. 30]).

- In the Southwest of England, there is a comparatively marked axis of interpoint similarities running from Cornwall via Devon and Somerset all the way to Wiltshire.
- In the Southeast of England, we note a triangle of relatively modest morphosyntactic similarities connecting Kent, London, and Suffolk.
- In the northern Midlands and the North of England, we find a web of strong interpoint similarities encompassing Nottinghamshire, Lancashire, Westmorland, Yorkshire, and Durham.
- The Central Scottish Lowlands exhibit a bolt of interpoint similarities involving parts of the urbanized "Central Belt" (Stuart-Smith 2004, 51): West Lothian, Midlothian, and East Lothian.

Just as network maps have a mirror image in reverse network maps, beam maps have a logically reverse counterpart in HONEYCOMB MAPS (see e.g. Goebl 2007, 11). So in Map C.4 (Appendix C, p. 174), polygon borders between dialects that are morphosyntactically dissimilar are marked by blueish and heavy lines (this echoes thin blueish interpoint beams in Map C.3), while polygon borders separating morphosyntactically similar dialects are reddish and thin (echoing heavy reddish interpoint beams in Map C.3).[3] We notice, then, marked interpoint dissimilarities (i) in the West Midlands (in particular around Warwickshire), (ii) between Denbighshire in North Wales and the neighboring measuring points, (iii) in the Southern Scottish Lowlands, and (iv) between measuring points in the Scottish Highlands (Sutherland, Ross and Cromarty) and in the Scottish Lowlands.

### 4.1.3   Two similarity profiles

So far, we have taken a rather global perspective in treating all measuring points in the dataset as being on equal par. We will now zoom in on individual measuring points; after all, at the level of the areal granularity selected in the presented study the dataset actually spawns thirty-four similarity distributions in which each measuring point is characterized by its relations to the other thirty-three measuring points. Similarity profiles can be cartographically projected to geography in SIMILARITY MAPS, a cartographic technique popular in the Salzburg School of Dialectometry. The idea is to generate a Voronoi-tesselated map in which the polygons are colored according to measuring points' similarity to some reference measuring point (whose Voronoi polygon appears in white). As with beam maps, warm (i.e. reddish) colors indicate relative similarities, while cold (i.e. blueish) colors depict relative dissimilarities. On the interpretational plane, Goebl explains that

---

[3] Just as Map C.3, Map C.4 is based on Euclidean similarities (*ES* values; see Section 2.2.5 [p. 30]).

each similarity map contains information on the geolinguistic modalities regarding the *position of a certain dialect within the whole inquiry grid, i.e. the complete map* [...] An analogous *non-linguistic* interpretation may help the reader understand the deeper meaning of the message conveyed by the similarity maps. The following examples show obvious analogies:

(i)   by analogy with the *telephone*: The mathematical reasoning underlying the similarity maps allows for considering every one of them as a general record of the phone calls (active and passive) of one of the $N$ participants within a telephone network. [...]

(ii)  by analogy with *diffusion*: Under the assumption that each reference point can be compared with a single "missionary" eager to diffuse a particular ideology or creed, the similarity maps show where and to what extent s/he succeeded.

(Goebl 2007, 140; emphases original)

Needless to say, Goebl's telephone metaphor in particular builds on a time-honored topos in dialectology – that "an isogloss presumably marks a line of weakness in the density of communication" (Bloomfield [1933] 1984: 340). We shall now exemplarily discuss two similarity profiles (and maps): one for Kincardineshire in the Northeastern Scottish Lowlands (Map C.5 [Appendix C, p. 175]), and the other one for Nottinghamshire in the English Midlands (Map C.6 [Appendix C, p. 175]).[4] Recall that we have seen before that Kincardineshire English does not exhibit many morphosyntactic similarities to other measuring points in the dataset, and radiates a strong signal of dissimilarity into map space (see Map C.2). In quantitative terms, Kincardineshire has a mean morphosyntactic distance of 7.17 Euclidean distance points to other dialects in the sample, which is a fairly high score. The similarity map in Map C.5 highlights Kincardineshire's marginal status: most of the map is painted in cold colors, and Kincardineshire entertains "warm," reddish relationships to only three measuring points in its immediate neighborhood: Angus, Perthshire, and West Lothian. The histogram in Map C.5, which has a positive skew, drives home Map C.5's message that there are many more measuring points to which Kincardineshire is dissimilar than to which it is similar. In terms of Goebl's interpretive metaphor, Kincardineshire does not make many phone calls, and it is a lousy missionary.

Nottinghamshire, by contrast, does not qualify as an outsider dialect (see Map C.6). The measuring point has behaved fairly inconspicuously in the maps we have seen so far, and its mean morphosyntactic distance to the other thirty-three measuring points in the dataset is 5.05 Euclidean distance points, slightly below the mean distance value of 5.41 that holds for the distance matrix as a whole. The histogram in Map C.6 is also more

---

[4] Both maps are VDM maps and thus based on Euclidean similarities (*ES* values; see Section 2.2.5 [p. 30]).

balanced than Kincardineshire's histogram. It stands to reason, then, that Map C.6 has many more reddish polygons than Kincardineshire's similarity map. Nottinghamshire entertains particularly close linguistic relationships to other counties in England (Warwickshire, Middlesex, and Northumberland being the exceptions), while it is dissimilar morphosyntactically from most measuring points in Scotland. Thus, Nottinghamshire makes regular phone calls to most of its brethren in England, but it does not talk a lot to its cousins in Scotland. As a general point, it bears mentioning that both Map C.5 and Map C.6 exhibit a geographic signal. The farther – in geographical terms – one strays from the reference polygon, the more blue the polygons tend to become.

## 4.2   Two regionally selective analyses

The goal in this section is to separately scrutinize aggregate morphosyntactic relationships in England, on the one hand, and in Scotland (including the Hebrides) on the other hand. The rationale for this more selective approach (which will be replicated in Section 5.3's number crunching approach) is that when attention is restricted to a subset of the data, some instructive details may come to the fore that would remain elusive in an analysis based on the entire dataset. Cartographically, this section will exclusively rely on network maps.

### 4.2.1   Aggregate morphosyntactic distances and similarities in England

FRED samples eighteen measuring points in geographic England, which yields a total of $18 \times 17/2 = 153$ measuring point pairings. According to Table 4.2, this regionally selective dataset is – not surprisingly – somewhat more homogeneous than the full 34-county dataset. Mean morphosyntactic distance is 4.43 Euclidean distance points, a figure that is comfortably below the mean distance of 5.41 points exhibited in the entire dataset and which is associated with a standard deviation of just .89. The minimum distance is 2.32 points (Somerset versus Wiltshire, both in the Southwest of England), and the maximum distance is 6.52 points (Suffolk, Southeast of England against Warwickshire, English Midlands). Unlike in the full dataset, the distance distribution (see Figure 4.2), while still a normal distribution, is positively skewed such that there are more smaller distances than larger distances.

The network map in Map C.7 (Appendix C, p. 176) projects aggregate morphosyntactic distances among English English dialects to geography. The map highlights the strong linguistic links interconnecting Southern English English dialects, especially Cornwall, Devon, Somerset, Wiltshire, London, and Kent. It also emphasizes the marked links that connect northern Midlands and Northern English English dialects, especially Shropshire,

| | |
|---|---|
| measuring point pairings | 153 |
| mean | 4.43 |
| standard deviation | .89 |
| minimum | 2.32 |
| median | 4.39 |
| maximum | 6.52 |
| skewness | .10 |
| kurtosis | −.47 |

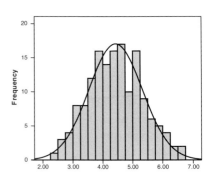

Table 4.2. *Aggregate morphosyntactic distances: summary statistics, measuring points in England only.*

Figure 4.2. Aggregate morphosyntactic distances: histogram, measuring points in England only.

Lancashire, Westmorland, and Yorkshire. Once again, this North–South opposition is in line with the literature (e.g. Trudgill 1990; Goebl 2007). Against this backdrop, it is curious that the network of morphosyntactic links depicted in Map C.7 bears a number of similarities to the primarily lexical connections noted by J. O. Halliwell in his 1847 *Dictionary of Archaic and Provincial Words* (cited in Ihalainen 1994, 210–212). Consider Figure 4.3, which is Ihalainen's visual summary of Halliwell's comments:

The arrows indicate that Halliwell connects the areas involved linguistically. The arrowhead indicates the direction of the connection. Thus, Cambridgeshire → Norfolk means that Cambridgeshire is related linguistically to Norfolk. (Ihalainen 1994, 211–212)

Although a number of counties which are part of the present study's measuring point portfolio are classified as unconnected by Halliwell (specifically so Lancashire, Nottinghamshire, Shropshire, and Leicestershire), the basic structure is fundamentally the same. There is, in both accounts, an axis that links the southern counties, i.e. Cornwall, Devon, Somerset, Wiltshire, and Kent. Second, both accounts point to strong links running from south to north in the East of England and connecting Kent, Suffolk, Yorkshire (via Nottinghamshire), and Durham. Obviously, not too much emphasis should be put on this comparison, which essentially compares apples (nineteenth-century variability that is primarily lexical in nature) to oranges (twentieth-century morphosyntactic variability), but the overlap nonetheless seems noteworthy. In any case, Map C.7 also emphasizes our earlier point that counties differ in their "centrality," i.e. in the extent to which they participate in network structures. For example, Yorkshire is fairly central in that it has robust morphosyntactic links to other counties. Other rather central counties include Cornwall, London, and Nottinghamshire. Conversely,

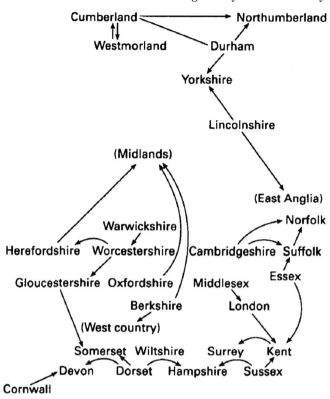

Figure 4.3. Connections among nineteenth century English English dialects, redrawn from Halliwell's *Dictionary of Archaic and Provincial Words* (Ihalainen 1994, figure 5.1). Reprinted with kind permission from Cambridge University Press.

there are a number of more marginal measuring points that have only weak links to other counties. The front-runners here include Middlesex, Suffolk, and – especially – Leicestershire and Warwickshire.

This takes us right away to the reverse network map in Map C.8 (Appendix C, p. 176). Middlesex, Suffolk, Leicestershire, and Warwickshire figure prominently when it comes to signals of linguistic difference among English English dialects. Succinctly put, Map C.8 demonstrates that there is a lot of morphosyntactic dissimilarity covering the West Midlands and neighboring measuring points, with the triangle Shropshire – Warwickshire – Leicestershire sitting in the epicenter of this dissimilarity tangle. Now, it is well-known that the West Midlands dialect has been a distinct dialect since Middle English times (Hughes and Trudgill 1996, 85). Today, the West Midlands dialect (especially the so-called *Black Country* dialect) is typically seen

## 80   Surveying the forest

| | |
|---|---|
| measuring point pairings | 78 |
| mean | 5.83 |
| standard deviation | 1.01 |
| minimum | 2.77 |
| median | 5.84 |
| maximum | 7.95 |
| skewness | −.26 |
| kurtosis | .17 |

Table 4.3. *Aggregate morphosyntactic distances: summary statistics, measuring points in Scotland and the Hebrides only.*

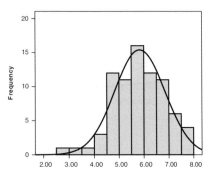

Figure 4.4. Aggregate morphosyntactic distances: histogram, measuring points in Scotland and the Hebrides only.

as being somewhat special (Clark 2004, 135), primarily on pronunciational grounds. The data presented here strongly suggest that there is also something about its morphosyntax that sets this area apart from other dialects. For a more detailed discussion of what distinguishes Leicestershire and Warwickshire from surrounding dialects according to the present study's dataset, the reader is referred to Section 7.1. Note, however, that in many of Orton et al.'s (1978) morphosyntax maps, the West Midlands region is also demarcated from surrounding measuring points; consider, for example, the case of *was/were* variation (maps M22–M25), negated forms of *can* (map M31), constituent ordering in dative constructions (map S1), or dialectal *did not do* periphrases (map S9).

### 4.2.2   Aggregate morphosyntactic distances and similarities in Scotland

FRED covers $N = 13$ measuring points in Scotland (including one measuring point for the Hebrides). This network yields a total of $13 \times 12/2 = 78$ measuring point pairings. According to Table 4.3, mean morphosyntactic distance in this subsample is 5.83 Euclidean distance points. This value is larger than the corresponding value in the full dataset (5.41), and considerably larger than the mean morphosyntactic distance between English English dialects (4.43). The minimum distance is 2.77 and can be observed between East Lothian and Midlothian, two neighboring measuring points in the Central Scottish Lowlands. The maximum distance in the subsample is 7.95 distance points (Kincardineshire, Scottish Lowlands versus Sutherland, Scottish Highlands). As in the full dataset, the distance distribution, while still a normal distribution, is negatively skewed such that there are more larger distances than smaller distances (see Figure 4.4).

Map C.9 (Appendix C, p. 177) highlights the geographic distribution of morphosyntactic similarities in the subsample. What is most striking about this map is the geographically extensive triangle of similarities connecting measuring points in the Central Scottish Lowlands to, first, the two measuring points in the Scottish Highlands (Sutherland and Ross and Cromarty), and second to the Hebrides. This is a triangle, then, that links young, non-traditional, non-Scots varieties of English to Scots varieties spoken in the Central Scottish Lowlands. There is a second, geographically less sprawling and less marked triangle linking Angus to Perthshire and West Lothian. West Lothian, lastly, is also part of an axis that connects to Midlothian and East Lothian. In regard to centrality and marginality, we note that with a mean morphosyntactic distance to the other counties of only 4.56 distance points, Midlothian is the most central county in the subsample. Conversely, with mean distances greater than 6, Banffshire, Dumfriesshire, and Kincardineshire are the most marginal counties in the sample. It stands to reason that these three measuring points are also implicated in the strong dissimilarity network depicted in the reverse network map in Map C.10 (Appendix C, p. 177).

## 4.3   On linguistic compromise areas and dialect kernels

This section addresses two overlapping but not identical issues. First, where may we find areas characterized by morphosyntactic compromise and exchange (Besch 1967) in the FRED network? Second, is there an empirical basis for positing morphosyntactic dialect kernels (see Gauchat 1903; Goebl 1982)? Technically, this section assesses two key statistical parameters – skewness and maximum similarity – of the present study's distance distribution portfolio, and projects these parameters to geography utilizing appropriate, Salzburg-style (see Goebl 2005, 507) cartographic techniques.

Our casual remarks in the previous sections on "marginal" and "central" counties in the FRED dialect network raise the question as to whether we are in a position to identify geolinguistic patterns that are indicative of linguistic compromise and exchange, in the sense of Besch's (1967) notion of *Sprachausgleich*. So far, we have judged the centrality or marginality of selected measuring points primarily on the basis of *mean* linguistic distances to other measuring points. We now utilize an analysis technique developed in Salzburg that can approach the issue more directly, and more comprehensively:

"linguistic compromise" is defined as the accumulation of linguistic exchange and (ad)mixture phenomena of all kinds that can exist over a shorter and/or longer distance. The result of the exchange is a linguistic intermixing which is strong to different degrees. Obviously, it is less important in those dialectal zones which participate little or not at all in the dynamics of interplay and exchange. This phenomenon can be detected statistically by the measurement of the symmetry of a given similarity distribution. Similarity distributions skewing to the left (negative skew, where most of the similarity values are concentrated below the arithmetic mean) tend to indicate isolated dialects, while similarity distributions skewing to the right (positive skew, where most of the similarity values are concentrated above the arithmetic mean) indicate expanding or well-integrated dialects. (Goebl 2006, 419)

To project skewness values to geography, the analyst assigns warm or cold color hues to individual measuring points. These hues are proportional to the skewness value of that measuring point's similarity distribution. Warm (i.e. reddish) colors depict negative similarity skewness (or positive distance skewness, depending on whether one is working with a similarity or distance matrix) and thus, by inference, weak linguistic compromise. Cold (i.e. blueish) colors indicate positive similarity skewness (or negative distance skewness) and hence, by inference, intense linguistic compromise. The cartographic outcome is a so-called SKEWNESS MAP, as in Map C.11 (Appendix C, p. 178). Thus, the distance distribution of the county Kincardineshire (measuring point 5) has the largest negative similarity skew and hence appears in criss-crossed bright red.[5] By contrast, the distance distribution of county Sutherland (measuring point 2) has the largest positive similarity skew and thus is depicted in criss-crossed deep blue. All this is another way of saying that most of the other thirty-three measuring points are linguistically rather distant to Kincardineshire, while there are more similarities than dissimilarities between Sutherland and the other thirty-three measuring points in the dataset. The big picture sketched in Map C.11, then, can be summarized as follows. In *England*, there are two epicenters of linguistic compromise. The first one encompasses the Northern measuring points (Westmorland, Durham, Lancashire, and Yorkshire) minus Northumberland (the Isle of Man is also a compromise data point, and can be argued to belong to the North of England in this connection). The second epicenter consists of Middlesex and London. In *Wales*, both measuring points are leaning towards linguistic compromise, though Glamorganshire markedly more so than Denbighshire. The *Scottish Lowlands* are mostly deep red, which is another way of saying that here we find only very weak linguistic compromise and exchange, the exceptions being Selkirkshire, Peebleshire, and Angus. Lastly, *the Scottish Highlands and the Hebrides* are an intense linguistic compromise area. The pattern, then, that emerges here is that we find morphosyntactic compromise and exchange primarily in (i) young varieties (for instance, in the Scottish Highlands), (ii) geographic transition areas such as the North, which geographically speaking may be seen as a transition zone between Southern English English dialects and

[5] Note that as a VDM map, Map C.11 is based on Euclidean similarities (*ES* values; see Section 2.2.5 [p. 30]).

Scots varieties, and (iii) dialects that (historically) have an affinity to the Standard language, or vice versa (Middlesex and London).

A related issue is the quest for "dialect kernels" (Gauchat 1903). Where is it that we may find the linguistic nuclei of dialect landscapes? Goebl (1982, 42–43) has suggested the following technique to approach this question empirically. First, the analyst calculates the similarity profile for each of the dialect objects under investigation; second, the maximal similarity value (or minimal distance value, depending on whether one is working with a similarity or distance matrix) for each of the objects is recorded; third, these values are projected to geography. The result is, in Goeblian parlance, a Choropleth map of the synopsis of the maximal values of $N$ similarity distributions (see Goebl 2006, 431), for which we will use the term KERNEL MAP as a shorthand. In kernel maps, warm color tones are assigned to measuring points with comparatively large similarity maxima (or low distance minima, as the case may be), and cold color tones to measuring points with comparatively low similarity maxima (or high distance minima). Interpretively, then, dialects whose Voronoi polygons appear in warm color tones can be likened to "mountains" – these are kernels which bear a lot of similarity to at least one other dialect. In keeping with the mountain range metaphor, cold color tones analogously correspond to "valleys," that is, transition zones where we do not find a lot of similarity to other dialects. In this spirit, Map C.12 (Appendix C, p. 178) is a kernel map that visualizes the distance minima distribution in the present study's dataset; as a VDM map, Map C.12 is based on Euclidean similarities (*ES* values; see Section 2.2.5 [p. 30]). In this map, measuring point 13 (Dumfriesshire) is the measuring point with the highest distance minimum: 5.49 Euclidean distance points, which is the measuring point's distance to Northumberland. Measuring points 28 and 29 (Somerset and Wiltshire), in contrast, are the two measuring points in the dataset with the lowest distance minima, 2.31 Euclidean distance points, which they happen to score with each other. In all, Map C.12 makes plain that in terms of morphosyntax, England has one major dialect kernel which comprises much of the Southwest of England (Cornwall, Devon, Somerset, Wiltshire) plus London. In Scotland, we find a more compact dialect kernel made up of measuring points 10 and 11 (Midlothian and East Lothian). In between, we find a transition zone with a particularly deep "valley" around measuring points 21 and 22 (Warwickshire and Leicestershire) in the English Midlands and measuring points 12 and 13 (Dumfriesshire and Selkirkshire) in the Southern Scottish Lowlands.

## 4.4   Dialectal similarities and distances to Standard English

This section explores aggregate morphosyntactic similarities and distances between the traditional British dialects sampled in FRED and, first, Standard conversational British English as represented in our reference corpus

| | |
|---|---|
| measuring point pairings | 34 |
| mean | 6.47 |
| standard deviation | .95 |
| minimum | 4.11 |
| median | 6.56 |
| maximum | 8.90 |
| skewness | −.05 |
| kurtosis | .61 |

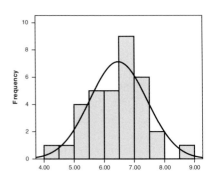

Table 4.4. *Aggregate morphosyntactic distances to Standard British English: summary statistics.*

Figure 4.5. Aggregate morphosyntactic distances to Standard British English: histogram.

tapping the British component of the *International Corpus of English*, and, second, Standard conversational American English as represented in our reference corpus based on the *Corpus of Spoken American English* (see Section 2.1.2).

We begin by stating that the distance between the two Standard varieties, British and American, is 3.92 Euclidean distance points. To put this figure into perspective, notice that this figure roughly corresponds to the morphosyntactic distance between the Hebrides and Ross and Cromarty. It is well below the mean dialectal distance in FRED (5.41 Euclidean distance points), and also comfortably below the mean score for English English FRED dialects (4.43 Euclidean distance points). This means that Standard British and American English are fairly close morphosyntactically, and that dialectal variability in Great Britain trumps variability between the two Standard varieties. This finding is certainly not entirely unexpected, yet it is still interesting given that the feature catalogue contains many features that also figure prominently in the sizable literature on British–American grammar differences – take, for example, genitive choice (e.g. Rosenbach 2003), future marker choice (e.g. Szmrecsanyi 2003), or verbal complementation (e.g. Mair 2002). Tables 4.4 and 4.5 provide some additional summary statistics. On the whole, the distance distribution is fairly similar in the case of both Standard varieties. We note especially that the mean distance between the Standard varieties and the FRED dialects is virtually identical (6.47 vs. 6.43). Both distance distributions are negatively skewed such that there are more larger distances than smaller distances (see Figures 4.5 and 4.6). The two distance distributions also correlate strongly ($r = .93$, $p < .001$). Actual per-measuring point distances are listed in Table 4.6.

What is the exact relationship between Standard British English and the traditional dialects sampled in FRED? In the FRED network as a whole, it is the Hebrides – recall here that Hebridean English is a comparatively

| | |
|---|---|
| measuring point pairings | 34 |
| mean | 6.43 |
| standard deviation | .86 |
| minimum | 4.31 |
| median | 6.56 |
| maximum | 8.45 |
| skewness | −.21 |
| kurtosis | .28 |

Table 4.5. *Aggregate morphosyntactic distances to Standard American English: summary statistics.*

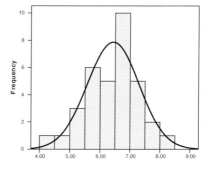

Figure 4.6. Aggregate morphosyntactic distances to Standard American English: histogram.

young variety of English – that exhibit the smallest morphosyntactic distance to Standard British English (4.11 Euclidean distance points; see Table 4.6). Conversely, Kincardineshire in the Scottish Lowlands is most distant morphosyntactically. If attention is restricted to measuring points in England, it is Westmorland that is most similar and Suffolk that is most distant. George Puttenham's well-known statement (1589: iii) that Standard English, or the "best" English, is "the vsuall speach of the Court, and that of London, and the shires lying about London within Ix. myles and not much aboue" therefore patently does not mesh with our data. Instead, it is in Westmorland – hundreds of kilometers away – where we find the variety of dialectal English most closely related to the morphosyntax of contemporary Standard British English. The similarity map in Map C.13 (Appendix C, p. 179) projects aggregate morphosyntactic similarities to geography such that (much as in Maps C.5 and C.6) a color slide distinguishes between dialectal measuring points that are extremely similar and extremely dissimilar to Standard English varieties: the bluer hues indicate dissimilarities while the redder hues indicate similarities. On a technical note, Maps C.13 and C.14 were generated by dividing the observable distance range into ten percentile bins such that each bin contains roughly the same number of observations. Each county's bin rank was then mapped on the red–green–blue color scheme, assigning a perfect blue hue to the highest bin rank, a perfect red tone to the lowest bin rank, and gradient red-blue color blends to the ranks in between. So, the pattern emerging from Map C.13 is that the Scottish Lowlands (except for Midlothian and East Lothian) as well as the English Midlands (in particular, Nottinghamshire and Leicestershire) display the largest distances to Standard British English. Conversely, the relatively young dialects in the Scottish Highlands and on the Hebrides are overall quite close – and so are the measuring points in the North of England.

Table 4.6. *Euclidean distances to Standard British English (source: ICE-GB) and Standard American English (source: CSAE) (ordered by distance to Standard British English).*

|  | distance to StBrE | distance to StAmE |
|---|---|---|
| Hebrides | 4.11 | 4.31 |
| Ross and Cromarty | 4.88 | 4.99 |
| Westmorland | 5.26 | 5.20 |
| Midlothian | 5.40 | 5.37 |
| Yorkshire | 5.47 | 5.93 |
| Lancashire | 5.49 | 6.21 |
| Warwickshire | 5.57 | 5.72 |
| Sutherland | 5.75 | 5.27 |
| East Lothian | 5.88 | 5.61 |
| Glamorganshire | 5.88 | 5.92 |
| Shropshire | 5.88 | 5.95 |
| London | 6.00 | 6.46 |
| Devon | 6.25 | 6.43 |
| Cornwall | 6.29 | 6.56 |
| Denbighshire | 6.45 | 5.66 |
| Somerset | 6.46 | 6.64 |
| Durham | 6.51 | 6.20 |
| West Lothian | 6.60 | 6.57 |
| Middlesex | 6.66 | 6.61 |
| Peebleshire | 6.68 | 6.60 |
| Wiltshire | 6.69 | 6.69 |
| Selkirkshire | 6.81 | 6.94 |
| Northumberland | 6.83 | 6.61 |
| Nottinghamshire | 6.91 | 7.34 |
| Isle of Man | 6.99 | 6.49 |
| Oxfordshire | 7.01 | 7.28 |
| Kent | 7.36 | 7.60 |
| Angus | 7.40 | 7.32 |
| Leicestershire | 7.40 | 7.61 |
| Suffolk | 7.46 | 7.25 |
| Perthshire | 7.47 | 6.97 |
| Dumfriesshire | 7.64 | 6.83 |
| Banffshire | 7.74 | 7.18 |
| Kincardineshire | 8.90 | 8.45 |

We now turn our attention to aggregate dialectal relations to Standard American English. Given the comparatively small morphosyntactic distance between Standard American and British English, this story necessarily has a similar arc to our previous account on dialectal relationships to Standard British English. With a distance of 4.31 Euclidean distance points (see Table 4.6), the measuring point that is most similar morphosyntactically to Standard American English is Hebridean English, exactly as with Standard British English. And again, it is Kincardineshire that is most distant from Standard American English. If only measuring points in England are considered, we also once again identify Westmorland as the most similar dialect, but – unlike in the Standard British English case – Leicestershire as the morphosyntactically most distant dialect. The corresponding similarity map (Map C.14) (Appendix C, p. 179) is very similar to what we have seen already for Standard British English. Some of the differences concern London, which is closer to Standard British English than to Standard American English, and Denbighshire in North Wales, which is considerably closer to Standard American English than to Standard British English. We also observe that all of the measuring points in Scotland except Selkirkshire and Ross and Cromarty are more similar to Standard American English than to Standard British English.

## 4.5   Chapter summary

This chapter aimed to sketch the big picture. In this spirit, we first explored aggregate morphosyntactic similarities and distances *among* British English dialects, and, second, distances *between* those dialects and Standard British and American English. We have seen that from the bird's eye perspective, English English dialects exhibit comparatively strong morphosyntactic similarities, with hotbeds of interpoint resemblance being located in the Southwest of England, the Southeast of England, and the North of England. By contrast, there is quite some heterogeneity among dialects spoken in Scotland. Having said that, the data suggest that Central Scottish Lowlands dialects are fairly similar to each other and also resemble varieties of English spoken in the Scottish Highlands. As for English English dialects, we highlighted the robust morphosyntactic links interconnecting Southwestern and Southeastern English English dialects, on the one hand, and discussed the links tying together Northern English English dialects on the other hand. At the same time, we have also identified a triangle of measuring points (Shropshire, Warwickshire, and Leicestershire) in the West Midlands that radiates a strong signal of dissimilarity into the rest of the dialect network. Moreover, this chapter has investigated how individual dialects differ in the *overall* extent to which they participate in network structures. For example, we have seen that Kincardineshire English is a rather marginal (i.e. loosely integrated) dialect that does not show many similarities to other dialects. Compare this to Nottinghamshire English, which is a fairly central dialect relatively similar to many other dialects. In this connection, we used an analysis technique designed to identify areas characterized by linguistic compromise and exchange and found – in short – that the North of England as well as young dialect regions in Wales and the Scottish Highlands are areas of more or less intense linguistic compromise and exchange. However, Lowland Scottish dialects really do not appear to compromise much morphosyntactically. As for dialect kernels, we have seen that England has one major dialect kernel which comprises much of the Southwest of England plus London while in Scotland, we find a more compact dialect kernel encompassing Midlothian and East Lothian, two measuring points in the

Central Scottish Lowlands. Lastly, in regard to the relationship between British English dialects and the two major Standard varieties (British and American) we noted that dialectal variation in Britain is considerably more endemic than variation between the two Standard varieties, and that the two Standard varieties are virtually equidistant morphosyntactically from the dialect varieties sampled in FRED. In the case of both Standard American English and Standard British English, we saw that dialects spoken in Scotland and some dialects spoken in the English Midlands stand out in being fairly distant from either Standard variety, while dialects spoken in the North of England are generally fairly close.

# 5    Is morphosyntactic variability gradient? Exploring dialect continua

We will now begin to push deeper into the geographic structure of linguistic variability in British English dialects. The matter that will concern us in this chapter is the extent to which the morphosyntactic dialect landscape in Great Britain can be thought of as being a dialect continuum – in other words, is linguistic distance proportional to geographic distance, such that dialect transitions are smooth as opposed to abrupt? Section 5.1 reviews the literature on dialect continua. Section 5.2 approaches the issue cartographically. Section 5.3 utilizes correlation analysis and regression techniques to quantify the extent to which linguistic distance is proportional to geographic distance. Section 5.4 is a chapter summary.

## 5.1    On dialect continua

There are two principal ways to think about dialect geographies (see Heeringa and Nerbonne 2001): the DIALECT AREA SCENARIO (an exploration of which is reserved for the following chapter), and the DIALECT CONTINUUM SCENARIO. Succinctly put, the dialect area scenario seeks to partition a given dialect landscape into internally homogeneous but mutually heterogeneous dialect areas. By contrast, the dialect continuum scenario posits that there are no sharp boundaries between dialects. Instead, linguistic distance is supposed to be directly proportional to geographic distance. In their extreme manifestations, the two scenarios are incompatible, for either we find sharp dialect boundaries, or we don't. Yet reality actually comes in shades of gray, and the present study operates on the assumption that the way in which geographic space conditions dialect variability has a continuum-like structure itself. At one end of this continuum, we find perfect dialect continua where linguistic transitions are maximally smooth; at the opposite end, we deal with perfectly regionalized dialect landscapes in which transitions between internally homogeneous dialect areas are maximally abrupt. The point is, though, that these poles are idealized prototypes, and that actual dialect relationships will typically fall somewhere in between. Hence in what follows, we premise that the

dialect area scenario and the dialect continuum scenario are two different, not necessarily contradictory but rather complementary analytical ways
of looking at the same empirical reality (see Goebl 1983; Chambers and
Trudgill 1998, 105; Heeringa 2004, 5 for a similar argument). Much as in
the realm of quantum mechanics light is *neither* a wave *nor* a particle but
exhibits both wave-like *and* particle-like properties, we offer that dialect
landscapes can be potentially both continuum-like and area-like at the same
time, the empirical question being the extent to which one of the two traits
prevails.

To reiterate, the key characteristic of dialect continua is the transi-
tional GRADUALNESS of dialect differences. Chambers and Trudgill neatly
illustrate this idea by the allegory of the traveler:

> If we travel from village to village, in a particular direction, we notice linguis-
> tic differences which distinguish one village from another. Sometimes these
> differences will be larger, sometimes smaller, but they will be CUMULA-
> TIVE. The further we get from our starting point, the larger the differences
> will become. The effect of this may therefore be, if the distance involved
> is large enough, that (if we arrange villages along our route in geographical
> order) while speakers from village A understand people from village B very
> well and those from village F quite well, they may understand village M
> speech only with considerable difficulty, and that of village Z not at all. Vil-
> lagers from M, on the other hand, will probably understand village F speech
> quite well, and villagers from A and Z only with difficulty . . . the cumulative
> effect of the linguistic differences will be such that the greater the geograph-
> ical separation, the greater the difficulty of comprehension. (Chambers and
> Trudgill 1998, 5; emphases original)

Needless to say, the view epitomized here is intellectually somewhat
indebted to the "wave theory" (*Wellentheorie*) of linguistic change (Schmidt
1872), according to which linguistic innovation diffuses "as a pebble-in-a-
pond effect, with a centre of influence (the point of impact of the pebble)
sending ripples outwards in all directions (the movement of the wave)"
(Chambers and Trudgill 1998, 166). Though the notion of sharp dialect
boundaries and attempts at rigid dialect classification reigned supreme in
the nineteenth century, many dialectologists eventually came to realize that
Schmidtian wave effects, with all the gradualness and "complex isogloss
patterns" (Hock and Joseph 2009, 341) they entail, often meshed better
with the data than alternative explanations, such as Schleicherian phylo-
genies (Schleicher 1863; see the next chapter for a discussion). Thus in
the 1930s, Bloomfield summarized the history of thought on this topic as
follows:

> Accordingly, some students now despaired of all classification and
> announced that within a dialect area there are no real boundaries. Even in

a domain such as that of the western Romance languages (Italian, Latin, French, Spanish, Portuguese) it was urged that there were no real boundaries, but only gradual transitions: the difference between any two neighboring points was no more and no less important than the difference between any two other neighboring points. (Bloomfield [1933] 1984: 341)

The gist of the dialect continuum scenario, then, is that "dialects differ from each other more radically the more remote they are from each other geographically" (Downes 1998, 18), an axiom that Nerbonne and Kleiweg (2007, 154) refer to as the "Fundamental Dialectology Principle." The more or less tacit assumption behind this sort of reasoning is that geographical proximity is a proxy for the likelihood of social contact and communicative interaction, and that "interaction becomes less frequent as a function of distance" (Johnstone 2009, 6; see also Nerbonne 2003; Gooskens 2005). Textbook examples of geographical dialect continua include the West Romance dialect continuum (see, e.g., Heinemann 2008), the West Germanic dialect continuum (see, e.g., Kremer 1979), or the Scandinavian dialect continuum (see, e.g., Chambers and Trudgill 1998, 11).

## 5.2   The cartographic take on dialect continua

This section probes the dialect continuum scenario cartographically. We first apply an exploratory statistical technique known as "Multidimensional Scaling" to the dataset, and subsequently visualize the results in appropriate plots and so-called "continuum maps."

### 5.2.1   *Multidimensional Scaling*

The first step towards visualizing dialect continua is a computational one – we process the dataset with the help of MULTIDIMENSIONAL SCALING (MDS), an analysis technique originally developed in psychometrics (Torgerson 1958). Embleton (1993) is commonly credited for introducing MDS to dialectology. In a nutshell, MDS seeks to reduce a higher-dimensional dataset to a lower-dimensional representation which is more amenable to visualization. In the present study, we will seek to scale down a $N-1$ dimensional distance matrix (in which each object, or dialect, is characterized by its distance to the other $N-1$ objects in the matrix) to a lower-dimensional representation in which each linguistic object has a coordinate in a small number of artificial MDS dimensions. Take, for example, the $34 \times 34$ dialects-only distance matrix discussed in Section 4.1 representing each one of the thirty-four British English dialects through its distance to the other thirty-three measuring points in the sample (and in so doing assigns thirty-three coordinates to each object). MDS can be used to scale down this high-dimensional coordinate system to one in which every measuring point has, for example, only two coordinates. This procedure would enable us, for the sake of easy interpretability, to depict dialectal variability on a two-dimensional plane. It is clear that this sort of dimension reduction may result in data loss. The reason is that variability in, say, two dimensions may not be able to capture the full extent of variability in, say, thirty-three dimensions. The good news is that MDS seeks to minimize this information loss, and that we can precisely quantify the amount of information lost.

A few more technical remarks are in order here. MDS exploits the mathematical truth that just as distances can be inferred from coordinates (e.g. the distance between two villages can be calculated from their longitude/latitude coordinates), so coordinates – in whatever dimensionality – can be inferred from distances (Heeringa 2004, 156). This is not the place to dwell on the algorithmical details behind this inference process (for an overview, see Kruskal and Wish 1978 and Heeringa 2004, 156–163). It should, however, be emphasized that the analyst can choose between a number of slightly different MDS algorithms. The *RuG/L04* package (module mds) and the statistics environment *R*, on which *RuG/L04*'s mds module is based, offer three MDS algorithms: (i) *Classical Multidimensional Scaling*, also known as *Principal Coordinates Analysis* (Torgerson 1958; Gower 1966; R Development Core Team 2010, 1152–1153); (ii) *Kruskal's Non-Metric Multidimensional Scaling* (Kruskal and Wish 1978; R Development Core Team 2010, 1842–1844); and (iii) *Sammon's Non-Linear Mapping* (Sammon 1969; R Development Core Team 2010, 1906–1907). The present study adopts Heeringa's (2004: 160–161) stance that we should prefer that algorithm whose Euclidean MDS coordinate-based distances exhibit the highest correlation with the original higher-dimensional distances in the distance matrix. This is another way of saying that we should opt for the algorithm that minimizes information loss best. So, we applied all three algorithms to the $34 \times 34$ distance matrix discussed in Section 4.1 as a test case to obtain a three-dimensional MDS solution. According to Heeringa's criterion, Kruskal's non-metric MDS appears to have an edge over the other two algorithms: Kruskal's method captures approximately 90 percent of the variance in the original linguistic distances ($R^2 = 89.3\%$; hence, the information loss incurred is about 10 percent only) while the other two algorithms capture only about 70 percent of the original variance (Classical MDS: $R^2 = 71.1\%$, Sammon's non-linear mapping: $R^2 = 72.4\%$). In the remainder of the chapter, we will therefore use Kruskal's non-metric MDS, although we hasten to add that the three MDS algorithms yield overall remarkably similar results.

*5.2.2   Some MDS plots*

We will now discuss a number of comparatively straightforward plots, mainly for the sake of familiarizing the reader with the use and analytical potential of MDS. Figures 5.1, 5.2, and 5.3 all locate FRED measuring points in

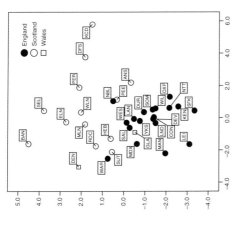

Figure 5.1. Two-dimensional MDS plot. Input: as-the-crow-flies distances. Proximity in the plot indicates spatial proximity. Shared variance with original distances: $R^2 = 99.9\%$.

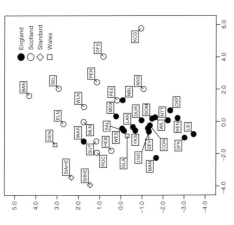

Figure 5.2. Two-dimensional MDS plot. Input: morphosyntactic distances (including distances to Standard English). Proximity in the plot indicates morphosyntactic similarity. Shared variance with original distances: $R^2 = 80.4\%$.

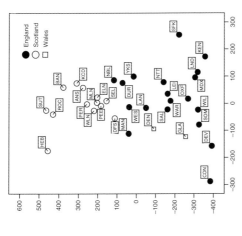

Figure 5.3. Two-dimensional MDS plot. Input: morphosyntactic distances (dialects only). Proximity in the plot indicates morphosyntactic similarity. Shared variance with original distances: $R^2 = 80.2\%$.

two-dimensional coordinate systems. The input to Figure 5.1 is a $34 \times 34$ distance matrix detailing not morphosyntactic but *geographic* as-the-crow-flies distances (in kilometers), which can be easily calculated from FRED county longitude/latitude coordinates using a spherical trigonometry formula. Figure 5.1 is, in essence, a visual argument that MDS works exactly as advertised: Fed with geographic distances, the technique locates measuring points in a way that corresponds perfectly to their location in actual map space (cf. Figure 2.1 [p. 20]). MDS is maximally successful in translating as-the-crow-flies distance into two-dimensional coordinates (shared variance between original distances and MDS distances: $R^2 = 99.9\%$). This should actually surprise no one given that as-the-crow-flies distances themselves derive from a two-dimensional reality. As in genuinely geographic maps, proximity between measuring points in Figure 5.1 indicates spatial proximity.

Moving on to the linguistic MDS plots, the empirical basis for the plot in Figure 5.3 is the $34 \times 34$ morphosyntactic distance matrix discussed in Section 4.1, while the plot in Figure 5.2 takes as input a $36 \times 36$ distance matrix about dialectal distances plus distances to Standard British and American English (see Section 4.4). In these plots, proximity between the measuring points is commensurate with linguistic similarity, and it should be emphasized that what matters interpretationally is not the absolute position of data points. Whether, say, Leicestershire ends up in the lower left corner or in the upper right corner is uninteresting. Instead, the interpretive meat of the plots is in the *position of data points relative to the position of the other data points in the plot*. The two linguistic MDS plots manage to account for approximately 80 percent of the variance in the original distances, which means that they account for about four-fifths of the story.

How do the three MDS plots bear on the issue of whether or not we are dealing with a morphosyntactic dialect continuum in Great Britain? To the extent that the arrangement of data points in the two linguistic plots (Figures 5.2 and 5.3) matches the arrangement in geographic map space (Figure 5.1), we would be justified in diagnosing a dialect continuum in which geographic distances are proportional to dialect distances. Now, the linguistic plots clearly do reflect some geographic structure: For instance, the English English measuring points (black dots) in Figures 5.2 and 5.3 are rather neatly segregated from non–English English measuring points, and within the English English cluster, we tend to find a North–South divide. Yet all in all, the overlap between the geographic plot in Figure 5.1 and the linguistic plots is clearly less than perfect. For one thing, the linguistic plots corroborate our earlier finding (see, e.g., Section 4.1.1) of strong and coherent morphosyntactic links in England and a somewhat looser linguistic network structure in Scotland. According to both Figure 5.2 and 5.3, the cloud of English English measuring points is substantially more compact than the cloud of measuring points in Scotland. Yet a cursory glance at Figure 5.1 is enough to remind us that in geographic terms, the reverse is true. Also, the linguistic plots exhibit a number of outliers such as Banffshire, Warwickshire, and Denbighshire. Precisely because of these contradictions and wrinkles, the interim diagnosis is that the morphosyntactic dialect landscape in Great Britain is apparently not a perfect continuum.

Let us add a brief discussion of the differences between the plot in Figure 5.3 (dialects only) and the plot in Figure 5.2 (dialects plus Standard varieties). First, notice that in regard to the relationships between the FRED measuring points, the plots are very similar but not identical. Thus it is not the case that the two additional measuring points in Figure 5.2 (that is, Standard British English and Standard American English) are simply added somewhere in Figure 5.3's arrangement. Instead, adding data points changes the equation, as it were, and results in a slight but wholesale change of the configuration of data points in plot space, a property of MDS that is known as "scale sensitivity" (see Nerbonne forthcoming a). Now, the Standard English data points in Figure 5.2 are located fairly closely to Ross and Cromarty, Warwickshire, and Denbighshire, which is as expected, given that these measuring points appear in deep blue ("highly similar") in the Standard English similarity maps discussed in Section 4.4 (Maps C.13 and C.14). Interestingly, however, the Hebrides are not located right next to the Standard varieties in Figure 5.2 even though we have seen in Section 4.4 that Hebridean English has the lowest morphosyntactic distance to both Standard British and Standard American English. So here we have a case of information loss where a two-dimensional MDS solution cannot do justice to a fact inherent in a higher-dimensional distance matrix.

We should stress along these lines that the share of variance accounted for by MDS can usually be boosted by adding additional MDS dimensions. For example, if the $36 \times 36$ distance matrix underlying the plot in Figure 5.2 is scaled in three (and not just two) dimensions, shared variance with the original distances increases by roughly ten percentage points to 89.5 percent. This is a substantial enhancement that one would not want to forgo if at all possible. Hence, Figure 5.4 is a three-dimensional scatterplot that seeks to visualize this particular MDS solution. The trouble is that three-dimensional scatterplots depicting more than a handful of data points look impressive, but are clearly less than highly readable. This being so, we need a better visualization technique – preferably one that is cartographic in nature – to depict three-dimensional MDS solutions. It is to this task that we turn next.

### 5.2.3  Introducing continuum maps

We will now turn to CONTINUUM MAPS, a signature visualization technique developed in Groningen (see Nerbonne et al. 1999; Heeringa 2004; Nerbonne forthcoming a). Continuum maps are per se two-dimensional

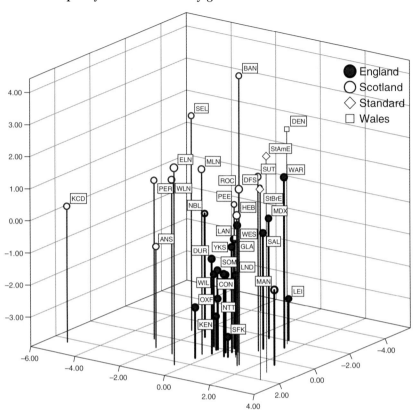

Figure 5.4. Three-dimensional MDS plot. Input: morphosyntactic distances (including distances to Standard English). Proximity in the plot indicates morphosyntactic similarity. Shared variance with original distances: $R^2 = 89.5\%$.

geographical maps which, quite ingeniously, draw on color coding to depict linguistic variation in three MDS dimensions. The analyst starts out by utilizing customary Voronoi tesselation (see Section 2.2.4) to assign each dialect site a convex polygon on the map. The next step scales down a higher-dimensional distance matrix to a three-dimensional MDS representation, in which each object has a coordinate in three MDS dimensions (much as shown in Figure 5.4). However, rather than plotting the result in three-dimensional – and hence visually badly digestable – plot space, the MDS coordinates are mapped to the red–green–blue color scheme, giving each of the Voronoi polygons in map space a distinct color hue. Notice here that in parallel to MDS plots, in continuum maps specific color hues assigned to individual data points are per se arbitrary and therefore interpretationally irrelevant (thus, whether, e.g., Leicestershire receives a red or green hue is uninteresting). What is important is a given data points's color hue relative to the hues of the other data points on the map. This is another way of saying that on the interpretational plane, *smooth color transitions between locations emphasize the continuum-like nature of the dialect landscape, whereas abrupt color transitions point to the necessity of alternative explanations.*

Maps C.15 through C.17 (Appendix C, pp. 180–181) translate the geographic MDS plots in Figures 5.1 through 5.4 into continuum maps. Map C.15 is based on scaling a distance matrix describing not linguistic distances but as-the-crow-flies geographic distances (in kilometers) between dialect sites, thus depicting, for reference purposes, a perfect continuum where transitions between measuring points are maximally smooth. Map C.17 takes as input the $34 \times 34$ morphosyntactic "dialects-only" distance matrix discussed in Section 4.1. Map C.16, finally, depicts the $36 \times 36$ distance matrix about dialectal distances plus distances to Standard British and American English (see Section 4.4). As for the explanatory-visual power of the maps, note that the continuum map in Map C.15 captures virtually all of the variance in geographic distances ($R^2 = 99.9\%$), while the two linguistic continuum maps (Maps C.16 and C.17) come with an information loss of about 10 percent ($R^2 = 89.5\%$ and $R^2 = 89.3\%$, respectively), which are rather tolerable values. In regard to the morphosyntactic relationships between the FRED measuring points, we observe that scale sensitivity notwithstanding, the two linguistic continuum maps are fairly similar (that is, the color hues assigned to individual measuring points are virtually identical), and this holds true in particular for measuring points in England. In Map C.16, Standard British English and Standard American English – which, as artificial measuring points, are placed (in an entirely arbitrary fashion) in boxes located in the North Sea, just off Scotland's coast – have darkish color hues. These mesh well with the dark hues assigned to measuring points such as, for example, Ross and Cromarty, Sutherland, and the Hebrides.

In all, the mosaic patterns exhibited in Maps C.16 and C.17, judged against the backdrop of Map C.15, confirm our earlier impression that the morphosyntactic dialect landscape in Great Britain is less continuum-like than it could be. It is true that there are some fairly nice micro-continua, especially so in the Southwest of England (where there is a nice, reddish continuum running from Cornwall over Devon, Somerset, and Wiltshire all the way to Oxfordshire) and in the Central and Northern Scottish Lowlands (notice the smooth greenish transitions between East Lothian, Midlothian, West Lothian, Perthshire, Angus, and Kincardineshire). Furthermore, dialects spoken in the North of England (Lancashire, Yorkshire, Westmorland, and Durham, all in reddish/brownish hues) fade easily, via Northumberland, into Southern Scottish Lowlands dialects such as Selkirkshire (blueish hues). Be that as it may, however, we are also looking at some rather abrupt transitions. For example, there is a somewhat rude break between the greenish Central Scottish Lowlands – comprising dialects spoken in West Lothian, Midlothian, and East Lothian – and blueish Southern Scottish dialects such as Peebleshire and Selkirkshire. In Scotland, Banffshire does not fit into the picture in that it is too blue, given its nearest neighbors. In Wales, it is Denbighshire that breaks ranks by being too violet. As for English English dialects, we must classify Middlesex (too violet given that its closest neighbor, London, is bright red), Leicestershire (too red), and Warwickshire (too violet) as outliers (for a more detailed discussion of why these measuring points have outlier status, we refer the reader to Section 7.1). In general, the linguistic continuum maps depict the Central England region as a rather noisy and patchy region, linguistically speaking.

At this point, it is instructive to pause for a moment, abandon the aggregate perspective, and reconsider the actual features on which the analysis is based. Why are measuring points assigned the color hues they are? Recall that we had said before that as such, color hues in continuum maps do not have a particular meaning since MDS only knows about distances and is completely agnostic about feature frequencies. This basic statistical truth notwithstanding, it is possible to use some correlational trickery to derive meaningful interpretations after the fact. To this purpose, the analyst may choose to correlate – via calculating, for example, Pearson correlation coefficients – frequency vectors with MDS dimensions to identify those features that are most robustly implicated in the overall dimensionality (Heeringa 2004, 266–271). When doing this on the basis of, for example, the $34 \times 34$ distance matrix and its lower-dimensional MDS solution on which Map C.17 empirically rests, we obtain the correlations indicated in the legend to Map C.17. Thus, we learn that reddish hues – which happen to dominate map space in England – correlate most robustly with increased text frequencies of multiple negation (feature [33], as in (1)), *don't* with 3rd person singular subjects (feature [40], as in (2)), the negator *ain't* (feature [32], as in (3)), GOT TO as a marker of epistemic and deontic modality (feature [26], as in (4)), and non-standard past tense *done* (feature [29], as in (5)). Incidentally, all of these "reddish" features turn out to have, when analyzed individually, some sort of significant or marginally significant geographic distribution according to the geographical significance instruments discussed in Chapter 3 (see, for instance, Table A.1 [Appendix A, p. 167]).

(1)    You *didn't* want *no* beer, you didn't think about beer anyway. [DUR001]

(2)    *She don't* mind nothing, she said. [WIL012]

(3)    Well, they made cider. *Ain't* going to say they made all that much. [SOM002]

(4)   Then of course you've *got to* squat the wagon up and just give 'em a tap on the nose or something [KEN004]

(5)   So what they *done*, they made it so that another teasel come there, another one come down there, you see, and in doing so that covered the lot. [WIL001]

Greenish hues, which especially characterize measuring points in the Central Scottish Lowlands, correlate first and foremost with increased text frequencies of the negative suffix *-nae* (feature [31], as in (6)), WASN'T (feature [37], as in (7)), archaic *ye* (feature [4], as in (8)), the relative particle *what* (feature [47], as in (9)), and non-standard WAS (feature [44], as in (10)).

(6)   I think he still carried on. Can*nae* mind of ever being laid off. [NBL003]

(7)   They *wasn't* very very big boats then – between five and six thousand ton they were then. [GLA005]

(8)   It's only about, take *ye* ten minutes to walk up there. [WIL011]

(9)   Seventeen and six a week, that was fifteen bob for the eggs; at last you'd have half a crown pocket money, and a dozen eggs, of course. A dozen eggs *what* you could sell for five bob at that time [ANS002]

(10)  We *was* busy when the commercial eh trade was good, we *was* busy really [NTT003]

Lastly, blueish hues (pervasive in some parts of Scotland but also defining outliers in England and Wales) correlate most consistently with elevated text frequencies of non-standard weak past tense and past participle forms (feature [28], as in (11)), lack of inversion and/or of auxiliaries in *wh*-questions and in main clause *yes/no*-questions (feature [55], as in (12)), non-standard past tense *come* (feature [30], as in (13)), *used to* as marker of habitual past (feature [20], as in (14)), and non-standard verbal *-s* (feature [39], as in (15)).

(11)  And I always remember, we *runned* up a bill, just in the teens of pounds. [CON009]

(12)  and he'd say, *When you coming back?* [LAN008]

(13)  Now Uncle Den doesn't drink much home but it were one time when he *come* home tight as a damn wheel. [CON005]

(14)  on every Sunday night they *used to* meet at the top of Alfreton Road and Darby Road what, Canning Circus every Sunday night they *used to* be there six o' clock till half past. [NTT016]

(15)  But I know*s* we we had eh two or three of them gramophones about just at one time. [OXF001]

### 5.2.4   Cartography: interim summary

This section has approached the issue of dialect continua cartographically and in doing so has uncovered a mixed picture. We have seen that Great Britain's morphosyntactic dialect landscape does exhibit some rather nice micro-continua, for example in the Central Scottish Lowlands region or in the Southwest of England. Nonetheless, at the same time we are dealing with a number of rather abrupt dialect transitions – for example, between Central Scottish Lowlands dialects and Southern Scottish Lowlands dialects. We would also like to reiterate here that Central England turns out to be a linguistically quite inhomogeneous region.

## 5.3   Quantification

The discussion in the previous section relied heavily on eyeballing visual representations of aggregate dialect relationships. While this line of analysis is certainly instructive, it can be nicely complemented by presenting precise continuum-hood measures. With exactly this goal in mind, this section marshals a number of correlation and regression analysis techniques to quantify the extent to which linguistic distance is proportional to several measures of geographic distance.

Methodically, we start out with an $N \times N$ linguistic distance matrix (which details pairwise linguistic distances) and create parallel language-external distance matrices (which detail pairwise language-external distances), one for each predictor to be tested. In the simplest case, each of these is subsequently correlated with the linguistic distance matrix by calculating, for example, a Pearson product-moment correlation coefficient. The language-external predictor that scores the highest coefficient is the best predictor of linguistic distances. More sophisticated research designs may involve, for example, regression analysis techniques, the results of which can be cartographically projected back to geography.

In this section, we endeavor to test four continuous language-external predictors for their explanatory potential:

- AS-THE-CROW-FLIES DISTANCE, in kilometers (see Section 5.3.1)
- LEAST-COST WALKING DISTANCE, in kilometers (see Section 5.3.2)
- LEAST-COST TRAVEL TIME, in minutes (see Section 5.3.3)
- LINGUISTIC GRAVITY, defined as two measuring points' population product divided by the square of travel time (see Section 5.3.4)

We reiterate that all of these measures can be seen as proxies of the likelihood of social contact and communicative interaction, as the underlying variable that is supposed to shape the diffusion of linguistic features in geographic space (Johnstone 2009, 6). The empirical question guiding this section is whether and to what extent this is true for the dataset at hand.

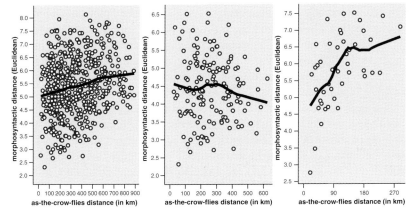

Figure 5.5. Morphosyntactic dialect distances versus as-the-crow-flies distances. Left: all $N = 34$ measuring points (linear estimate: $R^2 = 4.4\%$, $p < .001$). Middle: measuring points in England only ($N = 18$) (linear estimate: $R^2 = 0.5\%$, $p = .824$). Right: measuring points in the Scottish Lowlands only ($N = 10$) (logarithmic estimate: $R^2 = 33.3\%$, $p < .001$). Solid lines are LOESS curves estimating the overall nature of the relationship.

Throughout the following discussion, we will explore language-external determinants of morphosyntactic variability in the FRED dataset as a whole, though we will also in each case restrict our attention to (i) English English dialects and (ii) Scottish Lowland dialects (thus excluding younger, less traditional dialects in the Scottish Highlands and in Wales). The reason is that morphosyntactic variability in England is demonstrably conditioned differently than regional variability in the Scottish Lowlands.

### 5.3.1    As-the-crow-flies distance

Using a trigonometry formula on the FRED county coordinates (see Table 2.1), it is computationally trivial to calculate pairwise as-the-crow-flies distances between measuring points (these actually underlie the baseline MDS plot in Figure 5.1 and the baseline continuum map in Map C.15).[1] Thanks to its straightforwardness, as-the-crow-flies distance is the most common geographic distance measure in the dialectometry literature (e.g., Nerbonne et al. 1996; Goebl 2001; Gooskens and Heeringa 2004; Shackleton 2007).

In Figure 5.5, we find a series of three scatterplots which visually depict the relationship between pairwise morphosyntactic distances (on the vertical axes) and pairwise as-the-crow-flies distances (on the horizontal axis).

---

[1] The L04 software package provides a module (l12dst) that can do this job automatically.

The left plot is based on the entire dataset, the middle plot only considers pairings within England, and the right plot restricts attention to pairings in the Scottish Lowlands. Each dot represents one measuring point pairing. To illustrate: the lowermost dot in the left plot represents the pairing between the measuring points Wiltshire and Somerset, which is characterized by a morphosyntactic distance of 2.32 Euclidean distance points and an as-the-crow-flies distance of about 55 km. Recall, in this connection, that we assign coordinates to FRED counties by computing the arithmetic mean of all the location coordinates associated with a particular county (see Section 2.1.1); thus, for instance, the coordinates assigned to Wiltshire (longitude: $-2.03$, latitude: 51.26; see Table 2.1) are close to the village of Little Cheverell. The heavy lines are non-parametric locally estimated scatterplot smoothing (LOESS) curves estimating the relationship between morphosyntactic and as-the-crow-flies distances.

Observe now that in the dataset as a whole, as-the-crow-flies distances exhibit a significant and weakly positive linear correlation ($r = .210$). This means that increased as-the-crow-flies distance between two measuring points predicts increased morphosyntactic distance between them, as it should for all we know. Having said that, a linear regression indicates that as-the-crow-flies distances explain no more than about 4 percent of the variance in morphosyntactic distances ($R^2 = 4.4\%$), which is indeed not a lot. Restricting our attention regionally, it turns out that as-the-crow-flies distances do not correlate significantly at all with morphosyntactic distances in England. However, presuming a linear relationship we obtain a moderately strong correlation in the Scottish Lowlands that accounts for almost 30 percent of the morphosyntactic variance there ($R^2 = 28.9\%$). It should be added, along these lines, that excluding customary outliers (Banffshire, Denbighshire, Dumfriesshire, Middlesex, Leicestershire, and Warwickshire; see Section 7.1) from the analysis has the effect of increasing $R^2$ values across the board (all: $R^2 = 6.9\%$, England: $R^2 = 3.2\%$, Scottish Lowlands: $R^2 = 32.6\%$) and rendering the correlation between morphosyntactic distances and as-the-crow-flies distances positive ($r = .204$) even in England.

The above correlation coefficients and $R^2$ values all assume a linear relationship between as-the-crow-flies distances and morphosyntactic distances. A sizable body of dialectometrical research, however, shows that the relationship between geographic distance and linguistic distance is typically sublinear, not linear, such that the effect of a one-unit increase in geographic distance is smaller at large geographic distances than at smaller geographic distances (Nerbonne 2010 calls this "Séguy's Law," following Séguy 1971 who first noted this sublinearity). In other words: after a certain threshold, geography is not supposed to matter that much any more. Looking at Figure 5.5, a sublinear relationship does indeed appear to hold for the relationship between as-the-crow-flies and morphosyntactic distances in the Scottish Lowlands. In this region, the effect of geography seems to level off after a distance threshold of approximately 130 km. Quantitatively, a logarithmic estimate of the relationship fits the dataset better and accounts for $R^2 = 33.3\%$ of the variance in morphosyntactic distances.

### 5.3.2 Least-cost walking distance

Speakers do not have wings, so it is reasonable to assume that what really matters for dialect distances is the distance a human being would have to travel to get from point A to point B (see Gooskens 2005; Szmrecsanyi forthcoming). Ideally, because dialect genesis is historical one would like to draw on historical travel estimates à la Gooskens (2005) to explore this issue. Alas, in the case of Great Britain historical travel estimates that exactly match the FRED grid are hard to obtain. As a second-best solution, we opted to turn to Google Maps (http://maps.google.co.uk/), which has a route finder tool that allows the user to enter longitude/latitude pairings for two locations to obtain a least-cost travel route and an estimate of the total travel distance; for example, Google Maps estimates that the walking distance between Wiltshire and Somerset is 72 km (as-the-crow-flies distance: 55km). We queried Google Maps for all $34 \times 33/2 = 561$ dialect pairings, thus obtaining pairwise least-cost-travel distance estimates, and activated the route finder's "walking" option. The rationale was that matching linguistic data sourced from speakers born around the beginning of the twentieth century with travel estimates based on twenty-first-century transportation infrastructure is convenient but clearly suboptimal. Pedestrian routes (by contrast to routes utilizing twenty-first-century motorways, etc.), however, are unlikely to have changed much, so we reasoned that Google Maps' walking option would take us as close as possible to the reality of historical traveling.

The result is, however, disappointing. As can be seen from Figure 5.6 (whose plots look very, very similar to those in Figure 5.5), the relationship between walking distances and morphosyntactic distances is hardly stronger than the relationship between as-the-crow-flies distances and morphosyntactic distances. In the dataset as a whole, the share of variance explained is now 6.8 percent (as opposed to 4.4 percent), but this is a rather modest increase.[2]

### 5.3.3 Least-cost travel time

Originally intended as a third-best approach to operationalizing travel distance, we also queried Google Maps to obtain pairwise least-cost travel time estimates (in minutes) with no infrastructure restrictions, thus assuming

---

[2] Again, excluding our customary outliers (see Section 7.1) from the analysis increases $R^2$ values across the board (all: $R^2 = 9.9\%$, England: $R^2 = 5.8\%$, Scottish Lowlands: $R^2 = 34.0\%$).

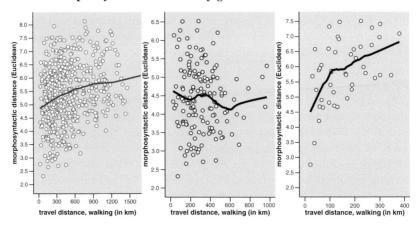

Figure 5.6. Morphosyntactic dialect distances versus walking distance estimates (in km) according to http://maps.google.co.uk/ (accessed April 2009). Left: all $N = 34$ measuring points (linear estimate: $R^2 = 6.8\%$, $p < .001$). Middle: measuring points in England only ($N = 18$) (linear estimate: $R^2 = 0.2\%$, $p = .718$). Right: measuring points in the Scottish Lowlands only ($N = 10$) (logarithmic estimate: $R^2 = 31.4\%$, $p < .001$). Solid lines are LOESS curves estimating the overall nature of the relationship.

travel by car using motorways, toll roads, and so on (to illustrate, Google Maps' least-cost travel time estimate for the route from Wiltshire to Somerset is 83 minutes). Now, in explaining morphosyntactic variance (see Figure 5.7), least-cost travel time does not fare spectacularly better than as-the-crow-flies distance or least-cost walking distance, but fare better it does. This is why we opt to report the correlations here, rather than throwing them away because the estimates are based on modern infrastructure.

The $R^2$ value for the dataset as a whole now approaches 8 percent, and in the Scottish Lowlands least-cost travel time accounts for almost 40 percent of the variance.[3] Observe also that in the dataset as a whole (left plot in Figure 5.7) as well as in the Scottish Lowlands subset (right plot in Figure 5.7), the relationship between least-cost travel time and morphosyntactic distances is very clearly sublinear (see Séguy 1971; Nerbonne forthcoming a).

That an operationalization of geographic distance that is calculated drawing on twenty-first-century infrastructure is no less, and actually slightly more, explanatory than a supposedly historically more accurate measure (least-cost walking distance) is, of course, a bit of a puzzle. After all, our

---

[3] Excluding our customary outliers (see Section 7.1) from the analysis increases $R^2$ values for the whole dataset ($R^2 = 11.4\%$) but not for the regionally selective subsets.

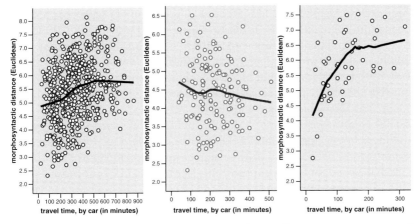

Figure 5.7. Morphosyntactic dialect distances versus travel time estimates, by car (in minutes) according to http://maps.google.co.uk/ (accessed October 2008). Left: all $N = 34$ measuring points (logarithmic estimate: $R^2 = 7.4\%$, $p < .001$). Middle: measuring points in England only ($N = 18$) (linear estimate: $R^2 = .7\%$, $p = .864$). Right: measuring points in the Scottish Lowlands only ($N = 10$) (logarithmic estimate: $R^2 = 39.4\%$, $p < .001$). Solid lines are LOESS curves estimating the overall nature of the relationship.

morphosyntactic distances derive from speakers that were typically born around the beginning of the twentieth century. We have no definite answer that could address this temporal mismatch. Nonetheless, we conjecture that least-cost travel time on twenty-first-century infrastructure is probably no true independent variable but follows itself certain (historical) contingencies of social contact. In other words, we submit that modern infrastructure may follow historical trade routes, migration patterns, or communicative channels.

### 5.3.4    Linguistic gravity

In a paper entitled "Linguistic Change and Diffusion: Description and Explanation in Sociolinguistic Dialect Geography," Trudgill (1974) proposed a gravity model to account for geographic diffusion. The model is intended

as a statement to the effect that the interaction ($M$) of a centre $i$ and a centre $j$ can be expressed as the population of $i$ multiplied by the population of $j$ divided by the square of the distance between them. (Trudgill 1974, 233)

As a testable hypothesis, this formula – which, as its name suggests, is inspired by Newton's famous inverse-square law of gravitation – postulates that the interaction between two dialects decreases with increasing geographic distance (in our parlance, that the morphosyntactic distance between two measuring points should increase with increasing geographic distance), but that this effect is counterbalanced by the size of speaker communities. Large speaker communities will tend to linguistically interact more than smaller speaker communities, all other things (and especially geographic distance) being equal. Observe, in this connection, that Groningen-style dialectometry has failed to detect a significant effect of linguistic gravity in Dutch dialects (see Heeringa et al. 2007; Nerbonne and Heeringa 2007). Will we find a gravity effect in our data?

Using Trudgill's formula, we calculated linguistic gravity scores for each of the 561 measuring point pairings in our database, feeding in least-cost travel time as the most explanatory geographic distance measure (see Section 5.3.3) and early-twentieth-century population figures (in thousands) as a proxy for speaker community size (specifically, we used early-nineteenth-century population figures, as published in the *Census of England and Wales, 1921* and the *Census of Scotland, 1921*; both documents are available online at http://histpop.org/). To illustrate, consider the pairing between Wiltshire and Somerset: the 1901 population product (in thousands) is $271.394 \times 434.945 = 118,041$, travel time squared (in minutes) is $83 \times 83 = 6,889$, so the linguistic gravity score calculates as $118,041/6,889 = 17.13$. Subsequently, we applied a *log*-transformation to the gravity scores to alleviate the effect of outliers. For example, the counties of Middlesex and London have a huge population product, even when drawing on early-twentieth-century population data, so their non-*log*-transformed linguistic gravity score is somewhat out of proportion. We submit that a *log*-transformation would probably be unnecessary were we operating at the level of individual FRED locations, and not on the level of FRED counties.

The scatterplots in Figure 5.8, which plot morphosyntactic distances against *log*-transformed linguistic gravity scores, show that indeed there is a linguistic gravity effect in the full dataset and in the Scottish Lowlands subset. In these samples, the sign of the effect also has the theoretically expected direction: Increased linguistic gravity scores predict decreased morphosyntactic distance, exactly as suggested by Trudgill. As with the other continuous distance predictors tested so far, however, linguistic gravity scores do not correlate significantly with morphosyntactic distances when attention is restricted to measuring points in England (see the middle plot in Figure 5.8).

The $R^2$ values yielded by linguistic gravity are the highest we have seen so far in this chapter. In the full dataset, linguistic gravity scores account for about a quarter ($R^2 = 24.1\%$) of the variance in morphosyntactic distances; in Scottish Lowlands dialects, they explain slightly less than half of

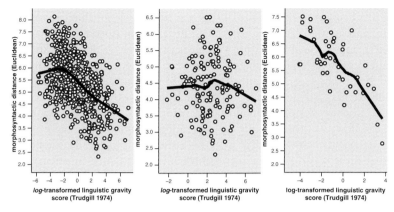

Figure 5.8. Morphosyntactic dialect distances versus *log*-transformed linguistic gravity scores (see Trudgill 1974). Left: all $N = 34$ measuring points (linear estimate: $R^2 = 24.1\%$, $p < .001$). Middle: measuring points in England only ($N = 18$) (linear estimate: $R^2 < .1\%$, $p = .589$). Right: measuring points in the Scottish Lowlands only ($N = 10$) (linear estimate: $R^2 = 46.5\%$, $p < .001$). Solid lines are LOESS curves estimating the overall nature of the relationship.

the variance ($R^2 = 46.5\%$). Once again, we can boost these values by excluding our customary outliers (see Section 7.1) from the analysis, in which case we obtain an $R^2$ value of 33.7 percent for the full dataset and 64.8 percent for the Scottish Lowlands subset (even in England, linguistic gravity would then account for 6.6 percent of the variance).

We wish to emphasize at this point that the linguistic gravity scores tested in this section are more than the sum of their component parts (that is, geographic distance and population size). Consider the full dataset: squaring least-cost travel time does not boost its explanatory power, which is less than 10 percent (see Figure 5.7). On the other hand, a linear regression using population products as the only predictor accounts for no more than 8 percent of the variance in morphosyntactic distances. As we have seen, however, using the gravity formula we can account for about a quarter of the variance. We conclude that linguistic gravity is by far the most potent continuous predictor of morphosyntactic distances tested in this chapter.

### 5.3.5    *Where do continuous predictors fail us?*

"Most potent" sounds big, but we hasten to add that in comparison to some previous research, the $R^2$ scores in this chapter are nothing to write home about. For example, Shackleton (2007), in his study of phonetic variation in the SED, reports an $R^2$ value of 49 percent for the relationship between phonetic and as-the-crow-flies geographic distances in England.[4] Spruit et al. (2009), in an atlas-based study on aggregate syntactic distances in Dutch dialects, calculate an $R^2$ value of 45 percent for the relation between syntax and geography (see Section 8.2 for a more detailed discussion). So at this point we may wonder where exactly the language-external, continuous distance measures tested here fail us explanatorily. To address this question, in what follows we draw on our best operationalization (*log*-transformed linguistic gravity scores) to deal with this issue cartographically. We begin by fitting three separate linear regression models predicting morphosyntactic distances from *log*-transformed linguistic gravity scores – one for the full dataset, one for the England only subset, and one for the Scottish Lowlands only subset. The three models account for morphosyntactic variance as indicated by the $R^2$ values in Figure 5.8. Conveniently for our purposes, linear regression models yield information on case-wise residuals as a gauge of the regression models' fitting errors. Eyeballing hundreds of residuals is a tedious task, so we draw on network maps (see Section 4.1.1) to visually represent the distribution of (unstandardized) residuals in geographic space (see Gooskens 2005). Thus in Maps C.18 to C.20 (Appendix C, p. 182), red links depict positive residuals; that is, dialect pairings whose morphosyntactic distance is greater than expected given a linguistic gravity score. Blue links indicate negative residuals; that is, cases where morphosyntactic distance is smaller than predicted based on the linguistic gravity score.

In the full dataset (Map C.18), positive "red" residuals – greater-than-expected morphosyntactic distances – emanate, for one thing, from certain outliers such as Denbighshire, Warwickshire, and Kincardineshire. More generally speaking, though, positive residuals characterize many of the trans-border links between Scotland and England, which is another way of saying that linguistic gravity does not work well across the border between England and Scotland. Negative "blue" residuals (i.e. smaller-than-expected morphosyntactic distances) characterize much of Southern England, some links in Northern England, and the Scottish Highlands. The signs of regression residuals derived from an England-only regression model, projected to geography in Map C.19, basically echo the England-only reverse network map in Figure C.8 (Section 4.2.1) – positive residuals are geographically concentrated around the West Midlands. Lastly, a Scottish Lowlands-only regression model generates the residuals visually depicted in Map C.20. Observe that negative residuals are concentrated in and around the Central Scottish Lowlands (so the Central Scottish Lowlands are closer morphosyntactically than expected), while Dumfriesshire and Banffshire

---

[4] This $R^2$ value refers to what Shackleton calls "Feature-Based Distances"; for "Variant-Based Distances," Shackleton reports a truly staggering $R^2$ value of 67 percent.

in particular entertain greater-than-expected morphosyntactic distances to other measuring points.

Interpretationally, of course, greater-than-expected morphosyntactic distances (red links) point to the possibility that a measuring point pairing transgresses some dialect area boundary, while smaller-than-expected morphosyntactic distances (blue links) may indicate membership in the same dialect area. This is an issue that we shall investigate more closely in the next chapter.

### 5.3.6  *Quantification: interim summary*

This section would seem to have suggested that as-the-crow-flies distance is a comparatively weak predictor of aggregate morphosyntactic variability, accounting for no more than about 4 percent of the variance in morphosyntactic distances in the full dataset. Least-cost travel time is a demonstrably better operationalization of geographic distance that can explain about 8 percent of the variance. We do not, however, begin to really get a grip on the data until we factor in size of speaker communities. Thus, utilizing Trudgill's (1974) linguistic gravity formula, we can account for about a quarter of the morphosyntactic variance in the full dataset. An interesting twist uncovered in this section is that while in England none of the continuous predictors turns out to be really explanatory, we can manage to explain up to about 50 percent of the morphosyntactic relationships in the Scottish Lowlands. In short: the Scottish Lowlands are fairly continuous morphosyntactically, but England is not.

## 5.4   Chapter summary

What is the travel experience Chambers and Trudgill's (1998) traveler would have when touring Great Britain's morphosyntactic dialect landscape? The exercise in continuum cartography undertaken in the first part of this chapter's empirical discussion suggests that he or she would, for sure, sometimes encounter smooth dialect transitions as advertised by a continuum scenario – for instance, in the Southwest of England or in the Central Scottish Lowlands. At the same time, though, the traveler would also notice rather abrupt transitions – for instance, between the Southern Scottish Lowlands and the Central Scottish Lowlands. She would moreover be faced with anomalies, such as the fact that Warwickshire is inexplicably different from the surrounding dialects. In short, morphosyntactic variability in British English dialects has a less than perfect continuum feel to it. The quantitative analysis undertaken in the second part of this chapter essentially confirms this verdict. The best continuous dialect distance predictors identified in this study are linguistic gravity scores in the spirit of Trudgill (1974), which combine least-cost travel time estimates with data about historical population sizes.

In the dataset as a whole, linguistic gravity scores account for about a quarter of the morphosyntactic variance, which is a statistically significant share but not one that is particularly sizable compared to shares reported in the atlas-based dialectometry literature. In other words, Great Britain's morphosyntactic dialect landscape is, on the whole, not very continuum-like. Having said that, however, we also noted that the Scottish Lowlands seem to be organized along the lines of a dialect continuum to a much larger degree than England is.

# 6 Classification: the dialect area scenario

The assumption we examined in the previous chapter was that linguistic distance between dialects is proportional to geographic distance between dialect sites. We concluded that this assumption is not perfectly borne out by the data. There is, however, an alternative view, according to which dialect landscapes may be geographically organized along the lines of geographically coherent, linguistically homogeneous, and clearly demarcated "areas within which similar varieties are spoken" (Heeringa and Nerbonne 2001, 375). In Section 6.1, we present a literature review of the history of thought on dialect areas. Section 6.2 proceeds deductively and explores the explanatory power of previous dialect partitions for the present study's dataset. Section 6.3 takes an inductive approach and marshals cluster analytical statistical analysis techniques to derive dialect groupings from the dataset. Section 6.4 summarizes this chapter's major findings.

## 6.1 On the notion of dialect areas

Attempts at regionalization, classification, and the quest for dialect areas all have a long and strongly entrenched tradition in dialectology. Indeed, for a long time the dialect area scenario was a great deal more popular among dialectologists than the more fuzzy – and arguably more modern – continuum view, which we discussed in the previous chapter. How come? Harnisch (2009, 275) notes that "traditional dialectology had an elementary interest in dialectal dissimilarity in so far as it attempted to explore the boundaries (isoglosses) of 'old' language spaces along which the variants of certain linguistic features or bundles of features differed." In pursuing this research agenda, traditional dialectology overlapped with folk beliefs that every language or dialect has, or ought to have, its sovereign territory (Auer 2004, 149–150). It goes without saying that this view is alive and kicking to this very day and permeates, in particular, folk thinking about dialect landscapes in countries such as Germany (Hock and Joseph 2009, 343). Bloomfield characterized the overlap between traditional dialectology and folk beliefs as follows:

The inhabitants of countries like England, Germany, or France, have always applied provincial names to rough dialect divisions, and spoken of such things as "the Yorkshire dialect," "the Swabian dialect," or "the Norman dialect." Earlier scholars accepted these classifications without attempting to define them exactly; it was hoped, later, that dialect geography would lead to exact definitions ... the question took on a sentimental interest, since the provincial divisions largely represent old tribal groupings: if the extension of a dialect, such as, say, the "Swabian dialect" in Germany, could be shown to coincide with the area of habitation of an ancient tribe, then language would again be throwing light on the conditions of a bygone time. (Bloomfield [1933] 1984: 340)

Crucially, Bloomfield went on to note that "[in] this respect, however, dialect geography proved to be disappointing" ([1933] 1984: 340), which is why, as we have seen in the preceding chapter, some dialectologists turned to the continuum view. Others "held fast to the national and provincial classifications, insisting, perhaps with some mystical fervor, on a terminology of cores and zones" (Bloomfield [1933] 1984: 341). Auer (2004, 150–160) presents a detailed account of how an interest in boundaries and neatly demarcated dialect areas has permeated German dialectology in particular from its inception in the nineteenth century. Many of the big names in nineteenth and early-twentieth-century German dialectology were, after all, more or less explicitly concerned with classification: Adelbert von Keller (Keller 1855, 21, cited in Schrambke 2009, 91); Georg Wenker, who initially sought to identify dialect boundaries (Wenker 1886, 189) but was disappointed in this endeavor (Auer 2004, 152); Ferdinand Wrede, in whose *Deutsche Dialektgeographie* series the notion of dialect boundaries figured prominently (see Schrambke 2009, 93–94 for a discussion); Karl Haag, who took an extensive interest in regionalization, endeavoring to explore the overlap between dialectal and old political boundaries (Haag 1898, 4, cited in Schrambke 2009, 98); and Karl Bohnenberger, who sought to establish a classificatory scheme for dialects (Bohnenberger 1928, discussed in Schrambke 2009, 101).

What is the theoretical basis for positing dialect areas and sharp dialect boundaries? Language-external factors (such as physical features, political boundaries, or settlement histories) may weaken communication networks, such that in the long term communities diverge, linguistically and otherwise, through a process of splitting (Sapir [1921] 2004: 123; Downes 1998, 19; Harnisch 2009, 291). The crucial term here is DIVERGENCE, which is defined as a "change in which languages or language varieties become more dissimilar" (Hinskens et al. 2000, 2). The typical scenario is that prior to divergence, the diverging varieties had formed a continuum

(Harnisch 2009, 275) – much as it is believed that there was, once upon a time, a Proto-Indo-European dialect continuum (Hock and Joseph 2009, 338–339) which historically diverged into clearly definable dialect or language areas. Notice here that notions such as splitting and divergence also ultimately underpin Schleicher's influential *Stammbaum* theory (Schleicher 1863), which offers that relationships between languages, or language varieties (Goebl 2006, 420) for that matter, can in principle be captured in phylogenetic language trees.

It follows from the foregoing discussion that one of the crucial differences between the dialect continuum view and the dialect area view is that the latter has a much stronger in-built (or inferred) *historical* component than the former. This is because language (or dialect) divergence is inherently historical, given that Schleicherian notions of phylogeny are ultimately all about language change in the long run. It should therefore surprise nobody that Edward Sapir, taking a long-term historical perspective on matters such as drift and language diversity, implicitly argues for the dialect area scenario and against the continuum scenario:

If all the speakers of a given dialect were arranged in order in accordance with the degree of their conformity to average usage, there is little doubt that they would constitute a very finely intergrading series clustered about a well-defined center or norm . . . If the speech of any member of the series could actually be made to fit into another dialect series [footnote omitted, BS], we should have no true barriers between dialects (and languages) at all. We should merely have a continuous series of individual variations extending over the whole range of a historically unified linguistic area, and the cutting up of this large area . . . into distinct dialects and languages would be an essentially arbitrary proceeding with no warrant save that of practical convenience. *But such a conception of the nature of dialectic variation does not correspond to the facts as we know them.* (Sapir [1921] 2004: 121–122; emphasis mine)

The stance that the present study takes on the issue of whether morphosyntactic variation in Great Britain is structured in terms of dialect areas or not is a strictly empirical, not ideological one. To the extent that (i) linguistic distances between dialects within a geographically coherent area are or approach zero while (ii) distances between dialects belonging to different areas are non-zero, regionalization is warranted (Heeringa and Nerbonne 2001, 377).

## 6.2 Quantifying the explanatory power of previous dialect partitions

We begin the empirical part of this chapter deductively, with the goal of quantifying the extent to which six selected previous regionalizations can explain the variance in morphosyntactic distances exhibited in the present study's dataset. We include four regionalizations reviewed in Section 1.2, and – for good measure – two Early English regionalizations, which will enable us to assess whether morphosyntactic variability in the FRED dataset echoes tribal areas in historical time.

**Dialects of Old English.** According to Baugh and Cable (1993, 52), the dialects of Old English can be classified into four groups: (1) West Saxon dialects (spoken in the Southwest of England today), (2) Kentish dialects (in the Southeast of England), (3) Mercian dialects (spoken between the Thames and the Humber), and (4) Northumbrian dialects (north of the Humber). This partition covers twenty-five of the thirty-four measuring points sampled in FRED (see Table 6.1). It does not, of course, cover the young dialects in the Scottish Highlands (the Hebrides, Ross and Cromarty, Sutherland) and Wales (Denbighshire, Glamorganshire), and it also does not cover some measuring points in the Scottish Lowlands (Angus, Banffshire, Kincardineshire, and Perthshire)

**Dialects of Middle English.** Baugh and Cable (1993, 185–186) identify five principal dialects of Middle English (again, see Table 6.1): (1) Southern other than Kentish, (2) Kentish, (3) East Midlands, (4) West Midlands (East and West Midlands dialects cover the region north of the Thames and south of the Humber), and (5) Northern (covering the area north of the Humber). This partition has the same coverage as Baugh and Cable's division of Old English dialects (See Table 6.1).

**Ellis' (1889) survey of English dialects.** As we saw in Section 1.2.2, Ellis distinguishes between six dialect areas: (1) Southern dialects, (2) Western dialects, (3) Eastern dialects, (4) Midland dialects, (5) Northern dialects, and (6) Lowland Scots dialects. Ellis' synopsis maps cover twenty-nine measuring points in the FRED network. Wales (Denbighshire, Glamorganshire) is not covered, nor are Scottish Highland varieties (the Hebrides, Ross and Cromarty, Sutherland) included.

**Trudgill's (1990) division of traditional dialects.** Drawing on phonetic and phonological SED evidence, Trudgill partitions England and parts of the Scottish Lowlands into six major dialect areas (see Section 1.2.3): (1) Scots, (2) Northern dialects, (3) Western Central (Midlands) dialects, (4) Eastern Central (Midlands) dialects[1], (5) Southwestern dialects, and (6) Southeastern dialects. The areal coverage of this partition (twenty-nine FRED measuring points) is exactly identical to Ellis' coverage (see above).

**Goebl's (2007) dialectometric account.** Based on lexical and morphosyntactic SED evidence, Goebl (2007) utilizes Cluster Analysis to divide

---

[1] Owing to FRED's areal coverage, in the subsequent statistical analysis we conflate Trudgill's Western Central Midlands and Eastern Central Midlands into a "Midlands" area.

Table 6.1. *Assigning FRED measuring points to Early English dialect areas according to the customary partitions in Baugh and Cable (1993).*

|  | Old English dialect area (Baugh and Cable 1993, 52) | Middle English dialect area (Baugh and Cable 1993, 186) |
|---|---|---|
| Angus | *n.a.* | *n.a.* |
| Banffshire | *n.a.* | *n.a.* |
| Cornwall | West Saxon | Southern |
| Denbighshire | *n.a.* | *n.a.* |
| Devon | West Saxon | Southern |
| Dumfriesshire | Northumbrian | Northern |
| Durham | Northumbrian | Northern |
| East Lothian | Northumbrian | Northern |
| Glamorganshire | *n.a.* | *n.a.* |
| Hebrides | *n.a.* | *n.a.* |
| Isle of Man | Northumbrian | Northern |
| Kincardineshire | *n.a.* | *n.a.* |
| Kent | Kentish | Kentish |
| Lancashire | Northumbrian | West Midlands |
| Leicestershire | Mercian | East Midlands |
| London | Kentish | Kentish |
| Middlesex | Kentish | East Midlands |
| Midlothian | Northumbrian | Northern |
| Northumberland | Northumbrian | Northern |
| Nottinghamshire | Mercian | East Midlands |
| Oxfordshire | Mercian | Southern |
| Peebleshire | Northumbrian | Northern |
| Perthshire | *n.a.* | *n.a.* |
| Ross and Cromarty | *n.a.* | *n.a.* |
| Shropshire | Mercian | West Midlands |
| Selkirkshire | Northumbrian | Northern |
| Suffolk | Mercian | East Midlands |
| Somerset | West Saxon | Southern |
| Sutherland | *n.a.* | *n.a.* |
| Warwickshire | Mercian | West Midlands |
| Westmorland | Northumbrian | Northern |
| Wiltshire | West Saxon | Southern |
| West Lothian | Northumbrian | Northern |
| Yorkshire | Northumbrian | Northern |

England plus the Isle of Man into eight dialect areas (see Section 1.2.4): (1) Northumberland, (2) Northern dialects other than Northumberland, (3) Western Central dialects, (4) Eastern Central dialects, (5) Northern Southwest dialects, (6) Central East dialects, (7) Southwestern dialects, and (8) Southeastern dialects. This partition covers nineteen FRED measuring points, leaving out Wales, the Scottish Lowlands, and the Scottish Highlands.

**Inoue's (1996) perceptual dialectology account.** By way of his experiment (see Section 1.2.8 for details ), Inoue (1996) uncovers five major areas: (1) Scotland, (2) Wales, (3) the North of England, (4) the English Midlands, and (5) the South of England. This division covers all thirty-four FRED measuring points.

Table 6.2. *The explanatory power of previous dialect partitions for the current dataset. Number of measuring points on which the analysis is based (N), and* PERMANOVA $R^2$ *value (% variance explained).*

|  | $N$ | $R^2$ | |
|---|---|---|---|
| dialects of Old English (Baugh and Cable 1993, 52) | 25 | 17% | * |
| dialects of Middle English (Baugh and Cable 1993, 186) | 25 | 24% | ** |
| Ellis (1889) | 29 | 30% | *** |
| Trudgill (1990) | 29 | 32% | *** |
| Goebl (2007) | 19 | 47% | * |
| Inoue (1996) | 34 | 24% | *** |

* sig. at $p < .05$, ** $p < .01$, *** $p \leq .001$.

We annotated every one of FRED's thirty-four measuring points for dialect area membership (which included a "not applicable" category for measuring points not covered) according to each of the above dialect partitions. This information, along with a $34 \times 34$ morphosyntactic distance matrix, was subsequently submitted to Permutational Multivariate Analysis of Variance Using Distance Matrices (PERMANOVA; see Anderson 2001),[2] which is analogous to MANOVA (Multivariate Analysis of Variance) but designed specifically to analyze distance matrices. The goal was to test how successful dialect area membership is in explaining continuous dialect distances between measuring points. For each dialect partition, the analysis produces significance values and an $R^2$ value (reported in Table 6.2), which indicates the share of the variance accounted for by a given partition.

All six partitions turn out to be statistically significant predictors, though Baugh and Cable's classification of Old English dialects is only just significant, and accounts for under 20 percent of the variance. The other five partitions explain between a quarter of the morphosyntactic variance (Middle English dialects and Inoue's perceptual dialectology experiment) and almost half of the variance (Goebl's Cluster Analysis on lexical and morphosyntactic grounds). We hasten to add that comparing the $R^2$ values in Table 6.2 is not entirely fair, since the PERMANOVA runs are not all based on exactly the same dataset – for example, when we test Inoue's classification on only the twenty-five measuring points also covered in Baugh and Cable (1993, 52) (thus excluding arguably "difficult" measuring points in, e.g., Scotland), Inoue's perceptual division will explain 29 percent (and not just 24 percent) of the variance in the dataset.

Still, we submit that the $R^2$ values in Table 6.2 can offer a rough orientation as to which partitions mesh particularly well with our dataset. The inevitable problem of differing coverages notwithstanding, then, we conclude that previous dialect divisions reported in the literature account for

---

[2] To conduct the analysis, we utilized the statistical software package R: library `vegan`, function `adonis` (http://vegan.r-forge.r-project.org/).

between a quarter to half of the morphosyntactic variability in FRED. In this connection, the modern, SED-based accounts (Goebl and Trudgill) tend to fare a lot better than "older" divisions, such as Ellis' account and, especially, the Early English dialect partitions. Therefore, the FRED dataset does not seem to exhibit a particularly strong signal of historical dialect genesis. It is also noteworthy that Ellis' and Trudgill's partitions, although exclusively based on accent (as opposed to grammatical) variation, still manage to explain about a third of the morphosyntactic variance in our morphosyntax dataset.

## 6.3    Deriving dialect areas inductively

By contrast to the top-down, literature-driven perspective adopted in the previous section, we will now seek to adopt an inductive, data-driven approach to explore whether heavy statistical artillery can manage to partition Great Britain's morphosyntactic dialect landscape into dialect areas.

### 6.3.1    Method: Hierarchical Agglomerative Cluster Analysis

The statistical tool of choice to regionalize dialect landscapes is HIERARCHICAL AGGLOMERATIVE CLUSTER ANALYSIS (henceforth: CA), a multivariate statistical technique popular in all those sciences that are concerned with classification and taxonomy (Sokal and Sneath 1963). This, of course, includes dialectometry (see e.g., Heeringa 2004; Goebl 2007). As Heeringa and Nerbonne (2001, 388) put it, "[i]f dialect areas exist, we can find them by applying clustering." In most general terms, CA seeks to reorganize a sample of objects into homogeneous groups, or clusters (Aldenderfer and Blashfield 1984, 7) that ideally lend themselves to meaningful interpretations. There are a number of ways to solve this reorganization task, and the hierarchical agglomerative variety is a very commonly used one. Hierarchical Agglomerative CA methods are bottom-up approaches that all dance to a tune which can be schematically summarized as follows (see Jain et al. 1999, 277):

(i)   Read in a $N \times N$ distance matrix. Treat each of the $N$ entities (in our case, dialect objects) in this matrix as a single-member cluster.
(ii)  Find the least dissimilar pair of clusters in the distance matrix. Merge these clusters into one cluster. Update the distance matrix accordingly, drawing on an algorithm to be specified by the user.
(iii) If there is only one cluster containing all $N$ dialect objects left, stop. Otherwise, go back to step 2.

Therefore, what CA does is to iteratively merge smaller clusters into larger clusters in a stepwise fashion, the end state being one cluster that contains all objects. The sequence of mergers can be depicted in a DENDROGRAM, which essentially works much like a family tree. This is why hierarchical agglomerative CA methods sit extremely well with the Schleicherian theme of phylogenetic language trees. The optimal number of clusters can be determined by diagramming the number of clusters against the so-called fusion coefficient, as in a scree graph, and spotting the "elbow" in the resulting graph – i.e. the point where the line is steep to the left, but non-steep to the right (see Aldenderfer and Blashfield 1984, 54). We are thus looking for an $N$-cluster solution that is not a lot less explanatory than an $N + 1$ cluster solution.

Classification and clustering are, alas, inherently subjective tasks (Jain et al. 1999, 290), and there are many ways in which the specifics of the agglomeration process can be furnished. The problem boils down to how the distance between clusters is judged and how the distance matrix is updated after each merger (see Jain et al. 1999, 275–277). Depending on the algorithm chosen, two smaller clusters may or may not end up in the same macro cluster, and this of course has ramifications for the final clustering outcome. In the present study, we marshal two matrix-updating algorithms that are fairly customary in the literature:

**Weighted Average** (henceforth WPGMA, shorthand for *Weighted Pair Group Method using Arithmetic averages*). WPGMA has some currency in the Groningen School of Dialectometry (e.g. Nerbonne et al. 2008 argue that WPGMA uncovers more geographic structure than competing algorithms). WPGMA calculates, in a very straightforward manner, the distance between two clusters as the distance between the means, without factoring in the number of elements in each cluster. Hence, the difference between two clusters is given by a comparatively simple formula: $d_{C_1,C_2} = \left(1/2 \times d_{a,C_1}\right) + \left(1/2 \times d_{b,C_1}\right)$, where $d_{C_1,C_2}$ is the distance between a new cluster $C_2$ (which merges the clusters $a$ and $b$) and an existing cluster $C_1$, $d_{a,C_1}$ is the distance between cluster $a$ and cluster $C_1$, and $d_{b,C_1}$ is the distance between cluster $b$ and cluster $C_1$ (Heeringa 2004, 149).

**Ward's Method** (also known as *Minimum Variance* method). Ward's Method (Ward 1963) is widely used because it tends to create small and even-sized clusters (Aldenderfer and Blashfield 1984, 43). Ward's Method is popular both in corpus linguistics (e.g. Gries and Wulff 2005) and in dialectometry (e.g. Heeringa and Nerbonne 2001; Goebl 2008). The algorithm is computationally intensive and seeks to minimize the error sum of squares (ESS; Kamvar et al. 2002) that results from each merger, in that the algorithm selects the merge operation that minimizes the ESS increase (Aldenderfer and Blashfield 1984, 43).

The possibility to conduct CA in more than one way is a headache, so how can we judge the quality of the results obtained by different matrix-updating algorithms? For one thing, interpretability plays a role. For example, some algorithms suffer from a nasty chaining effect (Jain et al. 1999, 276), which makes them useless in many circumstances. On a more quantitative plane, the analyst can calculate a *cophenetic correlation coefficient* (CPCC), which measures "the agreement between the distances as implied by the dendrogram and those of the original distance matrix" (Heeringa 2004, 151; see also Sokal and Rohlf 1962). To calculate the cophenetic distance between any two dialect objects, one first goes back to the dendrogram and identifies the smallest cluster (i.e. internal node) in which both objects are contained. Subsequently, the distance between the leaves and the containing node (see Nerbonne et al. 2008) is measured. This brings us to a further problem with CA: In addition to the issue of competing matrix-updating algorithms and how to compare clustering outcomes, simple clustering is unstable, no matter what algorithm is used. This is because small changes in the original distance matrix may result in major changes in the clustering outcome, a property that is not desirable. To mitigate this problem, the analysis in this chapter adopts a method known as "clustering with noise" (Nerbonne et al. 2008): the original distance matrix is clustered repeatedly (specifically, 10,000 times), adding some random amount of noise ($c = \sigma/2$) in each run. This exercise yields a cophenetic distance matrix that provides consensus – and thus more stable – cophenetic distances between dialect objects. The cophenetic distance matrix may serve as input to hard clustering, MDS, or any other statistical analysis technique that can process distance matrices.[3]

## 6.3.2   Clustering: a simple example

A simple example may illustrate the steps necessary to obtain a dialect division through Hierarchical Agglomerative CA. For now, we restrict our attention to only five counties sampled in FRED: East Lothian (ELN) in the Central Scottish Lowlands, Northumberland (NBL) in the North of England, Kent (KEN) in the Southeast of England, and Somerset (SOM) and Wiltshire (WIL) in the Southwest of England. This choice of measuring points yields the following $5 \times 5$ distance matrix specifying pairwise Euclidean morphosyntactic distances in the usual fashion (see Section 2.2.3 and Chapter 4):

|     | ELN  | KEN  | NBL  | SOM  | WIL |
|-----|------|------|------|------|-----|
| ELN |      |      |      |      |     |
| KEN | 7.00 |      |      |      |     |
| NBL | 5.68 | 5.31 |      |      |     |
| SOM | 5.96 | 3.51 | 4.58 |      |     |
| WIL | 6.17 | 3.98 | 4.57 | 2.32 |     |

[3] On a technical note, the visualization and statistical analysis techniques in this section draw on the *RuG/L04* package's `cluster`, `den`, and `mapclust` modules.

For the sake of inducing additional statistical robustness (see Nerbonne et al. 2008), we next submit this Euclidean distance matrix to repeated clustering with noise, using WPGMA as the matrix-updating algorithm. This exercise results in the following 5 × 5 *cophenetic* distance matrix:

|     | ELN  | KEN  | NBL  | SOM  | WIL  |
|-----|------|------|------|------|------|
| ELN |      |      |      |      |      |
| KEN | 6.45 |      |      |      |      |
| NBL | 6.45 | 5.28 |      |      |      |
| SOM | 6.45 | 4.09 | 5.29 |      |      |
| WIL | 6.45 | 4.09 | 5.29 | 2.67 |      |

Recall that the consensus cophenetic distances in this matrix are statistically tidied distances that specify the distance, as it were, one would have to travel *on average*, in various dendrograms, to get from one dialect to another dialect. Notice, now, that East Lothian turns out to be cophenetically equidistant from all other measuring points in the sample while Kent and Northumberland are equidistant from Somerset and Wiltshire.

Cophenetic distance matrices can be processed using any of the tools appropriate for "simple" distance matrices. This is another way of saying that we could now generate, for example, network maps or beam maps, or any other map type presented in Chapter 4. To learn more about dialect areas and sharp boundaries, we want to subject the cophenetic distance matrix to simple clustering (i.e. "hard" categorization). Hard clustering of the 5 × 5 cophenetic distance matrix discussed above drawing on WPGMA as a matrix-updating algorithm is documented in the following dendrogram:

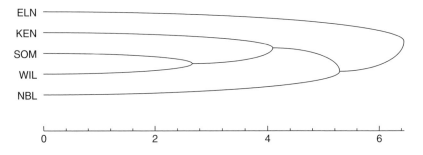

We adopt a top-down perspective (that is, we move from right to left in the dendrogram) and note that the most important division in our little dataset pits East Lothian against the other measuring points (which, notably, are all located in England), at a fusion coefficient of > 6 (see the ruler below the dendrogram). The least important division is between Somerset and Wiltshire (fusion coefficient: < 3). In other words, the WPGMA algorithm offers that the contrast between East Lothian and the other measuring points is far more crucial than the contrast between, for example,

Somerset and Wiltshire, which are classified as close relatives. Given the relatively minor split between Somerset and Wiltshire uncovered by WPGMA, the two locations may very well be taken to belong to one encompassing dialect area.

To which degree are the distances portrayed in this dendrogram in tune with the original Euclidean distances? The *cophenetic correlation coefficient* (CPCC), which measures the overlap between the original distances and cophenetic distances, is .96, which means that repeated clustering with noise utilizing the WPGMA algorithm does a pretty good job in preserving the variance in the original (Euclidean) distance matrix.

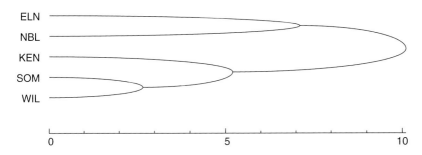

For reasons of comparison, we also report above a dendrogram that derives from repeated clustering and subsequent hard clustering of the dataset using Ward's method as matrix-updating algorithm. As can be seen, Ward's algorithm suggests a slightly different classification. Though it agrees with WPGMA that the split between Somerset and Wiltshire is minor, Northumberland is grouped with East Lothian, and the most crucial division pits these two measuring points against the three Southern English English measuring points. The CPCC coming with this particular clustering outcome is .80, and thus not as good, or as true to the data, as the WPGMA outcome. The bottom line is that choice of the matrix-updating algorithm matters.

### 6.3.3  *Analysis: dendrograms, cluster maps, and overlap with previous partitions*

Having covered the statistical technicalities, the task before us now is to analyze the FRED dataset from two angles – one, CA using the WPGMA algorithm; two, cluster analysis drawing on Ward's algorithm. In each case, we follow the previous chapter's precedent and explore dialect divisions in Great Britain against the backdrop of divisions deriving, trivially, from as-the-crow-flies geographic distances. We will also in each case quantify the overlap between our inductive clustering and some of the partitions previously reported in the literature (see Section 6.2).

*6.3.3.1*    WPGMA *clustering*

We thus begin by clustering not morphosyntactic but geographic as-the-crow-flies distances (in km) using the WPGMA algorithm. Figure C.1 (Appendix C, p. 183) is a dendrogram that visually depicts the hierarchical nature of geographic measuring-point relationships uncovered by WPGMA CA. The color coding (red, orange, green, blue) in the dendrogram derives from a 4-cluster solution which, according to the elbow criterion (see Section 6.3.1), is optimal. Concerning the overlap between cophenetic distances and the original as-the-crow-flies distances, the dendrogram in Figure C.1 yields a moderately robust CPCC value of .66. Map C.21 (Appendix C, p. 183) is a CLUSTER MAP that projects the 4-cluster solution depicted in Figure C.1's dendrogram to geography. A cartographic technique common in all strands of dialectometry (see, e.g., Heeringa 2004; Goebl 2007), cluster maps start out with a Voronoi tesselation of map space and subsequently assign the Voronoi polygons colors that match those in the source dendrogram.

In purely geographic terms, then, the most crucial division, according to WPGMA clustering, in geographic Great Britain pits counties north of Dumfriesshire and Northumberland (in blue) against counties south of Selkirkshire. The Southern group subsequently splits up into a green cluster encompassing counties in Central and Northern England plus Denbighshire and Dumfriesshire, and into a cluster comprising counties in Southern England plus Glamorganshire. Another significant division partitions the Southern group into a red group which unites counties in the Southwest of England plus Glamorganshire, and an orange group assembling counties in the Southeast of England: Kent, Suffolk, London, and Middlesex. Needless to say, the four clusters thus obtained are geographically perfectly coherent.

We proceed analogously for analyzing morphosyntactic dialect variability. Clustering the 34 × 34 morphosyntactic "dialects-only" distance matrix (see Section 4.1) using the WPGMA algorithm yields the dendrogram in Figure C.2 (Appendix C, p. 184) and the cluster map in Map C.22 (Appendix C, p. 184). In the case of morphosyntactic variability, a 6-cluster solution fits the dataset best. The CPCC value coming with the dendrogram in Figure C.2 is .66, exactly as with the geographic clustering discussed above. According to a PERMANOVA (see Section 6.2), the dialect grouping memberships depicted in Figure C.2 and Map C.22 account for about two-fifths ($R^2 = 41\%$, $p \leq$ .001) of the variance in morphosyntactic distances.

The first two splits in the dendrogram in Figure C.2 isolate two single-member clusters, Kincardineshire (in black) and Dumfriesshire (in light blue); we reserve a more detailed discussion of these outliers for Section 7.1. The remaining thirty-two measuring points are subsequently split up into a red cluster comprising measuring points in Southern England (Cornwall, Somerset, Wiltshire, Oxfordshire, London, and Kent), East Anglia (Suffolk), plus Durham in the North of England and the Isle of Man, and a largish blue-to-green cluster (Angus through Selkirkshire in the dendrogram).

The latter cluster is one notch further down the hierarchy partitioned into a small, dark-green cluster containing Banffshire and Selkirkshire as two geographically marginal measuring points in the Scottish Lowlands, and a larger cluster which, in a final step, breeds a somewhat tightly knit blue group containing measuring points in the Scottish Lowlands (Angus, Perthshire, West Lothian, Midlothian, East Lothian, and Peebleshire) plus Northumberland in Northern England, and a green group uniting measuring points all over the place except the Scottish Lowlands.

In all, it is fair to say that there is a good deal of geographic incoherence in this picture. Nonetheless, we may discern three major groupings:

- A geographically modestly coherent *red* cluster comprising most Southern English measuring points (Middlesex being the exception) plus Leicestershire and Nottinghamshire in Central England, Suffolk in East Anglia, and Durham in Northern England.
- A geographically incoherent *green* cluster that pools measuring points in the North of England with (i) measuring points in the West Midlands (Shropshire and Warwickshire), (ii) in Southern England (Middlesex), (iii) the traditional dialects spoken in Glamorganshire (South Wales), and (iv) pretty much all of the young, non-traditional varieties sampled in FRED (Denbighshire, Ross and Cromarty, Sutherland, Hebridean English). As an aside, we note that the green cluster is also the one in which Standard British English and Standard American English (see Section 4.4) are classed in an analysis (not reported here) that includes these measuring points.
- A dark-*blue*, geographically very coherent group uniting most of the (Central) Scottish Lowlands measuring points plus Northumberland.

Noise and geographical incoherence notwithstanding, this partition overlaps to some extent with the partition on purely geographic grounds discussed earlier (see Figure C.1 and Map C.21). The overlap can be quantified by calculating Adjusted Rand Indices (ARIs) (Rand 1971; Hubert and Arabie 1985), a measure of the similarity between two partitions which adjusts for chance overlap. ARIs have a maximum value of 1, which indicates a perfect overlap between two partitions.[4] Comparing Map C.21 to Map C.22 (geography versus morphosyntax), we obtain an ARI value of .13, which is not overwhelming. Where are the differences?

First, in morphosyntactic terms, the green cluster is not a well-defined region but rather a wastebasket group which – although it appears to be anchored in the North of England – contains outliers country-wide, such as the young dialects in the Scottish Highlands. Second, when turning back to the dendrograms we note that in the case of morphosyntax, the green

---

[4] We utilized the function adjustedRandIndex of the R package mclust (see http://cran.r-project.org/web/packages/mclust/mclust.pdf).

Table 6.3. *Adjusted Rand Indices (*ARIs*). (Partial) overlap between the* WPGMA *6-cluster solution and previous dialect divisions.* ARIs *closer to* 1 *indicate more overlap.*

|  | N | ARI |
| --- | --- | --- |
| dialects of Old English (Baugh and Cable 1993, 52) | 25 | .01 |
| dialects of Middle English (Baugh and Cable 1993, 186) | 25 | .10 |
| Ellis (1889) | 29 | .31 |
| Trudgill (1990) | 29 | .21 |
| Goebl (2007) | 19 | .08 |
| Inoue (1996) | 34 | .18 |

group is more related to the Scottish, blue group than to the red, Southern England group; geographically speaking, the reverse is true. Third, morphosyntax does not point to a split between measuring points in the Southwest of England and the Southeast of England, a split that is borne out by as-the-crow-flies distances and many previous dialect descriptions surveyed in Section 1.2.

How well does this clustering outcome dovetail with partitions previously reported in the literature (see Section 6.2)? Table 6.3 reports pertinent ARIs, which are moderate throughout. The WPGMA partition exhibits the largest overlap with Ellis' (1889) nineteenth-century survey of English dialects; Trudgill's (1990) partition also shows some overlap. The Early English partitions, by contrast, do not overlap well with the WPGMA partition. Again, we would like to caution the reader that a direct comparison of the $R^2$ values in Table 6.3 is problematic due to different areal coverages, but we clearly do see a tendency for WPGMA clustering to dovetail best with the two most customary dialect divisions.

### 6.3.3.2   Ward's Method

We now replicate the foregoing analysis. drawing not on WPGMA but on Ward's Method as matrix-updating algorithm. The dendrogram in Figure C.3 (Appendix C, p. 185) and the cluster map in Map C.23 (Appendix C, p. 185) document a cluster analysis run on the basis of as-the-crow-flies distances, to serve as the non-linguistic reference point for the discussion in this section. Observe that according to Ward's Method, Great Britain can be partitioned into three significant regions. A red region comprising the South of England and Central England plus the county of Glamorganshire in South Wales; a green region encompassing measuring points in the North of England plus the county of Denbighshire in North Wales plus the county of Dumfriesshire in Southern Scotland; and a blue region that unites measuring points in Scotland minus the county of Dumfriesshire. With a CPCC value of .69, the goodness of fit coming with this particular clustering outcome is comparable to WPGMA clustering on the basis of as-the-crow-flies distances. On the qualitative plane as well, the two algorithms overlap to a large extent – disagreements concern the opposition between Southwestern and Southeastern English measuring points, which Ward's Method does not emphasize as much as WPGMA, and the status of measuring points in Central England, which Ward's Method groups with Southern, not Northern, measuring points.

Against this backdrop, Figure C.4 (Appendix C, p. 186) and Map C.24 (Appendix C, p. 186) offer a regionalization on morphosyntactic grounds – specifically, on the basis of our by now customary $34 \times 34$ "dialects-only" distance matrix (see Section 4.1). For this dataset, Ward's Method can make do with a lean 3-cluster solution. The bad news is that Ward's method yields a CPCC value of only $r = .38$, which is a lot lower – and thus, less explanatory – than the corresponding value for the purely geographic partition, and also the morphosyntactic clustering utilizing the WPGMA algorithm. A PERMANOVA (see Section 6.2) suggests that dialect grouping memberships as derived by Ward's Method and depicted in Figure C.4 and Map C.24 explain about a fifth ($R^2 = 22\%$, $p \leq .001$) of the variance in morphosyntactic distances.

And again, we are dealing with some geographic incoherence, though arguably less so than in the case of WPGMA. The three dialect clusters suggested by Ward's Method are the following:

- We find, first, a geographically modestly coherent *red* cluster comprising most Southern English measuring points (Middlesex being the exception) plus Nottinghamshire in Central England, Suffolk in East Anglia, and Durham in Northern England. The only difference with the WPGMA red cluster (see Map C.22) is that according to Ward's Method, the red cluster does not include Leicestershire.
- We also obtain a geographically fairly coherent *green* group encompassing the majority of measuring points in Northern England (Westmorland, Yorkshire, Lancashire), the Isle of Man, Shropshire and Leicestershire in Central England, and Glamorganshire in South Wales.
- Lastly, Ward's method yields a *blue* cluster uniting all measuring points in Scotland plus Northumberland in Northern England plus Denbighshire in North Wales plus Warwickshire in Central England plus Middlesex in Southern England. Note that clustering a $36 \times 36$ distance matrix (not reported here) specifying dialectal distances plus distances to the Standard varieties (see Section 4.4) would also assign Standard British and Standard American English to the blue cluster.

This partition overlaps moderately with the partition according to Ward's Method on purely geographic grounds (ARI = .20). In comparison to the WPGMA division, Ward's wastebasket cluster is the blue cluster, which contains Scots varieties, young dialects (such as Hebridean English), and the usual traditional dialect outliers in England (i.e. Warwickshire and Middlesex; Section 7.1 has a more detailed discussion of these). Also unlike

Table 6.4. *Adjusted Rand Indices (*ARIs*). (Partial) overlap between Ward's 3-cluster solution and previous dialect divisions.* ARIs *closer to* 1 *indicate more overlap.*

|  | *N* | ARI |
|---|---|---|
| dialects of Old English (Baugh and Cable 1993, 52) | 25 | .14 |
| dialects of Middle English (Baugh and Cable 1993, 186) | 25 | .21 |
| Ellis (1889) | 29 | .54 |
| Trudgill (1990) | 29 | .44 |
| Goebl (2007) | 19 | .19 |
| Inoue (1996) | 34 | .53 |

WPGMA, Ward's Method classifies the Northern English green cluster as more closely related to the Southern English red cluster than to the Scottish cluster; recall here that WPGMA pits the red cluster (containing primarily measuring points in Southern England) against all the rest. Finally, Ward's Method groups the Standard varieties with the blue, Scotland-anchored cluster whereas WPGMA clustering classifies them into the green, Northern England-centered cluster.

As for the overlap with previous dialect divisions, it turns out that the clustering outcome according to Ward's Method is much more in line with previous dialect divisions than is the WPGMA clustering discussed in the previous section. Consider the ARIs in Table 6.4: again, we find that our dialect partition is most similar to the division by Ellis (1889), closely followed, however, by Inoue's (1996) perceptual dialectology experiment. Again, the two Early English partitions exhibit a rather low degree of overlap. In all, Ward's Method appears to uncover a partition that is more expected given the previous literature, and also one that captures a facet of the dataset that dovetails with perceptual dialectology experiments.

### 6.3.4    Interim summary

Both matrix-updating algorithms discussed in this section proceed inductively, and both support a tripartite division of Great Britain on morphosyntactic grounds. The first cluster of measuring points comprises primarily Southern England measuring points plus Nottinghamshire and Durham. There is substantial disagreement between the two clustering algorithms in regard to the scope of the second cluster, but it appears to be anchored in Northern England, encompassing as it does in both cases Westmorland, Lancashire, and Yorkshire as somewhat central measuring points. The third cluster of measuring points clearly has its center of gravity in Scotland, and although its boundaries are unclear it categorically includes the FRED measuring points in the Central Scottish Lowlands. Both algorithms produce clusters that are to varying degrees geographically (in)coherent, and much of this noise appears to be due to the unclear status of the usual outliers (i.e.

Warwickshire, Middlesex) and non-traditional dialects in the sample (e.g. Denbighshire). At any rate, we should like to emphasize that the so-called "Humber-Ribble line" (see, e.g., Wales 2006), which is often argued to be the most crucial linguistic boundary in England, does not play any role in any case. In like vein, this section's cluster analytic machinery has notably failed to detect a Central English Midlands area. As for the overlap with previous dialect divisions, we saw that the 3-cluster solution according to Ward's Method has a better fit with previous dialect divisions than the WPGMA 6-cluster solution. Both algorithms, however, agree that the division by Ellis (1889) comes closest to what is going on in the FRED dataset. Not surprisingly given their low overall explanatory power reported in Section 6.2, the two Early English partitions fare rather poorly.

## 6.4   Chapter summary

The aim of this chapter was to explore to what degree Great Britain's morphosyntactic dialect landscape can be thought of as being organized along the lines of internally more or less homogeneous and geographically more or less coherent dialect areas. We initially proceeded deductively and tested how successful previous dialect partitions are in predicting morphosyntactic dialect distances in FRED, and found that these explain between a quarter and a half of the variance in our dataset. We next moved on to inductively deriving dialect groupings from the dataset and utilized two hierarchical agglomerative clustering algorithms to this end. Both algorithms produce slightly different clustering outcomes, but both can be argued to boil the data down to a tripartite division of FRED measuring points: Scottish English dialects versus Northern English English dialects versus Southern English English dialects. While the dialect clusters are geographically not always perfectly coherent, they explain between about 20 and 40 percent of the aggregate morphosyntactic variance in the FRED dataset, which is more than we managed to explain drawing on continuous predictors in the previous chapter. At the outset of Chapter 5, then, we had suggested that dialect landscapes may exhibit both continuum and dialect area traits, the empirical question being to which extent one of the two traits prevails. We conclude, therefore, that while the FRED dialect landscape is not *perfectly* regionalized because of some geographic incoherence, the dialect area scenario is rather more powerful explanatorily than the dialect continuum scenario.

# 7    Back to the features

This chapter abandons the very aggregational, holistic perspective that has dominated the empirical discussion in the three previous chapters with the exception of Section 5.2.3, in which we correlated MDS dimensions with feature frequencies. Instead, we now adopt a more feature-centered and thus nicely complementary view, asking: How can the patterns we have seen so far be traced back to the distributional behavior of each of the morphosyntactic features on which the present study's analysis is based? Section 7.1 sets the scene by scrutinizing six measuring points (Banffshire, Denbighshire, Dumfriesshire, Middlesex, Leicestershire, and Warwickshire) that have struck us as exceptional to varying degrees in the previous chapters, and we will be interested in whether their status can be pinned down on text frequencies of individual morphosyntactic features. Section 7.2 adopts a more encompassing and systematic approach that marshals Principal Component Analysis to uncover feature bundles and to explore the layered nature of geographically conditioned variability in Great Britain. Section 7.3 is a chapter summary.

## 7.1    Revisiting the outliers

This section revisits six FRED measuring points (Banffshire, Denbighshire, Dumfriesshire, Middlesex, Leicestershire, and Warwickshire)[1] which, throughout the previous chapters, did not fit in the picture in various ways and to varying degrees. Recall also that in Chapter 5's series of regression and correlation analyses, excluding these six outliers from consideration substantially boosted the explanatory power of language-external predictors such as linguistic gravity, which amounts to further evidence that there is something odd about these measuring points. Thus, we will now endeavor to trace back the special status of these outliers to individual morphosyntactic features, by way of comparing each outlier's morphosyntactic profile to that of a well-behaved neighboring measuring point. Specifically, in

---

[1] Note that we do not include Kincardineshire in this discussion. Although the measuring point is clearly marginal and in many respects extreme (see especially Chapter 4), it is not consistently out of line with the large-scale patterns created by neighboring measuring points (see, e.g., the continuum map in Map C.17 [p. 181]).

each case we will conduct a series of fifty-seven Fisher's Exact Tests (Fisher 1954) on the basis of raw frequencies (one for each feature) to assess the significance of feature frequency differentials; in so doing, we will adopt a Bonferroni-corrected (Abdi 2007) $\alpha$ level of $p = 0.05/57 \approx .001$.

Right at the outset we wish to emphasize that the outlier status of the six measuring points does not necessarily have substantial linguistic reasons in all cases. It is certainly no accident that among the ten measuring points in FRED with the thinnest textual coverage, we find five of the above outliers (only Middlesex is a textually robustly documented measuring point). So, although we cannot be entirely sure, it is likely that a good deal of the noise generated by the outliers investigated in this section is due to poor sampling.

### 7.1.1    Banffshire

We have seen that Banffshire, the northernmost measuring point in the Scottish Lowlands sampled in FRED, behaves abnormally in a number of ways. Chapter 4 has indicated that Banffshire is a morphosyntactically marginal county that is not well connected to other measuring points in the FRED network. According to the continuum maps discussed in Chapter 5 (e.g., Map C.17 [p. 181]), Banffshire does not fit in with either the other Northern Scottish Lowlands measuring points or the Scottish Highlands measuring points. WPGMA cluster analysis (see, e.g., the dendrogram in Figure C.2 [p. 184]) has grouped Banffshire into a geographically incoherent mini-cluster where it lives with Selkirkshire, far away in the Southern Scottish Lowlands.

It is hard to trace Banffshire's outlier status back to frequencies of particular morphosyntactic features. Compared to Angus English, a geographically close measuring point, we find only one feature in Banffshire English whose text frequency is significantly different – the primary verb TO BE (feature [14]), which appears to be particularly frequent in Banffshire English. Upon close inspection, however, it turns out that most occurrences of the verb TO BE in FRED's Banffshire material are trivial copula usages (see (1)), as opposed to somewhat more exciting auxiliary uses or such like.

(1)    a.    he *was* the foreman in the crew. [BAN001]
       b.    my mother died when I *was* five [BAN001]
       c.    And always I *was* so proud of his needles, compared to the rough ones that the other girls had to fill. [BAN001]

Two frequency differentials that do not reach statistical significance according to the strict Bonferroni criterion but which nonetheless appear interesting concern feature [44] (non-standard WAS, as in (2)), which is not attested at all in the Banffshire material but which occurs thirty times *pttw* in Angus English ($p = .03$), and feature [31] (the negative suffix *-nae*) (as in (3)), which is only half as frequent in Banffshire English than in Angus English ($p = .04$).

(2)   you *was* finished with your horses Saturday dinner-time till Sunday morning [ANS001]

(3)   my father would*nae* look at that [BAN001]

We should point out – and this is possibly the most crucial factor – that FRED's textual coverage of Banffshire English is comparatively thin, with only one interview spanning 6,000 words of running text (the informant is female and was born in 1914; her family has been involved with salmon fishing). A sampling problem therefore cannot be ruled out and is, indeed, likely.

To recapitulate, Banffshire's outlier status is probably in large part due to poor sampling. To the degree that it is not, we saw that the primary verb TO BE is unusually frequent in Banffshire English, whereas non-standard WAS and the negative suffix *-nae* are conspicuously absent from the Banffshire material.

### 7.1.2   *Denbighshire*

On many occasions, we encountered Denbighshire in North Wales as a linguistically fairly odd measuring point. In Chapter 4, we saw that Denbighshire radiates a strong signal of dissimilarity to geographically neighboring measuring points (see Map C.2). The continuum plots and maps in Chapter 5 singled out Denbighshire as an outlier (see Map C.17, in which Denbighshire turns out as way too violet). Also, the Ward CA undertaken in Chapter 6 (see Map C.24) groups Denbighshire into the mixed-bag cluster that also encompasses measuring points in Scotland plus Warwickshire and Middlesex.

Let us reiterate here that Denbighshire is expected to be different, to some extent. By comparison to, for example, Glamorganshire English spoken in South Wales, Denbighshire English is a comparatively young dialect and not, technically speaking, a long-established mother-tongue dialect (see Section 4.1.1). On top of that we note that textual coverage in FRED of the measuring point Denbighshire is comparatively limited: 6,000 words of running text, 4 interviews, 1 location, 6 speakers. The interviewees fit FRED's sociological bill, however: two-thirds of the speakers are male; mean age is 87 years. In point of fact, the Denbighshire speakers are among the oldest speakers sampled in FRED. Be that as it may, thanks to a small textual basis sampling issues are likely.

As in the case of Banffshire, tracing back Denbighshire's outlier status to text frequencies of actual morphosyntactic features is tough. In comparison to Glamorganshire English, Denbighshire's morphosyntactic profile is characterized by only two Bonferroni-significant feature frequency differentials. For one thing, *used to* as marker of habitual past (feature [20], as in (4)) is very popular in the Denbighshire texts (229 occurrences *pttw* as opposed to only 43 occurrences *pttw* in the Glamorganshire material). Second, the synthetic *s*-genitive (feature [9], as in (5)) is significantly more frequent in the Denbighshire material (16 occurrences *pttw*) than in the Glamorganshire material (3 occurrences *pttw*).

(4)   He *used to* go and help the men in the kiln, loading a lorry, but he'd only load about five barrows, and then somebody would call him. [DEN003]

(5)   they go to John Bright School, which was where the *posh people's children* went, you know, but now this one has come on equal parity with the other one. [DEN004]

In the light of these rather uninterpretable frequency differentials, therefore, we conclude that sampling problems are the most likely cause for the special status of measuring point Denbighshire.

## 7.1.3   Dumfriesshire

Dumfriesshire is the southernmost FRED measuring point in Scotland. In the preceding chapters, Dumfriesshire has attracted our attention for two reasons. First, Section 4.2.2 demonstrated that Dumfriesshire is a fairly marginal measuring point which entertains relatively high mean Euclidean distances to other measuring points. Along similar lines, Section 4.3 has shown that Dumfriesshire is the measuring point in the FRED network that exhibits the highest distance minimum to other measuring points. According to the analysis of regression residuals conducted in Section 5.3.5 (see Map C.20), linguistic gravity scores cannot begin to explain these high distances. Second, the WPGMA CA undertaken in Chapter 6 (see Map C.22) isolates Dumfriesshire in a single-member outlier cluster.

We should point out that while textual coverage in FRED of the measuring point Dumfriesshire is certainly not extensive (10, 000 words of running text in one interview with two speakers), it is not terribly low. The profile of the two informants sampled is inconspicuous as well: a husband (a retired farmer) and wife (who does not talk a lot), with the husband having been born in 1910. What, then, are the features that might make Dumfriesshire English special? A comparison to two immediately neighboring measuring points (Selkirkshire or Peebleshire) would be statistically pointless due to the fact that these measuring points themselves do not have extensive textual coverage, so let us compare Dumfriesshire's morphosyntactic profile to that of West Lothian English (textual

Table 7.1. *Bonferroni-significant feature frequency differentials between Dumfriesshire English and a geographically close neighbor, West Lothian English.*

|      |                                                                                                          | normalized frequency (*pttw*) Dumfriesshire | normalized frequency (*pttw*) West Lothian |
|------|----------------------------------------------------------------------------------------------------------|:-------------------------------------------:|:------------------------------------------:|
| [31] | the negative suffix *-nae*                                                                               | 0                                           | 37                                         |
| [18] | the future markers WILL/SHALL                                                                            | 26                                          | 8                                          |
| [39] | non-standard verbal *-s*                                                                                  | 41                                          | 6                                          |
| [55] | lack of inversion and/or of auxiliaries in *wh*-questions and in main clause *yes/no*-questions          | 14                                          | 0                                          |
| [20] | *used to* as marker of habitual past                                                                     | 213                                         | 15                                         |
| [34] | negative contraction                                                                                     | 15                                          | 1                                          |
| [30] | non-standard past tense *come*                                                                           | 13                                          | 1                                          |

coverage: 18,000 words of running text), a measuring point in the Central Scottish Lowlands approximately 110 km away. Customary testing for significant frequency differentials yields a set of seven features (see Table 7.1) that set apart Dumfriesshire English from West Lothian English (and, by inference, from other dialects in its neighborhood). Most significantly, the negative suffix *-nae* (feature [31], as in (6)), the well-known Scotticism, is absent in the Dumfriesshire material but frequent in the West Lothian material.

(6)   And our shift still did*nae* get in, so then eh, the union, eh, called in the management [WLN005]

The other six features in Table 7.1 are all more frequent in the Dumfriesshire material than in the West Lothian material: the future markers WILL/SHALL (feature [18], as in (7)), non-standard verbal *-s* (feature [39], as in (8)), lack of inversion and/or of auxiliaries in *wh*-questions and in main clause *yes/no*-questions (feature [55], as in (9)), *used to* as marker of habitual past (feature [20], as in (10)), negative contraction (feature [34], as in (11)), and non-standard past tense *come* (feature [30], as in (12)).

(7)   We'*ll* attend to it. [DFS001]

(8)   I say*s*, I have dozens of them. [DFS001]

(9)   Ye ken what they are? [DFS001]

(10)   And they *used to* make what they called charpins. [DFS001]

(11)   Aye! *Isn't* it, aye. [DFS001]

(12)   and I remember one night he *come*, he'd been round the country hawking and he *come* home, and eh, the wife had a, what they called the cheaty boxes. [DFS001]

Notice also that in regard to the frequency of most of the features in Table 7.1, Peebleshire and Selkirkshire – Dumfriesshire's immediate neighbors in the FRED network – take the middle road between Dumfriesshire and West Lothian. It is only in terms of *used to* as a marker of habitual past, lack of inversion, and non-standard past tense *come* that the text frequencies in the Dumfriesshire material are truly extreme.

In all, the most persuasive causes for why the measuring point Dumfriesshire behaves abnormally include (i) the total absence of the negative suffix *-nae*, (ii) the comparatively high frequency of non-standard verbal *-s*, and (iii) the popularity in Dumfriesshire English of non-standard past tense *come*.

## 7.1.4 *Middlesex*

According to our data, Middlesex is not an entirely well-behaved Southern England measuring point. Section 4.2.1 has shown that Middlesex belongs to a set of marginal measuring points that have only weak links to other counties, radiating a robust signal of morphosyntactic dissimilarity into the network. In the continuum perspective (Section 5.2.3; see Map C.17), Middlesex quite clearly is an outlier. In a similar vein, the dialect area view identifies Middlesex as a special case: WPGMA clustering (Section 6.3.3) groups Middlesex into a heterogeneous cluster also encompassing measuring points in the Scottish Highlands, Wales, and Northern England; Ward clustering (Section 6.3.3) assigns Middlesex to a cluster principally consisting of measuring points in Scotland. At the same time, Middlesex's renegade status seems to be empirically substantial, for Middlesex is a measuring point whose textual coverage in FRED is rather satisfactory: two interviews spanning 32,000 words of running text, one location (Pinner), but no more than two male speakers (born in 1897 and 1905, respectively), both of whom have a working-class background.

To address the strange behavior of measuring point Middlesex, let us make a comparison to measuring point London, which is the closest neighbor to Middlesex geographically and a fairly well-behaved Southern English English measuring point. Customary testing for significant feature frequency differentials uncovers five features (Table 7.2) which make a significant difference between Middlesex's and London's morphosyntactic profiles. Four of these are underrepresented in Middlesex English vis-à-vis London English: the primary verb TO DO (feature [13], as in (13)), the primary verb TO HAVE (feature [15], as in (14)), *them* (feature [6], as in (15)), and *us* (feature [5], as in (16)). There is one feature that is significantly more frequent in the Middlesex material than in the London material, namely the primary verb TO BE (feature [14], as in (17)).

(13)    And, uh, there was a time, when, well, a few of us *did* kick up a bitta fuss about it, you know [LND002]

Table 7.2. *Bonferroni-significant feature frequency differentials between Middlesex English and a geographically close neighbor, London English.*

|  |  | normalized frequency (*pttw*) Middlesex | normalized frequency (*pttw*) London |
|---|---|---|---|
| [13] | the primary verb TO DO | 48 | 109 |
| [15] | the primary verb TO HAVE | 75 | 112 |
| [6] | *them* | 13 | 31 |
| [5] | *us* | 5 | 16 |
| [14] | the primary verb TO BE | 394 | 338 |

(14)   and he *had* stomach trouble [LND007]

(15)   In *them* days, you couldn't leave a job without this release form [LND002]

(16)   'Cause *us* kids used to pinch the sweets like hell, so that, that wasn't very profitable. [LND005]

(17)   Of course, there *was* no houses there then. [MDX002]

It is hard to speculate about the reasons for the primary verb frequency differential (features [13], [14], and [17]). In regard to feature [6] (*them*), recall that according to SED (Orton et al. 1978, map M83 [LAE]) evidence, *them* for *those* is supposed to be rare in the Southeast of England, so the real outlier here may actually be London English. However, in regard to feature [5] (*us*) map M75 in Orton et al. (1978) (LAE) suggests that the variation between *with our eyes* and *with us eyes* is subject to isoglosses that are close to, or actually cut through, the London/Middlesex region – thus, this particular frequency differential makes some sense given the literature.

All in all, then, the features that appear as most strongly implicated in the outlier status of measuring point Middlesex include *them*, *us*, and the three primary verbs.

### 7.1.5   Leicestershire

Leicestershire in Eastern Central England (see Trudgill 1990, map 9) was not the worst outlier in the preceding chapters, but the measuring point is definitely a bit odd. Section 4.2.1 identified Leicestershire as a marginal measuring point that has only weak links to other counties; Leicestershire, in point of fact, sits in the epicenter of a dissimilarity tangle that emits a strong signal of dissimilarity into the network. In Section 4.4, we additionally saw that Leicestershire entertains comparatively large distances to Standard English. Moreover, according to Section 5.2.3's continuum maps (see Map C.17), Leicestershire is rather different from its neighbors.

Table 7.3. *Bonferroni-significant feature frequency differentials between Leicestershire English and a geographically close neighbor, Nottinghamshire English.*

|  |  | normalized frequency (*pttw*) Leicestershire | normalized frequency (*pttw*) Nottinghamshire |
|---|---|---|---|
| [39] | non-standard verbal -*s* | 2 | 49 |
| [45] | non-standard WERE | 120 | 12 |
| [6] | *them* | 24 | 63 |
| [29] | non-standard past tense *done* | 10 | 1 |

Textual coverage in FRED of Leicestershire tends towards the bottom end of acceptability: The measuring point is documented by two interviews (1 location, three speakers) spanning 6,000 words of running text. All three interviewees appear to have a NORM profile. All are male; one was born in 1903 and has a working-class background. The exact age of the other two speakers is unknown, but they are rather elderly. In any case, Leicestershire's behavior may very well be a statistical accident due to thin textual coverage. Assuming for the moment that there are substantial reasons for the measuring point's outlier status, let us check Leicestershire's morphosyntactic profile against the backdrop of the profile of its closest neighbor, Nottinghamshire. Table 7.3 reports four features that are significantly more or less frequent in the Leicestershire material than in the Nottinghamshire material. Two fairly generic and supra-regional dialect features – specifically, non-standard verbal -*s* (feature [39], as in (18)) and *them* (feature [6], as in (19)) – are underrepresented in Leicestershire English. By contrast, non-standard WERE (feature [45], as in (20)) and non-standard past tense *done* (feature [29], as in (21)) – are both overrepresented in Leicestershire English, by a factor of 10 : 1.

(18)   I said to him I said, Grandfather, I say*s*, I'm I'm fed up with the railway [NTT015]

(19)   all *them* teams as played there then [NTT016]

(20)   It *were* H. T. Buster the name on him, he *were* the headmaster. [LEI001]

(21)   well we we *done* no more than what other kids used to do [LEI002]

In regard to non-standard WERE, observe that the SED material does suggest a good deal of regional variation in the Leicestershire/Nottinghamshire area (Orton et al. 1978, maps M20–M25 [LAE]).

In short, Leicestershire appears to be special thanks primarily to (i) the rarity of non-standard verbal -*s* and *them*, and (ii) the popularity of non-standard WERE and non-standard past tense *done*.

### 7.1.6 *Warwickshire*

Warwickshire is a measuring point in England's West Midlands region that, in the foregoing analyses, raised our eyebrows in the following ways:

- Throughout Chapter 4, Warwickshire emerged as surprisingly dissimilar to many measuring points in its immediate vicinity (see Map C.8).
- In the continuum perspective (see Map C.17), Warwickshire is a clear outlier.
- As with Middlesex, Ward clustering (Section 6.3.3) categorizes Warwickshire into a wastebasket cluster combining measuring points in Scotland, Wales, and England.

Recall now that dialects in the West Midlands have a reputation of being special (see Section 4.2.1). We are thus left to wonder whether Warwickshire's special status in the FRED network is substantially real or due to a sampling problem. Note that textual coverage in FRED of the measuring point Warwickshire is merely one interview with one speaker encompassing 8,000 words of running text. The interviewee is an elderly male (exact age unknown) who served in the army until 1947, and who then started "working on the market." One of Warwickshire's immediate neighbors in the FRED network that is itself well behaved is Shropshire. Using our customary instrument of testing feature frequencies for Bonferroni-significant differences uncovers two features that set Warwickshire's morphosyntactic profile apart from Shropshire's. First, we note that *wh*-relativization (feature [46], as in (22)) is extremely frequent in the Warwickshire material (87 occurrences *pttw* versus 27 occurrences *pttw* in the Shropshire material). This finding is interesting, since according to Orton et al. (1978, map S5) (LAE) *wh*-relativization should not be particularly widespread in the West Midlands. Second, *us* (feature [5], as in (23)) is unpopular in the Warwickshire material (1 occurrence *pttw* versus 13 occurrences *pttw* in the Shropshire material). This one is less surprising, as *us* as a subject pronoun replacing standard *me* is known to be variable in the West Midlands area (see Orton et al. 1978, map M74 [LAE]).

(22)    they have these dining rooms there with a chap standing in the winter *whose* name was Bill Kemp [WAR001]

(23)    we were all *us* children at the age of three, *us* little uns, were tutored at The Finger Chapel. [SAL006]

In summary, Warwickshire's outlier status is probably at least in part a function of its small textual coverage in FRED. In terms of actual features, we saw that the Warwickshire material displays an unusually high frequency of *wh*-relativization.

## 7.2   The quest for feature bundles: Principal Component Analysis

The previous discussion has sought to single out individual features that may be responsible for the fact that a handful of measuring points in our sample behave in an interesting manner. In this section, we embark on a more encompassing, dataset-wide investigation to explore feature bundles and global co-occurrence patterns. The goal is to identify linguistic structure in the aggregate perspective (Nerbonne 2006), taking into joint consideration *all* measuring points and *all* features. Two specific questions guide the analysis in this section. On the linguistic/structural plane, to what extent do high text frequency of some features predict high or low text frequencies of other features? And on the geographical plane, how do features gang up to create layered areal patterns?

To address these questions, we utilize PRINCIPAL COMPONENT ANALYSIS (PCA) (Hotelling 1933), a well-established and elegant multivariate dimension reduction technique that transforms a set of high-dimensional vectors (in our case, 57-dimensional feature frequency vectors) into a set of lower-dimensional vectors (so-called "principal components"), which we will interpret as feature bundles. In crosslinguistic Greenberg-style typology (Greenberg 1963), such bundles correspond to *biconditional implications*, also known as *equivalences*. Similar to MDS, PCA's dimension-reduction process is designed to preserve as much information from the original dataset as possible (Dunteman 1989, 7). PCA is a fairly popular and well-understood technique (see Dunteman 1989, 8); in linguistics, PCA and related techniques are the tool of choice in multidimensional studies of register variation (see, e.g., Biber 1988). In dialectology, PCA and a close cousin, *factor analysis*, are also quite common (see, e.g., Shackleton 2005; Nerbonne 2006; Wieling et al. 2007; Leinonen 2008).

This is not the place to discuss in detail the statistical technicalities underpinning PCA (the interested reader is referred to Dunteman 1989),[2] but we will briefly discuss the workings of PCA from an end-user's perspective. PCA takes as input what we have called an $N \times p$ frequency matrix (see Section 2.2.2). The FRED county-level $34 \times 57$ frequency matrix that has served this study quite well so far has a fairly dismal so-called subject-to-item ratio (Costello and Osborne 2005, 4), which poses a problem for PCA. So for the purposes of this section, we need to increase the level of

---

[2]   To conduct PCA, we utilized the statistical software package SPSS (www.spss.com): module FACTOR, method "Principal Components," Varimax rotation.

| com- ponent | variance explained | cum. variance explained |
|---|---|---|
| 1 | 13.0% | 13.0% |
| 2 | 7.9% | 20.9% |
| 3 | 6.4% | 27.3% |
| 4 | 4.1% | 31.4% |
| 5 | 3.7% | 35.1% |
| 6 | 3.7% | 38.8% |
| 7 | 3.3% | 42.1% |
| 8 | 3.1% | 45.3% |
| 9 | 2.8% | 48.0% |
| 10 | 2.6% | 50.7% |
| 11 | 2.5% | 53.1% |
| 12 | 2.3% | 55.5% |
| 13 | 2.2% | 57.7% |
| 14 | 2.2% | 59.8% |
| 15 | 2.1% | 61.9% |
| 16 | 2.1% | 64.0% |
| 17 | 2.0% | 66.0% |
| 18 | 1.9% | 67.9% |
| 19 | 1.9% | 69.7% |
| 20 | 1.8% | 71.5% |

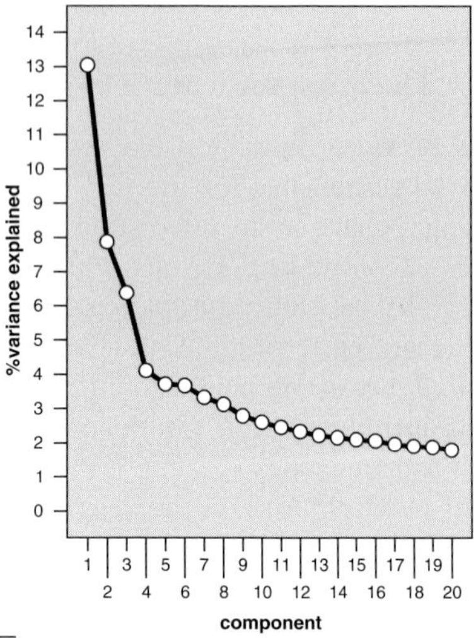

Figure 7.1. Principal Component Analysis. Left: Components extracted and variance explained. Right: Scree plot (variance explained by component number).

areal granularity, which is another way of saying that we will resort to the FRED location level, processing a 158 × 57 frequency matrix. This larger matrix, which has a more acceptable subject-to-item ration of 2.8, describes 158 FRED locations (that is, villages and towns) by 57-dimensional feature frequency vectors.

From this matrix, we had PCA extract twenty components ("feature bundles"), using a customary Eigenvalue threshold to determine the statistically optimal number of components. The twenty components cumulatively account for 71.5% of the variance in the original 158 × 57 frequency matrix; component 1 accounts for 13.0% of the variance, component 2 for 7.9%, and so on (see Figure 7.1). What is the exact nature of these components, and precisely how do they relate to each other? Leino and Hyvönen (2008) explain that

PCA finds the direction in the data which explains most of the variation in the data. This is the first principal component. After this each consecutive component explains the variation left in the data after the variation explained by the previous components has been removed. (Leino and Hyvönen 2008, 178)

Thus, lower-numbered components are always more explanatory and more important (and more often than not also more interpretable) than higher-numbered components. This is why principal components provide "a layered view of the variation" (Leino and Hyvönen 2008, 186), from more crucial to less crucial. But as a rule not all statistically warranted components will also have a meaningful, substantially significant linguistic interpretation, and the analyst – faced with a trade-off between explanatory power, interpretability, and parsimony – will want to consider only the first $n$ components. We generated a scree plot (Figure 7.1) to help decide on a reasonable number of principal components to retain (see Dunteman 1989, 22–23). The scree plot in Figure 7.1 shows that the first four components buy us a lot in terms of variance explained, but that from the fourth principal component onwards the gains in explanatoriness are comparatively meagre. Hence we chose to retain the first $n = 4$ principal components and subsequently applied Varimax rotation (Kaiser 1958), a popular method to increase interpretability of the components (see Dunteman 1989, 48–50 for the technicalities).

In terms of interpretation, there are two avenues to explore principal components[3] and hence feature bundles. The analyst may concentrate, first, on *the nature of the feature interdependencies* revealed by PCA, or, second, on how feature interdependencies gang up to create *cross-dialect patternings*, which are possibly geographically cohesive. As for the first mode of interpretation (focus on the interdependencies themselves), PCA yields a $p \times n$ (rotated) component-loading matrix that reports COMPONENT LOADINGS for each of the features subject to analysis. Component loadings are similar to correlation coefficients and indicate how strongly individual features are associated with a particular component. Loadings range from $-1$ (a perfect negative association) to $+1$ (a perfect positive association). Appendix B reports the full $57 \times 4$ component-loading matrix generated from the FRED location level $158 \times 57$ frequency matrix. On the basis of this matrix, we may take an interest in, say, the first component (the PC1 column) and rank features according to their loadings on PC1. Doing exactly that, we find, among other things, that feature [33] (multiple negation) has a quite strong positive loading on PC1 (.70), and so does feature [32] (the negator *ain't*; .64). Conversely, feature [14] (the primary verb TO BE) has a negative loading on PC1 ($-.19$). All this is another way of saying that frequencies of multiple negation and of the negator *ain't* are interdependent (i.e. the features tend to co-occur) and thus form a feature bundle, which is captured in PC1. At the same time, the text frequencies of both features are negatively correlated to text frequencies of the primary verb TO BE, a feature that tends to be infrequent when

---

[3] We acknowledge that since we applied Varimax rotation, we should strictly speaking no longer refer to the rotated components as "principal" components (see Leino and Hyvönen 2008, 178), but for the sake of brevity and readability we will nonetheless do so.

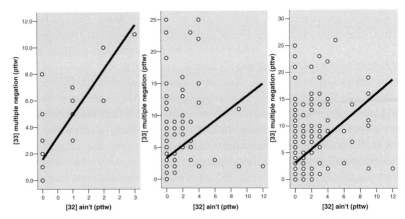

Figure 7.2. Text frequencies of feature [33] (multiple negation) versus text frequencies of feature [32] (the negator *ain't*) (*pttw*, no *log*-transformation). Left: county level (*N* = 34). Middle: location level (*N* = 162). Right: individual FRED texts (*N* = 347). Solid lines are linear regression estimates (county level: *r* = .800; location level: *r* = .304; text level: *r* = .405). All correlations are significant at *p* < .05.

multiple negation and *ain't* are frequent. This interdependency is likewise captured in PC1.

To illustrate, and to increase confidence in the method, consider Figure 7.2, whose diagrams plot text frequencies of feature [33] against frequencies of feature [32] on three levels of granularity: FRED counties, FRED locations, and FRED texts/interviews (which approximate the level of individual speakers). In all cases, we indeed find a positive correlation between text frequencies of the two features, exactly as predicted by the component loadings reported in Appendix B. Conversely, the scatterplots in Figure 7.3 plot frequencies of feature [33] against frequencies of feature [14], and here we find a *negative* correlation throughout – again, as predicted by the component loadings in Appendix B. That these interdependencies scale across three levels of granularity is good news, for it means that the feature interdependencies uncovered by PCA are not some aggregation artifact but are real all the way to the level of individual dialect speakers.

Are particular feature bundles more popular in some regions than in other regions? This is the second issue that PCA can explore. Whereas component loadings measure the importance of individual linguistic features in particular principal components, the analyst may also elect to calculate so-called COMPONENT SCORES to shed light on the distribution of bundles across measuring points. Component scores measure the strength of particular components in particular dialects as a function of each feature's frequency

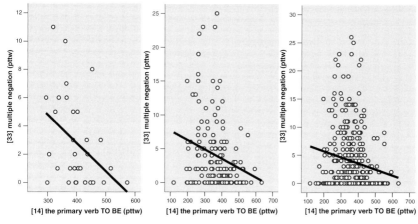

Figure 7.3. Text frequencies of feature [33] (multiple negation) versus text frequencies of feature [14] (the primary verb TO BE) (*pttw*, no *log*-transformation). Left: county level (*N* = 34). Middle: location level (*N* = 162). Right: individual FRED texts (*N* = 347). Solid lines are linear regression estimates (county level: *r* = − .403; location level: *r* = − .235; text level: *r* = −.178). All correlations are significant at *p* < .05.

value in that dialect and the feature's component loading in a given component. Component scores may thus uncover how particular feature bundles have a geographical distribution (see Shackleton 2010, 9). We used the so-called "regression method" to calculate component scores – one for every component under analysis – for each of the thirty-four FRED measuring points. To investigate areal patterns, component scores can be projected to geography in COMPONENT SCORE MAPS.

In the discussion that follows, we will discuss, one by one, the first four principal components that characterize the FRED dataset. To investigate the features that define each component, we will report (1) features with positive loadings > .32, which is a customary threshold (Costello and Osborne 2005, 4), as well as (2) up to three features with the lowest negative loadings. Features that load even higher or lower on other components will be skipped. Observe, moreover, that we will adopt a common practice in PCA interpretation (see Dunteman 1989, 51) by selecting one feature with a particularly high loading (typically the highest loading) to label the principal component in question.

### 7.2.1 *Principal component 1: the non-standard* come *component*

The first principal component (PC1) always captures the overall most important pattern of aggregate variability (Leino and Hyvönen 2008, 178), and in

Table 7.4. *Principal component 1: rotated component loadings.*

| [30] | non-standard past tense *come* | .72 |
|---|---|---|
| [33] | multiple negation | .70 |
| [29] | non-standard past tense *done* | .66 |
| [32] | the negator *ain't* | .64 |
| [43] | absence of auxiliary BE in progressive constructions | .60 |
| [39] | non-standard verbal *-s* | .59 |
| [44] | non-standard WAS | .52 |
| [1] | non-standard reflexives | .51 |
| [40] | *don't* with 3rd person singular subjects | .50 |
| [55] | lack of inversion and/or of auxiliaries in *wh*-questions and in main clause *yes/no*-questions | .41 |
| [47] | the relative particle *what* | .40 |
| [50] | unsplit *for to* | .34 |
| [28] | non-standard weak past tense and past participle forms | .33 |
| [48] | the relative particle *that* | −.14 |
| [14] | the primary verb TO BE | −.19 |
| [46] | *wh*-relativization | −.31 |

our case PC1 accounts for 13.0 percent of the total variance in the dataset. In all, thirteen features load robustly on PC1, and the list in Table 7.4 reads like a Who's Who of the usual suspects which are recurrent in the literature on dialect morphosyntax in Great Britain. Consider that seven of the features boast maps in SED-based interpretation atlases. Observe also that the vast majority of the features have, as we saw in Chapter 3, an individually significant geographic distribution. Because the morphosyntactic feature with the highest loading (.72) on the component turns out to be non-standard past tense *come* (feature [30], as in (24)), we choose to dub PC1 the "non-standard *come* component."

(24)    I were taken into the hospital and they eh, it was eh malaria and bronchitis, with one doctor, one nurse made me o- one of the doctors told me to get up, so I got up but I was that s- weak I had to sit down again and the, the n- the nurse that *come* in said, You stop there 'til doctor comes, he *come* the next day and they took blood tests [NTT002]

Non-standard past tense *come* has two central properties that it shares with most other features in the PC1 bundle. First, by virtue of leveling the contrast between the Standard English past tense form *came* and present tense and past participle forms *come*, the feature is invariant and arguably also simplifying (in the sense of Szmrecsanyi and Kortmann 2009) in nature. Second, non-standard past tense *come* is a very dialectal feature in that it is not attested in the Standard English reference corpora analyzed in the present study (see Table A.1 [Appendix A, p. 167]).

    The other features that characterize PC1 and whose usage frequencies thus correlate positively with frequencies of non-standard past tense *come* include multiple negation (feature [33]), as in (25) (note that multiple negation is likewise absent from Standard English); non-standard *come*'s cousin, non-standard past tense *done* (feature [29]), as in (26) (which, exactly like non-standard *come*, is absent from Standard English and invariant in nature); the negator *ain't* (feature [32]), as in (27) (absent from Standard English and invariant); absence of auxiliary BE in progressive constructions (feature [43]), as in (28) (absent from Standard English and invariant because it does away with highly variable BE forms); non-standard verbal *-s* (feature [39]), as in (29) (absent from Standard American English, infrequent in Standard British English, and invariant); non-standard WAS (feature [44]), as in (30) (absent from Standard American English, infrequent in Standard British English, and invariant); non-standard reflexives (feature [1]), as in (31) (absent from Standard American English, infrequent in Standard British English, and invariant); *don't* with 3rd person singular subjects (feature [40]), as in (32) (absent from Standard English and invariant); lack of inversion and/or of auxiliaries in *wh*-questions and in main clause *yes/no*-questions (feature [55]), as in (33) (invariant also, because the feature skips possibly inflecting auxiliaries); the relative particle *what* (feature [47]), as in (34) (absent from Standard English and invariant vis-à-vis *wh*-relative pronouns); unsplit *for to* (feature [50]), as in (35) (absent from Standard English); and non-standard weak past tense and past participle forms (feature [28]), as in (36). Non-standard weak forms are not really invariant in nature (on the contrary), but we stress that they are demonstrably absent from Standard English.

(25)   If you *ain't* got it in writing, they *don't* take *no* notice. [KEN002]

(26)   I forget what I *done*. [DEV007]

(27)   But *ain't* the case this year; *ain't* many about this year – very scarce. [SOM024]

(28)   And *they choosing* the varieties, so that we could have a continuity of the early ones before Christmas [CON010]

(29)   And I *goes* out again on Friday [SFK006]

(30)   And, 'course, they *was* all getting ready to go home [LND006]

(31)   then there would be the coach for the workers *theirself* and that [DEV010]

(32)   I said I do hope he *don't* send me over with another one. [KEN010]

(33)   She says, *how long you've been out?* [NTT002]

(34)   And the lady *what* was driving, she said, Excuse me young man [SOM032]

(35)   others jumped up *for to* give them a hand [CON005]

(36)   And I never *knowed* that man work from that day till when he passed away. [MDX001]

We note that the above set of features overlaps fairly well with the set of features implicated in the red MDS dimension (see Section 5.2.3, Map C.17).

Table 7.4 also lists the three features with the highest *negative* component loadings on PC1 – features, in other words, which are repelled by the non-standard *come* component: the relative particle *that* (feature [48]), as in (37); the primary verb TO BE (feature [14]), as in (38); and *wh*-relativization (feature [46]), as in (39).

(37)   that was the name *that* it got [KEN003]

(38)   And I *were* barking, just like a dog, you see. [SOM032]

(39)   I knew the lad *who* the farm belonged to [CON009]

The news value coming with this negative feature set is limited. It stands to reason that higher text frequencies of the relative particle *what* (which, as we have seen, is positively associated with PC1) should predict lower text frequencies of alternative relativization strategies, such as the particle *that* or *wh*-relativization. It is no big surprise either that the verb TO BE – which, after all, exhibits an abundance of different, strongly suppletive verb forms – loads negatively on a component that is overall characterized by a prevalence of invariant features.

Map C.25 (Appendix C, p. 187) is a component score map that projects mean component scores per FRED county to Voronoi-tesselated map space.[4] Yellowish hues indicate higher component scores (and thus, increased popularity of the PC1 feature bundle) while blueish hues indicate lower component scores. As is immediately obvious from the map, the non-standard *come* component has a very cohesive geographic distribution: It is popular in the South of England (Cornwall, Devon, Somerset, Wiltshire, Oxfordshire, Middlesex, London, Kent, and Suffolk) plus Nottinghamshire and Leicestershire in Central England, but it tends to be unpopular everywhere else – and increasingly so the more north one goes. In fact, component scores and geographic latitudes show 29.4 percent shared variance ($r = -.542$, $p < .001$); there is also some shared (14.4%) variance between longitudes and PC1 component scores ($r = .380$, $p < .001$). Given that most features in the non-standard *come* component are very dialectal, it should surprise no one that there is in addition a good deal of shared variance between component scores and distances to Standard English, as calculated in Section 4.4 (Standard American English: $r = .571$, $p < .001$, $R^2 = 32.6\%$, Standard British English: $r = .336$, $p = .052$, $R^2 = 11.3\%$). Specifically, high

---

[4] The component score maps in this chapter were generated by dividing the observable component score range into ten percentile bins such that each bin contains roughly the same number of observations. Each county's bin rank was then mapped on the red–green–blue color scheme, assigning a perfect yellow hue to the highest bin rank, a perfect blue hue to the lowest bin rank, and gradient yellow-blue color blends to the ranks in between.

Table 7.5. *Principal component 2: rotated component loadings.*

| | | |
|---|---|---|
| [13] | the primary verb TO DO | .80 |
| [15] | the primary verb TO HAVE | .80 |
| [6] | *them* | .68 |
| [25] | marking of epistemic and deontic modality: HAVE TO | .58 |
| [34] | negative contraction | .58 |
| [53] | zero complementation after THINK, SAY, and KNOW | .56 |
| [39] | non-standard verbal -*s* | −.18 |
| [44] | non-standard WAS | −.32 |

non-standard *come* component scores correlate with increased distances to Standard English.

In all, then, we have seen that the most crucial component of aggregate morphosyntactic variability in Great Britain is what we have named the non-standard *come* component. It encompasses thirteen features that tend to be broadly dialectal and invariant in nature. This feature bundle is particularly popular in the South of England, and we note that the South–North continuum thus inherent in the non-standard *come* component has not gone unnoticed in recent feature-by-feature studies (e.g. Kortmann 2004b, 2009; Herrmann 2005). That the pattern is robust in the face of multivariate feature variance, however, is remarkable.

### 7.2.2   *Principal component 2: the* DO *and* HAVE *component*

The second principal component identified by PCA, and hence the second layer of aggregate morphosyntactic variability in our dataset, explains 7.9 percent of the overall variance. The top loaders on this component (see Table 7.5) include the primary verb TO DO (feature [13], as in (40)) and the primary verb TO HAVE (feature [15], as in (41)). This is why we shall refer to PC2 as the "DO and HAVE component."

(40)   And when the graft *do* grow, I've known them to burst off if they grows too quick [SOM002]

(41)   So we never *had had* nothing happen [SOM028]

The primary verbs DO and HAVE, which when used as auxiliaries are periphrastic markers, are of course textually frequent (mean frequency in FRED: 103 hits *pttw* and 130 hits *pttw*, respectively; see Table A.1 [Appendix A, p. 167]). DO and HAVE are also not necessarily heavily dialectal phenomena (although there are, of course, non-standard usages such as DO as a tense and aspect marker), and so it stands to reason that DO and HAVE are frequent in the Standard English reference corpora as well (again, see Table A.1, Appendix A). This profile DO and HAVE share with the other features robustly loading on the DO and HAVE component: *them* (feature [6]), which captures both standard usages of *them* (as in *I saw them*) and non-standard usages (as in (42)); HAVE TO as a periphrastic marker of epistemic and deontic modality (feature [25], as in (43)), a feature which partially overlaps with feature [15] (the primary verb TO HAVE); negative contraction (feature [34], as in (44)); and zero complementation after THINK, SAY, and KNOW (feature [53], as in (45)), which is common to spoken English in general.

(42)   going over *them* docks used to be awful [DUR003]

(43)   It *has to* be done perfect. [WES004]

(44)   They *won't* do repairs at the pensioner's bungalows [LAN011]

(45)   I don't think they do it now. [SOM036]

Further, we note that two broadly dialectal features that are implicated in the non-standard *come* component load *negatively* on, and thus are repelled by, the DO and HAVE component: Non-standard verbal -*s* (feature [39], as in (46)), and non-standard WAS (feature [44], as in (47))

(46)   Built up, you know*s*. [SOM005]

(47)   No, they *was* getting theirselves buried in. [LAN011]

The geographic distribution of the DO and HAVE feature bundle can be seen from Map C.26 (Appendix C, p. 187). The three FRED counties exhibiting the highest PC2 component scores are Somerset in the Southwest of England (observe that Somerset is known for unorthodox usages of the verb DO, which as we have seen is a top loader on PC2), the Hebrides, and Selkirkshire in the Southern Scottish Lowlands. The three counties with the lowest PC2 scores are Middlesex in Southeastern England, and Lancashire and Northumberland in Northern England. All in all, then, the DO and HAVE component is based in a geographically quite cohesive area in the North of England and in the Southern Scottish Lowlands (East Lothian, Selkirkshire, Westmorland, Durham, and Yorkshire), though emphatically not in Northumberland and Lancashire. In addition, the component is in vogue in the Hebrides and in Somerset.

By way of an interim summary, we have seen that PC2 (the DO and HAVE component) spans frequent features that are not particularly dialectal; in Section 3.2, we have defined such features as non-salient features whose variation is statistical, rather than categorical, in nature. In other words, the feature bundle keeps a low dialectal profile. Three features associated with the component (DO, HAVE, and HAVE TO) have a periphrastic feel to them. Geolinguistically, the DO and HAVE component appears to be restricted to the North of England and the Southern Scottish Lowlands, as well as to Somerset and the young dialect spoken in the Hebrides.

Table 7.6. *Principal component 3: rotated component loadings.*

| [37] | WASN'T | .83 |
|------|--------|-----|
| [42] | existential/presentational *there is/was* with plural subjects | .80 |
| [14] | the primary verb TO BE | .61 |
| [36] | *never* as past tense negator | .33 |
| [26] | marking of epistemic and deontic modality: GOT TO | −.20 |
| [45] | non-standard WERE | −.23 |
| [23] | the present perfect with auxiliary HAVE | −.36 |

### 7.2.3   Principal component 3: the BE component

We move on to the third layer of aggregate morphosyntactic variability (PC3), which accounts for 6.4 percent of the variance in the dataset. As we will see presently, this component has a lot to do with the verb BE, so we take the liberty to label PC3 the "BE component." As can be seen from Table 7.6, the feature with the highest loading on the component is feature [37] (WASN'T, as in (48)).

(48)   they *wasn't* begging, they all had something [DFS001]

Our original motivation for including in this study feature [37], which is about the frequency of standard as well as non-standard usages of past tense negative WASN'T, was that dialects of English tend to do two things with past tense BE, according to the literature (Britain 2002, 19). They either generalize to *was* across all persons, a phenomenon we check for via feature [44] (a feature that is, as we have seen, implicated in PC1), or generalize to *weren't* in negative contexts but to *was* in affirmative contexts. The latter pattern is known as the *was–weren't* split. The component at hand does plainly not appear to capture variation along the lines of the *was–weren't* split. Observe, however, that feature [45] (non-standard WERE, as in (49)), loads negatively on the component, so it seems that the BE component is really about the first of the two patterns discussed above: *was* leveling.[5]

(49)   Oh, I *were* about, eh, fifteen or sixteen. [ANS003]

Another robustly loading feature is feature [42] (existential/presentational *there is/was* with plural subjects, as in (50)), a non-standard feature that of course brings with it non-standard usage of BE.

---

[5] A close look at the component loadings < .32 in Appendix B admittedly complicates the picture. We learn that feature [44] (non-standard WAS, as in *three of them* was *killed*) has a positive loading on PC3 (.32) (though feature [44] loads even more strongly [.52] on PC1). This fits the *was* leveling bill. Having said that, it also emerges that feature [38] (WEREN'T, as in *they* weren't *hungry*) is likewise positively associated with PC3 (.29), which it should not. Still, the *was* leveling explanation appears to be the most parsimonious one all things considered.

(50)   Different colours, yes that's right, some had blue and some had striped waistcoats and black trousers and, oh *there was* various. [NBL008]

Also among the features positively associated with PC3 we find feature [14], as in (51)), which measures frequencies of standard or non-standard, auxiliary or main verb, and negative or affirmative usages of BE. In short, then, the BE component is also about high text frequencies of BE in general.

(51)   I remember that *being* built now [NBL006]

The only feature in the component-loading matrix not directly related to BE and still loading positively on PC3 is feature [36] (*never* as past tense negator, as in (52)). The feature is usually thought of as a pervasive and rather supraregional dialect phenomenon, yet here we learn that its frequency correlates with frequencies of a number of other (typically BE-related) features.

(52)   and they *never moved* no more [CON005]

Two features besides feature [45] (non-standard WERE) have a tendency not to co-occur with BE component features: feature [36] (marking of epistemic and deontic modality: GOT TO, as in (53)), and feature [23] (the present perfect with auxiliary HAVE, as in (54)).

(53)   I've *got to* start straight away of course [NBL007]
(54)   Might *have worked* at the Choppington brickyard [NBL003]

Closer inspection of the component-loadings in the component-loading matrix reveals that the present perfect with auxiliary HAVE's direct non-standard competitor, feature [22] (the present perfect with auxiliary BE, as in *I'm come down to pay the rent*) also has a moderately negative loading $(-.10)$ on PC3. We therefore conjecture that the BE component may be somewhat hostile to present perfect usages in general.

What about geographic patterns? Consider Map C.27 (Appendix C, p. 188). Although the picture is not entirely clear-cut, there is a tendency towards the BE component feature bundle being more popular in Great Britain's North than in the South. Among the PC3 top scorers, we accordingly find Northumberland, Durham, and Yorkshire in Northern England, Kincardineshire, Angus, and Dumfriesshire in the Scottish Lowlands, and the Isle of Man. Having said that, we also note that there is a geographically very well-defined region centered on the Central Scottish Lowlands (comprising Perthshire, West Lothian, Midlothian, East Lothian, Peebleshire, and Selkirkshire) that does not buy into the BE component at all.

Summing up, the BE component defines a feature bundle that is characterized by features relating to the verb BE. In geographic terms, this feature bundle is diagnostic of dialects in the North of Great Britain save the Central Scottish Lowlands.

Table 7.7. *Principal component 4: rotated component loadings.*

| [19] | WOULD as marker of habitual past | .71 |
|------|----------------------------------|-----|
| [10] | preposition stranding | .56 |
| [57] | double object structures after the verb GIVE | .33 |
| [34] | negative contraction | −.21 |
| [35] | auxiliary contraction | −.28 |
| [41] | standard *doesn't* with 3rd person singular subjects | −.46 |

### 7.2.4   Principal component 4: the WOULD component

The fourth and final principal component that we will be concerned with in this chapter accounts for 4.1 percent of the aggregate variability in the dataset. The feature that is most strongly associated (see Table 7.7) with PC4 is WOULD as marker of habitual past (feature [19], as in (55)), which is an excellent reason to refer to PC4 as "the WOULD component."

(55)    As I say, he *would* go away, he was out some time, go away about three in the morning, depending on the tides [BAN001]

Text frequencies of WOULD, then, turn out to dovetail with text frequencies of feature [10] (preposition stranding, as in (56)) and feature [57] (double object structures after the verb GIVE, as in (57)). It is fair to say that none of these features is particularly dialectal.

(56)    You had a different board *which* you put your dummies *on*. [BAN001]

(57)    I *gave* [my mother] [nine out of that] [DEN003]

Turning to negative loaders, Table 7.7 details that where we find high text frequencies of WOULD as marker of habitual past, preposition stranding, and double object structures, we tend not to find much negative contraction (feature [34], as in (58)) or auxiliary contraction (feature [35], as in (59)). This is another way of saying that the WOULD component is not fond of contraction in general.

(58)    I *won't* mention their names [SAL009]

(59)    I have known when we*'ve not* known where our next meal was coming from [SAL029]

Standard *doesn't* with 3rd person singular subjects (feature [41], as in (60)) also loads negatively on PC4. We do not have a good explanation for this particular interdependence.

(60)    *He doesn't* know where Farley is, and I'm not going up with him [SAL020]

On the geographic plane, Map C.28 (Appendix C, p. 188) illustrates that the WOULD component is characteristic of a number of measuring points in Scotland; Kincardineshire and Dumfriesshire are, in fact, the top scorers on the WOULD component. There is also a WOULD component hotbed in Central England (Shropshire, Warwickshire, and Leicestershire).

Summing up, our discussion has suggested that the WOULD component is positively associated with features that do not strike us as especially dialectal. These features – specifically, WOULD as marker of habitual past, preposition stranding, and double object structures – tend to co-occur in a number of measuring points in Scotland and in Central England.

## 7.3   Chapter summary

With an interest in viewing aggregate morphosyntactic variability against the backdrop of the distributional behavior of individual linguistic features, this chapter had two goals.

First, we were interested in why a number of measuring points in our sample (Banffshire, Denbighshire, Dumfriesshire, Middlesex, Leicestershire, and Warwickshire) turn out as outliers. We concluded that it is hard to trace Banffshire's and Denbighshire's outlier status back to abnormal text frequencies of specific features. Rather, in the case of these two measuring points we are very likely to be dealing with sampling problems due to thin textual coverage. By contrast, we saw that in the Dumfriesshire material the negative suffix -*nae* is conspicuously absent; in the case of Middlesex, it seems that primary verb frequencies are to blame for the measuring point's capriciousness; in the Leicestershire material, non-standard verbal -*s* is comparatively infrequent while non-standard WERE and non-standard past tense *done* is comparatively frequent; and as for Warwickshire, *wh*-relativization is much too frequent given Warwickshire's geographic location.

In the second part of the chapter, we utilized Principal Component Analysis to identify linguistic structure (i.e. feature bundles and co-occurrence patterns) in the aggregate perspective. We identified four major principal components ("layers") that underpin morphosyntactic variability in the dataset. The most crucial layer – which we dubbed the "non-standard *come* component" – bundles many of the usual suspects in the dialectology literature (e.g. multiple negation, past tense *done*, *ain't*) and creates a very neat South–North continuum. We also identified (in decreasing order of importance) a "DO and HAVE component," which combines relatively frequent and not particularly dialectal features, and which is especially diagnostic of dialects in the North of England and the Southern Scottish Lowlands; a "BE component," which is sensitive to features that relate in some way or another to the verb BE and which enjoys currency in the North of Great Britain except in the Central Scottish Lowlands; and a "WOULD component," which is important in Central England and in parts of Scotland and which unites three features: WOULD as marker of habitual past, preposition stranding, and double object structures.

# 8     Summary and discussion

In this book, we have sought to address the spatial nature of large-scale morphosyntactic variability in British English dialects. This chapter pulls together the study's major findings. We first summarize the empirical facts in Section 8.1, and subsequently move on to a detailed discussion of the role that geography plays in structuring morphosyntactic variability in Great Britain (Section 8.2).

## 8.1   Summary: morphosyntactic variability in British English dialects

Chapter 1 outlined three major research questions which guided the present study. The big, overarching question was whether corpus-derived and frequency-based patterns of aggregate syntactic and morphological variability – calculated on the basis of the joint frequency variance of fifty-seven morphosyntactic features in spontaneous speech, as sampled in the *Freiburg Corpus of English Dialects* (FRED) – exhibit a geolinguistic signal. The short answer to this question is "yes." The long answer goes as follows.

Among other things, we saw in Chapter 3 that according to a relatively conservative statistical gauge, fourteen – or about 25 percent – of the fifty-seven morphosyntactic features covered in this study are, on an individual basis, geographically distributed in FRED. The identities of the features that make it into Table 8.1, which provides an exhaustive list, should not cause major surprises (though maybe a few little ones) given the literature on grammatical variability in the British Isles (we discussed Britain 2010 as an example in this connection). What about the other forty-three features? While these are geolinguistically inconspicuous when considered in isolation, we nonetheless included them in the subsequent empirical analyses. The a-priori rationale for this inclusion harks back to a methodological cornerstone in dialectometry according to which non-geographic variability will cancel out in the aggregate view, and that even geographically seemingly irrelevant features contribute to and are indispensable for an accurate description of the big picture (see, e.g., Goebl and Schiltz 1997; Nerbonne 2006); we will revisit this issue in more detail

Table 8.1. *Morphosyntactic features with a geographically significant distribution in FRED.*

| | |
|---|---|
| feature [1] | **non-standard reflexives** <br> (e.g. *they didn't go* theirself) <br> ⇨ frequent in the South of England |
| feature [9] | **the *s*-genitive** <br> (e.g. *my father*'s *presence*) <br> ⇨ frequent in the English Midlands, North Wales & the Isle of Man |
| feature [14] | **the primary verb TO BE** <br> (e.g. *I* was *took straight into this pitting job*) <br> ⇨ frequent in Scotland, increasingly less frequent as one moves south |
| feature [20] | ***used to* as marker of habitual past** <br> (e.g. *he* used to *go around killing pigs*) <br> ⇨ frequent in the Southeast of England & English Midlands, increasingly less frequent as one moves north |
| feature [26] | **marking of epistemic and deontic modality: GOT TO** <br> (e.g. *I* gotta *pick up the book*) <br> ⇨ frequent in the South of England, & English Midlands, increasingly less frequent as one moves north |
| feature [29] | **non-standard past tense *done*** <br> (e.g. *you came home and* done *the fishing*) <br> ⇨ frequent in the South of England; increasingly less frequent as one moves north |
| feature [30] | **non-standard past tense *come*** <br> (e.g. *he* come *down the road one day*) <br> ⇨ frequent in the South of England & Scottish Lowlands, rare in the North of England & Scottish Highlands |
| feature [31] | **the negative suffix *-nae*** <br> (e.g. *I can*nae *do it*) <br> ⇨ restricted to the Scottish Lowlands & Northumberland |
| feature [32] | **the negator *ain't*** <br> (e.g. *people* ain't *got no money*) <br> ⇨ frequent in the South of England, increasingly less frequent as one moves north |
| feature [33] | **multiple negation** <br> (e.g. *do*n't *you make* no *damn mistake*) <br> ⇨ frequent in the South of England, increasingly less frequent as one moves north |
| feature [40] | ***don't* with 3rd person singular subjects** <br> (e.g. *if this man* don't *come up to it*) <br> ⇨ observable in the Southwest & Southeast of England, but rare elsewhere |
| feature [49] | ***as what* or *than what* in comparative clauses** <br> (e.g. *we done no more* than what *other kids used to do*) <br> ⇨ frequent in some parts of the English Midlands, the Isle of Man & the Scottish Highlands |
| feature [56] | **the prepositional dative after the verb GIVE** <br> (e.g. *she gave [a job] [to my brother]*) <br> ⇨ rare in the Scottish Lowlands & the far North of England |
| feature [57] | **double object structures after the verb GIVE** <br> (e.g. *she gave [my brother] [a job]*) <br> ⇨ frequent in the Southeast of England, the English Midlands, & in Wales |

in Section 8.2 below. Our reasoning was vindicated in Chapter 7, where we saw that even features that appear to be distributed non-geographically when analyzed in isolation may help to create geographically more or less focused layers of morphosyntactic variability in conjunction with other features.

We then went on to calculate an overall measure of morphosyntactic distance and similarity between FRED measuring points, drawing on the well-known Euclidean distance measure that defines pairwise dialect distances as the square root of the sum of all fifty-seven pairwise feature frequency differentials (Chapter 2 explicated the details). Sure enough, the cumulative weight of evidence amassed in this book suggests that the distribution of aggregate morphosyntactic distances and similarities in British English dialects is indeed sensitive to geography, in that dialects which are close geographically are more likely to be similar morphosyntactically, all other things being equal. This generalization – also known as the "Fundamental Dialectology Principle" (Nerbonne and Kleiweg 2007, 154) – holds true even though the FRED dataset exhibits a good deal of noise and geographical incoherence.

Chapter 4 was devoted to an exploration of the many aspects that characterize the relationship between morphosyntactic variability and geography in our dataset. Besides surveying the distribution of aggregate dialect distances and similarities, Chapter 4 was particularly concerned with

- the issue of linguistic compromise and exchange (*Sprachausgleich*) areas (we found that the North of England and young dialects in Wales and the Scottish Highlands are areas of intense linguistic compromise and exchange);
- the notion of dialect kernels (we saw that England has one major dialect kernel which comprises much of the Southwest of England plus London; in Scotland, we find a more compact dialect kernel encompassing Midlothian and East Lothian);
- and the relation between dialectal, non-standard English and Standard English (one of the conclusions was that the two Standard varieties, British and American, are equidistant morphosyntactically from the dialect varieties sampled in FRED).

Chapters 5 and 6 approached the book's second research question, which addresses a venerable issue in theories about language and space: Is Great Britain's morphosyntactic dialect landscape organized along the lines of dialect areas, such that we observe internally homogeneous but mutually sharply demarcated speech areas (along the lines of Schleicher 1863)? Or, alternatively, are we dealing with a dialect continuum scenario in the spirit of Schmidt (1872), without sharp dialect boundaries because linguistic distance is directly proportional to geographic distance? At the outset, we stressed that the present study is not seeking "either"/"or" answers to these questions. Instead, we sought to view the way in which geographic space conditions dialect variability as having a continuum-like structure itself. At one end of this continuum, we find perfect dialect continua where linguistic transitions are maximally smooth; at the opposite end, we deal with perfectly regionalized dialect landscapes where transitions between internally homogeneous dialect areas are maximally abrupt. It is clear that these poles are idealized prototypes, and that reality will fall somewhere in between. The book thus investigated the very same dataset first from the perspective of the dialect continuum pole (Chapter 5), and subsequently from the angle of the dialect area scenario (Chapter 6).

In so considering this an empirical question, we wheeled out heavy statistical artillery (principally, Multidimensional Scaling and Cluster Analysis) and found that the aggregate morphosyntactic variability in the FRED dataset is fully compatible neither with the dialect area scenario, nor with the dialect continuum scenario. Chapter 5 demonstrated that while there are nice morphosyntactic micro-continua in the Southwest of England and in the Central Scottish Lowlands, there are fairly abrupt linguistic transitions between, for example, the Southern Scottish Lowlands and the Central Scottish Lowlands. Recall further that in numerical terms, this study's measure of morphosyntactic distance and various measures of geographical distance exhibit, in the dataset as a whole, up to about 24 percent of shared variance (notice here that in a perfect dialect continuum, the amount of shared variance should approach 100 percent). Interestingly, we presented evidence that geography-based dialect continuum predictors appear to fare much better in Scotland than in England, subject to the additional twist that across the board, linguistic gravity scores in the spirit of Trudgill (1974), which use a Newtonian formula to factor in historical population sizes in addition to geographic distance, outperform simple distance predictors. At any rate, when we subsequently tested previous dialect area partitions for their explanatory power in Chapter 6, we found that these explain between one-quarter and one-half of the variance in the FRED dataset; not unexpectedly, the Anglo-Saxon dialect division according to Baugh and Cable (1993, 52) did worst, and two modern, SED-based divisions (Trudgill 1990; Goebl 2007) worked best. The remainder of Chapter 6 set out to extract a data-driven, inductive dialect area partition from the FRED dataset, and this exercise essentially yielded a tripartite division (Scottish English dialects versus Northern English English dialects versus Southern English English dialects). Remarkably, in no case did we obtain direct positive evidence for a well-defined Midlands (Central England) dialect area (see, e.g., Trudgill 1990) on morphosyntactic grounds. Throughout this book, however, we did find noise and geographically erratic dissimilarities galore in the Central England region, and to the extent that "extensive crosshatching of isoglosses rather than the more orderly bundled or parallel isoglosses that are characteristic of more settled regions" (Thomason 2001, 107) is diagnostic of language or dialect contact, we may tentatively suggest that the FRED dataset's Central England area is a high-contact transition zone between Northern English English and Southern English English dialects. Be that as it may, the dialect areas (or, more neutrally, dialect groupings) for which we did obtain positive evidence were, alas, to varying degrees not geographically coherent. Quantitatively, inductive partitioning yields divisions that account for between 20 and 40 percent of the aggregate morphosyntactic variance in the dataset, which is another way of saying that the dialect area scenario is slightly more powerful explanatorily than the dialect continuum scenario. That said, we are basically left with the conclusion that the way morphosyntactic dialect variability in Great Britain is structured geographically – continua or areas? – is complex and multifaceted.

To come to terms with this sophistication, we now present a further cartographic projection to geography on Map C.29 (Appendix C, p. 189). As a synopsis map of sorts, Map C.29 marries Cluster Analysis (the analytical technique of choice for dialect area partitions, classification, and taxonomy; see Section 6.3.1) and Multidimensional Scaling (the statistical tool to project dialect continuumhoods to geography; see Section 5.2.1). Map C.29 thus combines the dialect area view and the dialect continuum view in one and the same projection.[1] What is the interpretational bonus? First, compared to a genuine continuum map, Map C.29 accentuates, via differential colorization, differences between dialects that belong to different, inductively identified clusters or dialect groupings; this is the job carried out by Cluster Analysis in the genesis of the projection. Second, compared to a genuine cluster map, Map C.29 emphasizes the gradient nature of dialect grouping memberships (this is the task that Multidimensional Scaling performs), such that some measuring points are depicted, by way of purer color tones, as "better," more prototypical members of some dialect grouping. Other measuring points, which on a "yes"/"no" basis may belong to some cluster-analytically derived grouping, but only just barely, will receive more blended color tones. With this information in mind, the picture that emerges from Map C.29 essentially boils down to the tripartite division from Chapter 6 – we find an orange group of dialects mainly in the South of England; a violet-blueish group of dialects located mainly in the North of England (plus measuring points in the Scottish Highlands); and a greenish cluster of Scottish Lowlands dialects. The point, however, is that the orange and violet-blueish England-centered groups are fairly homogeneous internally: Here,

---

[1] Note that Map C.29 represents the outliers discussed in Section 7.1 as language islands – small diamonds – so as not to disturb the overall picture. Technically, the projection was created as follows. We initially applied repeated clustering with noise ($i = 10,000, c = \sigma$, clustering algorithm: Ward's Method) to the original $34 \times 34$ distance matrix (see Nerbonne et al. 2008 and Section 6.3.1 for an explanation). Next, the resulting cophenetic distance matrix was subjected to three-dimensional Multidimensional Scaling in the usual fashion, and the Voronoi polygons were colorized accordingly.

we do not find a lot of internal color variance (read: not a lot of morphosyntactic variability), probably thanks to a long-term process of region-internal dialect leveling (defined as "a change toward greater similarity of dialects" [Thomason and Kaufman 1988, 30]). By contrast, then, the greenish Scottish Lowlands group exhibits a good deal of internal gradience; in point of fact, the greenish group emerges as a fairly well-behaved dialect continuum internally, and this is why the continuum predictors tested in Chapter 5 work rather nicely in Scotland but not so well in England. Thus, the point that we are driving at is that England's internal morphosyntactic dialect landscape is organized along the lines of a Schleicherian dialect area scenario, while Central Scotland's morphosyntactic dialect landscape appears to obey the laws of a Schmidtian dialect continuum. That said, we emphasize that even in this interpretational twilight, geography demonstrably retains a good deal of explanatory power (though see Section 8.2 below).

Our third major research question mandated an exploration of feature subsets, and so we examined the extent to which individual features gang up to create areal (sub)patterns. Thus, Chapter 7 complemented the aggregational-abstractive and holistic perspective in Chapters 4 to 6 with an investigation of the distribution of the linguistic features, one by one, on which the analysis in this book is based. For one thing, we investigated the degree to which the geolinguistic behavior of six notorious outliers in our study (Banffshire, Denbighshire, Dumfriesshire, Middlesex, Leicestershire, and Warwickshire) can be traced back to frequencies of particular morphosyntactic features. The second part of the chapter relied on Principal Component Analysis to identify four major principal components – i.e. feature bundles or "layers" – that help create geolinguistic structure in aggregate comparison. The most important such bundle, which we dubbed the "non-standard *come* component," assembles a comparatively large number of well-known dialect features (such as multiple negation, past-tense *done*, *ain't*) and generates a very neat South–North continuum geographically, such that the features loading on the component are frequent in the South but not in the North of Great Britain. The other three layers uncovered in Chapter 7 included (i) the "DO and HAVE component," which differentiates measuring points in the North of England and the Southern Scottish Lowlands; (ii) the "BE component," which is geographically diagnostic of measuring points in the North of Great Britain; and (iii) the "WOULD component," which characterizes measuring points in Central England and parts of Scotland. In short, the main insight afforded by Principal Component Analysis is that in a feature-centered perspective, the most important, sweeping dimension of variability in Great Britain is a South–North continuum; other geolinguistic patterns are only ornament. We thus unearthed a macro pattern which replicates recent feature-by-feature analyses on a micro scale (consider, e.g., Kortmann 2004b, 2009; Herrmann 2005).

It is precisely in the context of this South–North continuum that the handful or so of relatively young dialects included in the present study's measuring point portfolio (Denbighshire in North Wales, the Hebridean Islands, Ross and Cromarty and Sutherland in Scotland) have notably clustered with Northern British English (and/or Northern *English* English) dialects, rather than with Southern English English dialects. The cluster maps on Map C.22 (p. 184) and C.24) (p. 186), for example, amply illustrate this allegiance. Now, what we informally call "young" dialects here can in more technical parlance be referred to as "shifted" varieties – that is, varieties that used to be language-shift varieties at some point in the recent historical past – defined as varieties "that develop when English replaces the erstwhile primary language(s) of a community" and that have "adult and child L1 and L2 speakers forming one speech community" (Mesthrie 2006, 383), but which no longer have significant numbers of L2 speakers. Crucially, language shift implicates language contact, and there is reason to believe that in general high-contact varieties are progressive and simplifying, due to the "lousy language-learning abilities of the human adult" (Trudgill 2001, 372). Low-contact varieties, in contrast, tend to be conservative (e.g., Trudgill 2004b; Szmrecsanyi 2009; Szmrecsanyi and Kortmann 2009). Now, Southern English English and particularly Southwestern English English dialects (Britain 2010) are known to have been fairly distinctive and conservative since Middle English times (Thomason and Kaufman 1988, 274), and the bulk of innovations finding their way into Standard English between Middle English and Present-Day English have originated in Northern English dialects (see, e.g., Anderwald 2005, 130). As a matter of fact, in a long-term historical perspective Northern English English dialects are actually high-contact dialects themselves thanks to substantial contact with Old Norse in Anglo-Saxon times (for instance, Thomason and Kaufman 1988, 274), although we hasten to add that nowhere in this study did we actually see geolinguistic patterns in any way reminiscent of the so-called "Danelaw," an area in Central and Northern England under Danish rule during parts of the Old English period (see, e.g., Graham-Campbell 2001). But in any event, given the differential contact histories of Southern versus Northern dialects it makes sense indeed that the young, high-contact dialects considered in the present study coincide with Northern rather than Southern dialects morphosyntactically.

## 8.2 Is geography overrated?

So, we concluded in the previous section that the FRED dataset produces a geolinguistic signal. Yet compared to previous atlas-based dialectometry this signal is, in a number of ways, somewhat frail. Inevitably, we are confronted with frequency noise; the inductively derived dialect areas discussed in Chapter 6 are geographically not entirely coherent; and the continuum

Table 8.2. *Shared variance (R²) between as-the-crow-flies distances and linguistic distances in selected studies.*

| | variability in ... | data source | linguistic level | $R^2$ | |
|---|---|---|---|---|---|
| Alewijnse et al. (2007) | Bantu varieties | atlas | pronunciation | 21% | a |
| Houtzagers et al. (2010) | Bulgarian dial. | dictionary | pronunciation | 24% | a |
| Spruit et al. (2009) | Dutch dial. | atlas | pronunciation | 47% | |
| Spruit et al. (2009) | Dutch dial. | atlas | lexis | 33% | |
| Spruit et al. (2009) | Dutch dial. | atlas | syntax | 45% | |
| Shackleton (2007) | Eng Eng dial. | atlas | pronunciation | 49% | b |
| Nerbonne and Siedle (2005) | German dial. | atlas | pronunciation | 32% | a |
| Gooskens and Heeringa (2004) | Norwegian dial. | atlas | pronunciation | 5% | c |
| present study: total | BrE dial. | corpus | morphosyntax | 4% | |
| present study: England | BrE dial. | corpus | morphosyntax | 1% | |
| present study: Scottish Lowlands | BrE dial. | corpus | morphosyntax | 33% | |

[a] $R^2$ value calculated on the basis of *r* value reported in Nerbonne (forthcoming a)

[b] $R^2$ value refers to "Feature-Based Distances" (Shackleton 2007, 45–47)

[c] $R^2$ value calculated on the basis of *r* value reported in Gooskens (2005)

predictors tested in Chapter 5 turn out to be not as explanatory as may have been expected, given previously published data. To cut a long story short, we have seen that geography is important, but it is not all-important.

To back up this point with more empirical substance, Table 8.2 lists the amount of shared variance ($R^2$) between as-the-crow-flies geographic distances and linguistic distances as reported in a number of studies, including the present one; recall that higher $R^2$ scores indicate more explanatory power of geography.[2] Therefore in the FRED dataset as a whole, as-the-crow-flies geographic distances turn out to account for about 4 percent of aggregate morphosyntactic variance (see Section 5.3.1). Somewhat remarkably, among English English measuring points the amount of shared variance is no more than 1 percent, while among Scottish Lowlands dialects the $R^2$ score is a considerable 33 percent – a discrepancy that reiterates the previous section's verdict that geolinguistically, England and the Scottish Lowlands are organized differently.[3] Consider now, against this backdrop, the $R^2$ values obtained in previous atlas-based (or dictionary-based) dialectometrical research. The bulk of research in this vein has reported much higher $R^2$ scores. Two such studies merit particular attention in the context of the

[2] Notice that in the FRED dataset, as-the-crow-flies geographic distance is explanatorily inferior to, e.g., linguistic gravity scores, but for the sake of comparability Table 8.2 restricts attention to the former.

[3] We would also like to reiterate here that excluding the customary outliers (see Section 7.1) from the analysis increases $R^2$ values substantially.

present study. For one thing, Shackleton (2007) (see Section 1.2.6) studies aggregate phonetic variability in English English dialects (unlike the present study, Shackleton 2007 does not cover Welsh and Scottish dialects) and finds that as-the-crow-flies distances account for a whopping 49 percent of the variance in phonetic distances. In a similar vein, Spruit et al. (2009) investigate, among other things, syntactic variability in Dutch dialects (in contrast to the present study, Spruit et al. are not concerned with morphology) and report an $R^2$ value of 45 percent. We conclude that previous analysts have looked at both syntax (though not at *morpho*syntax) and at variability in England (though not in Great Britain) and have, in both cases, found geography to be a more powerful predictor of linguistic variability than we did. This discrepancy is obviously in need of discussion, and in what follows we will offer three possible explanations.

*Is Great Britain different?*
Some may think that *the dialect landscape in Great Britain may be organized differently, with less reference to geography, than elsewhere.* It is true that the presence of two dialect kernels and the ensuing contrast between English English and Scottish English varieties render linguistic variability in Great Britain a special case (though not that special – consider the German dialect landscape, with its multiple contrasts between Swiss German, Austrian German, and German German). Yet there is no a-priori reason to assume that a bi-kernel situation like this should necessarily depress the explanatory potential of geography. What is more, the argument fails to explain why, according to the present analysis, morphosyntactic variability in England exhibits less than 1 percent of shared variance with geography whereas Shackleton (2007), who studies phonetic variability, obtains an $R^2$ value of 49 percent. In short, the assumption that Great Britain is somehow special is less than fully convincing.

*Is morphosyntax different?*
Some researchers would contend that *(morpho)syntactic variability in general is different from (read: less* raumbildend *than) pronunciational or lexical variability.* This explanation has more merit, given a long-held suspicion by typologists, syntacticians, and even dialectologists (see, e.g., Wolfram and Schilling-Estes 1998; Löffler 2003; Lass 2004) that morphosyntax and grammar are less diffusable geographically than, for instance, pronunciation (see our discussion in Section 1.1). There are two problems with this assumption, however. For one thing, on empirical grounds the analysis of aggregate syntactic differences in the Dutch language area presented in Spruit et al. (2009) yields a substantial overlap between syntactic and geographic distances (see Table 8.2). Second, in a more theoretical perspective a perusal of the literature calls into question the axiom that (morpho)syntax is hostile to geographic diffusion. It is certainly true that according to the

famous borrowing scale discussed in Thomason and Kaufman (1988), structural features (i.e. grammar and phonology) are not borrowed as easily as low-level lexical and maybe phonetic features.[4] If we assume that borrowing is necessarily implicated in diffusion (see Winford 2003 for a discussion), this would naturally lead one to predict that geography is less explanatory in terms of grammar than in terms of pronunciation. We concur, however, rather with Heine and Kuteva (2005, 1), who point out that the putative indiffusability of grammar in situations of language contact is no more than a prejudice that ultimately goes back all the way to Ferdinand Saussure and Edward Sapir. What is true for language contact must also be true for dialect contact, and hence there is no good reason why morphosyntax and grammar should not diffuse geographically.

*Are atlas-based measurements inaccurate?*
We now turn to the most convincing explanation, which is concerned not with substance but with methodology: *Compared to corpus-based and frequency-centered approaches, atlas-based approaches overestimate the importance of geography.* For two reasons, this is the most cogent scenario.

First, we stress that feature selection (see Section 3.2) does matter a great deal. To put this into sharper empirical focus, Figure 8.1 displays a series of three scatterplots which visually depict the relationship between pairwise morphosyntactic distances (on the vertical axes) and pairwise as-the-crow-flies distances (on the horizontal axis). The left plot, which we have already seen in Figure 5.5 [p. 101], depicts morphosyntactic distances as calculated – in the present study's usual fashion – on the basis of frequencies of *all* fifty-seven features discussed in Chapter 3. The middle plot's morphosyntactic distance calculation restricts attention to features that load positively on Chapter 7's non-standard *come* component – in other words, the middle plot considers only features that are implicated in a South–North continuum. Similarly, the right plot in Figure 8.1 considers only those fourteen morphosyntactic features which have, on an individual basis, a significant geographic distribution (see our discussion at the beginning of Section 8.1). With the middle and right plots depicting stronger correlations (notice the steeper regression lines), our point is that drawing on specific feature subsets comprising material that is somehow more relevant geographically boosts the explanatory power of geography; in the case of the feature subsets plotted in Figure 8.1 we see increases from about 4 percent in the default case to about 8 and 15 percent, respectively. In this connection, it is fair to ask to what extent compilers of linguistic atlases, the data source tapped by those

---

[4] In a similar vein, Winford (2003, 97) offers that "syntactic structure very rarely, if ever, gets borrowed" (although he adds that "lexical borrowing can act as a conduit for structural innovation in ... (morpho)syntax"; 2003, 99).

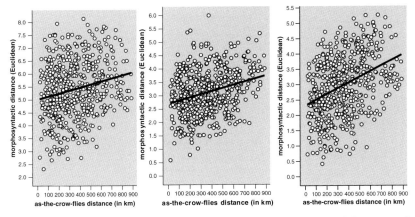

Figure 8.1. Morphosyntactic dialect distances (selected feature sets) versus as-the-crow-flies distances. Left: all $N = 34$ measuring points, all 57 features (see Figure 5.5) (linear estimate: $R^2 = 4.4\%$, $p < .001$). Middle: all $N = 34$ measuring points, 13 morphosyntactic features which load positively on principal component 1 (see Section 7.2.1, Table 7.4) (linear estimate: $R^2 = 8.0\%$, $p < .001$). Right: all $N = 34$ measuring points, 14 morphosyntactic features which are geographically significant on an individual basis (see Section 8.1) (linear estimate: $R^2 = 14.6\%$, $p < .001$). Solid lines depict linear regression estimates.

studies in Table 8.2 that report high $R^2$ values for geography, really draw on all available features (as mandated by the dialectometric creed), instead of just those features that seem geographically "interesting" in some way (in which case a comparatively strong showing of geography is to be expected). The answer, plain and simple, is that atlases are *of course* biased towards geographically distributed features; after all, worthwhile dialect cartography depends on interesting geographic distributions (see Glaser forthcoming on this point). Nonetheless, this bias has ramifications for atlas-based dialectology research, a fact that we need to keep in mind while interpreting quantitative results.

Second, we suspect also that the more or less violent data reduction (where, e.g., continuous variables, such as frequency of use, are summarized into categorical variables) that is the hallmark of most survey and atlas projects systematically overrates geography. Wälchli (2009) shows that data reduction is a problem for typological analysis, for instance when typologies are established on the basis of atlas databases such as the *World Atlas of Language Structures* (WALS; Haspelmath et al. 2005). Much the same is true, we submit, for dialectometry based on dialectological atlas databases.

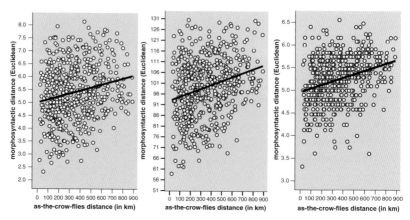

Figure 8.2. Morphosyntactic dialect distances (various levels of data reduction) versus as-the-crow-flies distances. Left: logged frequencies, all measuring points, all features (cf. Figure 5.5) (linear estimate: $R^2 = 4.4\%, p < .001$). Middle: rank by frequency, all measuring points, all features (linear estimate: $R^2 = 7.1\%, p < .001$). Right: two frequency bins, all measuring points, all features (linear estimate: $R^2 = 9.2\%, p < .001$). Solid lines depict linear regression estimates.

As discussed in Chapter 1, atlas data are (typically) categorical and rely on a second-hand "attested" vs. "not attested" distinction mediated by fieldwork-ers. This sort of data reduction, then, may exaggerate the explanatory power of geography because linguistic contrasts and distinctions appear more pronounced than they actually are. We understand that this is a strong charge to bring; where is the evidence? Consider the plots in Figure 8.2, which once again depict the relationship between as-the-crow-flies geographic distances and morphosyntactic distances in the FRED dataset. As in the previous figure, the left plot is a reference plot whose morphosyntactic distance measurements are based on graded feature frequencies. Figure 8.2's middle plot depicts morphosyntactic distances which have been calculated on the basis of a frequency rank measure; for any given morphosyntactic feature, the measuring point with the highest text frequency receives rank 1, the measuring with the lowest frequency receives rank 34, and so on. This is a mild form of data reduction in that information about the exact scope of frequency differences between two neighboring ranks is lost. The right plot in Figure 8.2 calculates morphosyntactic distances subject to more substantial data reduction: Measuring points are categorized, for each individual morphosyntactic feature, into two frequency bins, a low-frequency bin and a high-frequency bin.[5] In other words, the right plot in Figure 8.2 essentially transforms the dataset's graded frequency signal into a reductionist "high"/"low" signal (akin to a "yes"/"no" signal). Thus, data reduction seems to increase the explanatory power of geographic distances – in the given case study plotted in Figure 8.2, from about 4 percent to about 7–9 percent (again, notice that the regression lines become steeper towards the right in Figure 8.2). The reason for this boost is that data reduction exaggerates contrasts and removes noise, and we suggest that atlas-based dialectometry suffers from this sort of distortion.

It turns out that an "intelligent" combination of outlier removal, data reduction, and feature selection will boost the explanatory power of as-the-crow-flies distance in the FRED dataset to about $R^2 \approx 25$ percent, a score which is within normal parameters of variation in Table 8.2. But at what price? The answer to this question basically boils down to what the most appropriate method is for assessing how dialects "actually are." This is a question that has no easy answer, and dialectologists are not exactly drowning in research addressing this issue (though we believe that perceptual dialectology experiments in the spirit of Inoue 1996; Preston 1999; and Niedzielski and Preston 1999 may be our best bet for a relatively objective answer). Yet in the absence of other evidence, we should maintain that feature selection and data reduction are essentially a form of academic fraud: Geographically insignificant features and frequency noise are part of linguistic reality, and any big-picture account should have to deal with these things, instead of disposing of them for the sake of neatness.

---

[5] The binning is based on percentile groups, such that each group contains approximately the same number of cases. For every individual feature, the low-frequency bin contains measuring points whose observed frequency in regard to some feature is below the 50th percentile, and the high-frequency bin contains measuring points exhibiting frequencies above the 50th percentile.

# 9   Outlook and concluding remarks

This book has advocated an approach to the analysis of naturalistic dialect data which holistically focuses on the forest and not so much on the individual trees. We called this approach CORPUS-BASED DIALECTOMETRY, or CBDM for short, and what takes center stage in CBDM is the graded differentiation of linguistic variability. This is another way of saying that CBDM is not concerned with the mere presence or absence of linguistic features in particular locations, and does not settle for merely analyzing lists of attested linguistic variants, or some such thing. Instead, the analysis in this book was based on intrinsically graded text frequencies, feature by feature, in a naturalistic dialect corpus.

The methodology's commitment to contextualized, authentic speech data (which takes the cultural and interactional nature of dialect discourse seriously) and its focus on geography as a fundamentally social factor (which approximates the likelihood of communicative contact) should appeal in particular to those geolinguists with a sociolinguistic background (or sociolinguists with an interest in geolinguistics). Quantitative variationists, linguistic anthropologists, or qualitative-interactional sociolinguists – we all stand to gain from learning more about how speech habits are patterned spatially.

It should also be emphasized, in this connection, that the breadth of the findings uncovered in this book would be hard to come by in any single-feature study, no matter how interesting the feature. The holistic study of many features in many dialects, married with computational analysis techniques and attractive visualization and cartographic projection techniques, advances dialectological scholarship and yields insights and generalizations which would remain elusive to the analyst who is beholden to the philologically orthodox study of a particular dialect feature in one or two particular dialects.

Let us go on to sketch some directions for further research. First, there remain a number of methodological issues to be worked out, most notably the vexed issue of how to calibrate frequency measurements and how to evaluate the status of linguistic features that are not distributed geographically. We touched on this question in the previous chapter and suggested that future

164

analysis should tap into perceptual dialectology research, for the sake of validating dialect distances with perceptual data (in the spirit of, e.g., Gooskens and Heeringa 2004).

Second (and along similar lines), it would be highly desirable to be in a position to explore empirically the impact that factors relating to language ideology and speaker identity may have on dialect variation. Auer (2004), for example, argues that "imagined" borders can robustly shape dialect continua. So alongside "objective" language-external distance measures, such as as-the-crow-flies distance or least-cost travel time, it would be a real boon to dialectometrical research (corpus-based *or* atlas-based) to find a viable operationalization of "felt" or "cognitive" distance.

Third, observe that the data source we used in this book (the *Freiburg Corpus of English Dialects*) was by design biased towards non-mobile old rural males born around the beginning of the twentieth century, which is why, for example, longitudinal change was fairly irrelevant to the present study. Yet, CBDM is not intrinsically limited to the analysis of fairly traditional dialect speech. It can just as well be applied to variability in modern dialects and accents. And this is a desideratum that is high on the agenda. David Britain has noted that "there are huge gaps in our knowledge of the present-day grammars of varieties in England" (2010, 53), and we believe that CBDM is a methodology that advertises itself for addressing these gaps from the bird's-eye perspective, in tandem with more traditional variationist analysis methods designed to cover the jeweler's-eye perspective.

Lastly, note that CBDM is not in any way limited to the analysis of morphosyntactic phenomena. Phonetics (through, e.g., acoustic measurements), phonology, lexis, and even pragmatics are all in principle amenable to dialectometrical analysis using a corpus-based approach. There is even the intriguing possibility of aggregating not "surfacy" feature frequencies but "deep" feature conditionings through probabilistic modeling of language variation and usage frequencies. Contextualized variation research along these lines, which combines quantitative measurements of linguistic variability with qualitative discourse-analytic inquiry (along the lines of, e.g., Mair 2006), simply cannot be done on the basis of decontextualized atlas or dictionary data, whereas CBDM can easily accommodate research into language use in context. As for suitable databases, notice that CBDM can be applied to *any* corpus in which we find geographic variability. This includes not only dialect corpora in the traditional, narrow sense, but also corpora sampling geographically non-contiguous regional language varieties (such as the *International Corpus of English*; see Greenbaum 1996). In short, there are a great many research opportunities just waiting to be tapped.

# Appendix A: the feature catalogue–summary statistics

Table A.1 provides a number of instructive summary statistics. For each individual feature, we report:

(i)   which dataset was utilized (FRED$_{full}$ vs. FRED$_{abridged}$) to extract text frequencies (see Section 3.3.2);

(ii)  the number of raw hits of the feature in this dataset;

(iii) the corresponding mean normalized frequency per ten thousand words (*pttw*) of the feature;

(iv)  as a summary measure of FRED-internal dispersion, the standard deviation ($\sigma$) associated with the normalized frequency figure on the county level ($N = 34$ measuring points);

(v)   whether the feature has a significant geographic distribution in the dataset as a whole ($N = 34$ measuring points) according to the frequency-distance correlation coefficient (henceforth: FDCC statistic) (see Section 3.4);

(vi)  whether the feature has a significant geographic distribution, according to the FDCC statistic, if attention is restricted to measuring points in England ($N = 18$);

(vii) whether the feature has a significant geographic distribution according to *Moran's I* (see Section 3.4);

(viii) mean normalized frequencies *pttw* in Standard British English, according to the ICE–GB-based reference corpus (see Section 2.1.2);

(ix)  mean normalized frequencies *pttw* in Standard American English, according to the CSAE-based reference corpus (see Section 2.1.2).

Table A.1. *The 57-feature catalogue: some summary statistics*

| | British English dialects (FRED) | | | geographic significance (FRED)[b] | | | Standard English benchmarks | |
|---|---|---|---|---|---|---|---|---|
| dataset[a] | raw hits | mean freq. *pttw* | st.dev. | FDCC total | FDCC England | *Moran's I* | freq. *pttw* AmE | freq. *pttw* BrE |
| [1] F | 158 | 0.6 | 0.6 | * | ° | ° | 0 | 0 |
| [2] F | 1,282 | 5.2 | 2.5 | | | | 5 | 10 |
| [3] F | 185 | 0.8 | 1.0 | | | | 0 | 0 |
| [4] F | 440 | 1.8 | 8.7 | | | ° | 0 | 0 |
| [5] F | 3,302 | 13.5 | 6.8 | | | | 4 | 8 |
| [6] F | 14,721 | 60.1 | 21.9 | | | | 59 | 51 |
| [7] F | 109 | 0.4 | 0.4 | ° | ° | | 0 | 1 |
| [8] F | 1,404 | 5.7 | 4.4 | | | | 4 | 7 |
| [9] F | 1,115 | 4.6 | 3.6 | | | * | 4 | 6 |
| [10] F | 853 | 3.5 | 1.7 | | | ° | 8 | 6 |
| [11] F | 1,145 | 4.7 | 2.8 | | | | 1 | 6 |
| [12] F | 407 | 1.7 | 2.0 | | | | 1 | 0 |
| [13] F | 25,231 | 103.0 | 27.0 | | | | 162 | 211 |
| [14] F | 90,778 | 370.5 | 62.9 | * | | | 282 | 358 |
| [15] F | 31,829 | 129.9 | 20.9 | ° | | | 115 | 115 |
| [16] F | 412 | 1.7 | 2.0 | | | | 0 | 2 |
| [17] F | 628 | 2.6 | 1.7 | | | | 15 | 7 |
| [18] F | 4,155 | 17.0 | 8.3 | | | | 6 | 42 |
| [19] A | 2,119 | 42.2 | 23.4 | | | | 5 | 4 |
| [20] A | 3,857 | 76.8 | 54.6 | * | * | | 3 | 6 |
| [21] A | 1,648 | 32.8 | 16.9 | ° | | | 52 | 62 |
| [22] F | 503 | 2.1 | 2.6 | | | | 0 | 0 |
| [23] A | 1,571 | 31.3 | 15.8 | | | | 27 | 40 |
| [24] F | 821 | 3.4 | 2.8 | | | ° | 4 | 3 |
| [25] F | 6,553 | 26.7 | 10.4 | | | | 21 | 16 |
| [26] F | 1,571 | 6.4 | 3.5 | ° | | * | 3 | 1 |
| [27] F | 339 | 1.4 | 1.8 | | | | 0 | 0 |
| [28] F | 262 | 1.1 | 1.4 | | | | 0 | 0 |
| [29] F | 649 | 2.6 | 2.6 | * | ° | | 0 | 0 |
| [30] F | 663 | 2.7 | 2.5 | * | | | 0 | 0 |
| [31] F | 648 | 2.6 | 27.3 | * | ° | * | 0 | 0 |
| [32] F | 205 | 0.8 | 0.7 | * | | * | 0 | 0 |
| [33] F | 1,170 | 4.8 | 3.1 | * | | * | 0 | 0 |
| [34] F | 5,260 | 21.5 | 9.7 | | | | 21 | 46 |
| [35] F | 946 | 3.9 | 4.2 | | | | 8 | 25 |
| [36] F | 2,225 | 9.1 | 4.0 | | | | 0 | 0 |
| [37] F | 2,400 | 9.8 | 4.8 | | | | 3 | 10 |
| [38] F | 971 | 4.0 | 2.3 | | | | 2 | 4 |
| [39] F | 3,234 | 13.2 | 12.2 | | | | 0 | 2 |
| [40] F | 122 | 0.5 | 0.4 | * | ° | * | 0 | 0 |
| [41] F | 192 | 0.8 | 1.6 | ° | | | 7 | 11 |
| [42] F | 1,834 | 7.5 | 4.0 | | * | | 6 | 0 |
| [43] F | 134 | 0.5 | 0.5 | ° | | | 0 | 0 |
| [44] A | 435 | 8.7 | 8.0 | | | | 0 | 1 |

(continued)

Table A.1. *(continued)*

| dataset[a] | raw hits | British English dialects (FRED) mean freq. *pttw* | st.dev. | geographic significance (FRED)[b] FDCC total | FDCC England | *Moran's I* | Standard English benchmarks freq. *pttw* AmE | freq. *pttw* BrE |
|---|---|---|---|---|---|---|---|---|
| [45] A | 304 | 6.1 | 20.8 | | | | 0 | 1 |
| [46] A | 734 | 14.6 | 18.6 | | | | 4 | 37 |
| [47] A | 149 | 3.0 | 2.8 | ° | | | 0 | 0 |
| [48] A | 787 | 15.7 | 9.1 | | | | 27 | 44 |
| [49] F | 241 | 1.0 | 0.8 | * | | | 0 | 0 |
| [50] F | 175 | 0.7 | 1.4 | | ° | | 0 | 0 |
| [51] F | 379 | 1.5 | 1.4 | | | | 2 | 3 |
| [52] F | 563 | 2.3 | 1.8 | | | | 2 | 2 |
| [53] F | 5,125 | 20.9 | 9.4 | | | | 21 | 64 |
| [54] F | 506 | 2.1 | 2.1 | | * | | 2 | 10 |
| [55] F | 330 | 1.3 | 2.4 | | | | 31 | 31 |
| [56] F | 143 | 0.6 | 0.7 | * | | ° | 1 | 2 |
| [57] F | 1,571 | 6.4 | 2.8 | ° | | * | 3 | 6 |

[a] F: full dataset, A: abridged dataset

[b] significance codes: * significant at $p \leq .001$, ° marginally significant at $p \leq .05$

# Appendix B: component-loading matrix

Table B.1 reports the 57 × 4 component-loading matrix generated from the FRED location level 158 × 57 frequency matrix. This matrix is the basis for the discussion in Section 7.2.

Table B.1. *Principal Component Analysis: rotated component-loading matrix (displayed: first four principal components)*

| feature | PC 1 | PC 2 | PC 3 | PC 4 |
|---------|------|------|------|------|
| [1]  | .51   | −.03 | −.07 | .02   |
| [2]  | .00   | .31  | .06  | −.09  |
| [3]  | −.02  | .02  | −.17 | .09   |
| [4]  | .12   | .05  | −.05 | .10   |
| [5]  | .07   | .24  | .22  | .06   |
| [6]  | −.01  | .68  | .17  | −.03  |
| [7]  | −.06  | .07  | −.01 | .03   |
| [8]  | .00   | .02  | .10  | .13   |
| [9]  | .26   | .06  | .08  | .02   |
| [10] | .09   | .20  | .16  | .56   |
| [11] | .01   | .10  | −.08 | .15   |
| [12] | .28   | .09  | −.15 | .05   |
| [13] | .14   | .80  | −.06 | −.01  |
| [14] | −.19  | −.05 | .61  | .21   |
| [15] | .06   | .80  | .03  | .30   |
| [16] | .07   | .06  | .03  | −.04  |
| [17] | .11   | .12  | −.01 | .03   |
| [18] | .07   | .16  | −.04 | −.08  |
| [19] | .07   | .21  | −.03 | .71   |
| [20] | .25   | .26  | .12  | .21   |
| [21] | −.13  | .30  | −.09 | .08   |
| [22] | .08   | .06  | −.10 | .04   |
| [23] | −.02  | .11  | −.36 | .11   |
| [24] | .01   | .09  | .14  | .15   |
| [25] | .10   | .58  | .26  | .25   |
| [26] | .27   | .24  | −.20 | −.18  |
| [27] | .24   | −.05 | .07  | −.10  |
| [28] | .33   | .01  | .09  | .10   |
| [29] | .66   | .13  | −.10 | .07   |
| [30] | .72   | .03  | .12  | .11   |
| [31] | −.11  | −.06 | −.01 | .04   |
| [32] | .64   | .16  | −.10 | −.13  |
| [33] | .70   | .22  | .10  | .18   |
| [34] | .13   | .58  | .53  | −.21  |
| [35] | −.19  | .14  | .01  | −.28  |
| [36] | .30   | .29  | .33  | .20   |
| [37] | .05   | .21  | .83  | −.01  |
| [38] | −.04  | .21  | .29  | .09   |
| [39] | .59   | −.18 | .25  | .26   |
| [40] | .50   | .13  | −.12 | −.16  |
| [41] | −.26  | .17  | −.09 | −.46  |
| [42] | .06   | .07  | .80  | .06   |
| [43] | .60   | .03  | .03  | −.16  |
| [44] | .52   | −.32 | .32  | .32   |
| [45] | .29   | .20  | −.23 | .10   |
| [46] | −.31  | −.06 | −.03 | .13   |
| [47] | .40   | .18  | −.15 | −.05  |
| [48] | −.14  | .04  | .11  | .02   |
| [49] | .18   | .00  | .20  | .00   |
| [50] | .34   | .28  | −.13 | −.07  |

(continued)

Table B.1. *(continued)*

| feature | PC 1 | PC 2 | PC 3 | PC 4 |
|---------|------|------|------|------|
| [51] | .07 | −.01 | .23 | .16 |
| [52] | .03 | .15 | .02 | −.02 |
| [53] | .11 | .56 | .15 | .01 |
| [54] | .03 | .06 | .03 | .04 |
| [55] | .41 | .04 | .22 | .00 |
| [56] | .07 | .01 | −.18 | .02 |
| [57] | .12 | .08 | .15 | .33 |

# Appendix C: color maps

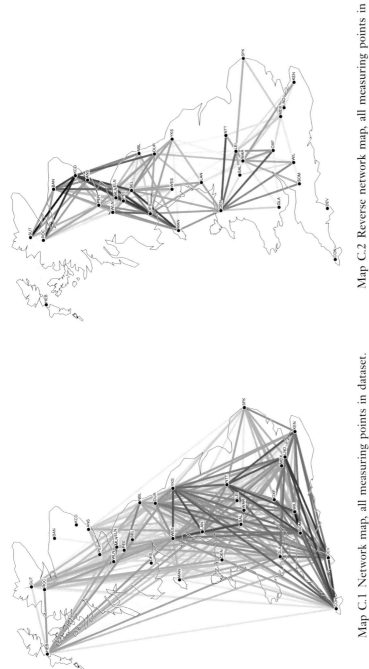

Map C.1 Network map, all measuring points in dataset. Links depict morphosyntactic similarities. Link blueness is directly proportional to dialectal similarity.

Map C.2 Reverse network map, all measuring points in dataset. Links depict morphosyntactic dissimilarities. Link blueness is directly proportional to dialectal dissimilarity. Distance limit: 250 km.

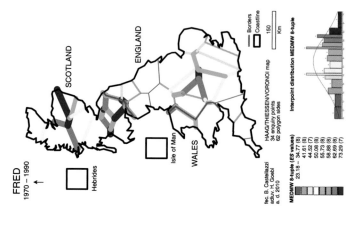

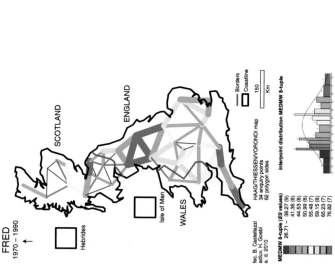

Map C.3 Beam map. Neighbors that are close morphosyntactically are connected by warm and heavy beams. Neighbors that are distant are connected by cold and thin beams.

Map C.4 Honeycomb map. Morphosyntactically distant neighbors are separated by cold and thick boundaries. Similar neighbors are separated by warm and thin boundaries.

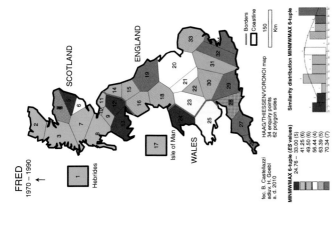

Map C.5 A similarity map for Kincardineshire (in white; measuring point 5, Scottish Lowlands). Warmer tones indicate relative morphosyntactic similarities. Colder tones indicate relative morphosyntactic dissimilarities.

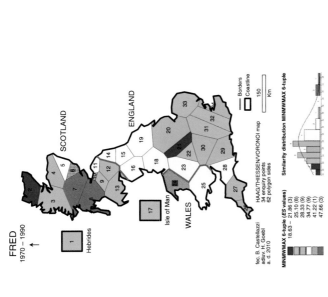

Map C.6 A similarity map for Nottinghamshire (in white; measuring point 20, English Midlands). Warmer tones indicate relative morphosyntactic similarities. Colder tones indicate relative morphosyntactic dissimilarities.

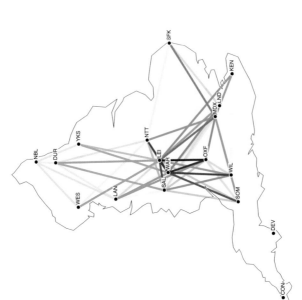

Map C.8 Reverse network map, measuring points in England only. Links depict morphosyntactic dissimilarities. Link blueness is directly proportional to dialectal dissimilarity. Distance limit: 250 km.

Map C.7 Network map, measuring points in England only. Links depict morphosyntactic similarities. Link blueness is directly proportional to dialectal similarity.

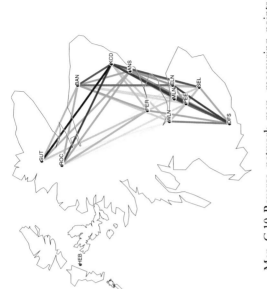

Map C.10 Reverse network map, measuring points in Scotland and the Hebrides only. Links depict morphosyntactic dissimilarities. Link blueness is directly proportional to dialectal dissimilarity. Distance limit: 250 km.

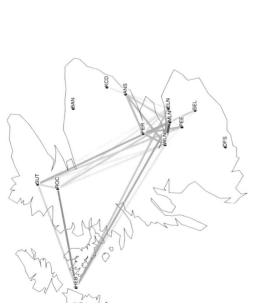

Map C.9 Network map, measuring points in Scotland and the Hebrides only. Links depict morphosyntactic similarities. Link blueness is directly proportional to dialectal similarity.

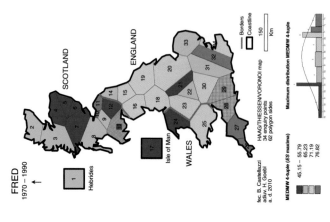

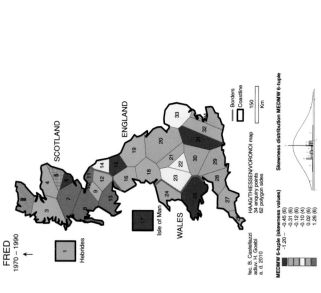

Map C.11 Skewness map: synopsis of the skewness values of the similarity distributions in the dataset. Colder tones indicate increasingly larger positive skewness values and, by inference, *Sprachausgleich*.

Map C.12 Kernel map: synopsis of the maximal values of the similarity distributions in the dataset. Warmer tones indicate measuring points with comparatively large similarity maxima and, by inference, dialect kernels.

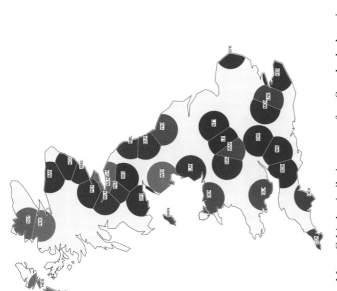

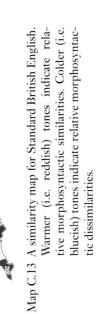

Map C.13 A similarity map for Standard British English. Warmer (i.e. reddish) tones indicate relative morphosyntactic similarities. Colder (i.e. blueish) tones indicate relative morphosyntactic dissimilarities.

Map C.14 A similarity map for Standard American English. Warmer (i.e. reddish) tones indicate relative morphosyntactic similarities. Colder (i.e. blueish) tones indicate relative morphosyntactic dissimilarities.

Map C.15 A perfect continuum map for reference purposes. Input: as-the-crow-flies distances. Similar color shades indicate spatial proximity. Shared variance with original distances: $R^2 = 99.9\%$.

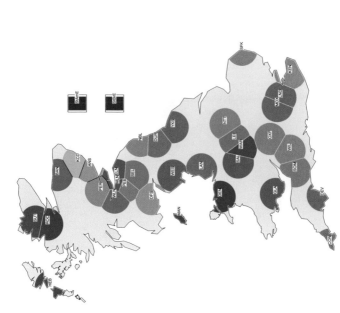

Map C.16 Continuum map. Input: morphosyntactic distances (including distances to Standard English). Similar color shades indicate morphosyntactic similarity. Shared variance with original distances: $R^2 = 89.5\%$.

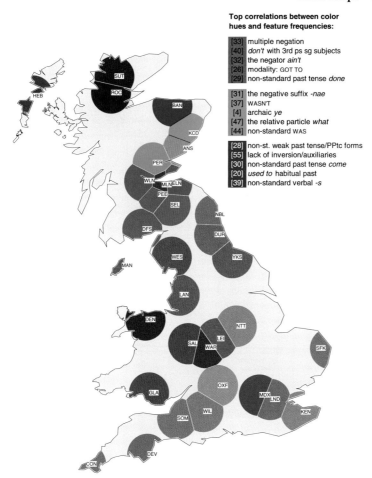

**Top correlations between color hues and feature frequencies:**

[33] multiple negation
[40] *don't* with 3rd ps sg subjects
[32] the negator *ain't*
[26] modality: GOT TO
[29] non-standard past tense *done*

[31] the negative suffix *-nae*
[37] WASN'T
[4] archaic *ye*
[47] the relative particle *what*
[44] non-standard WAS

[28] non-st. weak past tense/PPtc forms
[55] lack of inversion/auxiliaries
[30] non-standard past tense *come*
[20] *used to* habitual past
[39] non-standard verbal *-s*

Map C.17. Continuum map. Input: morphosyntactic distances. Similar color shades indicate morphosyntactic similarity. Shared variance with original distances: $R^2 = 89.3\%$.

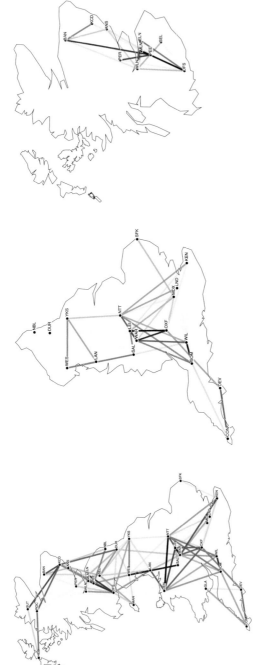

Map C.18 Visualizing regression residuals: network map, full dataset. Red links: morphosyntactic distance is greater than predicted. Blue links: morphosyntactic distance is smaller than predicted. Distance limit: 250 km.

Map C.19 Visualizing regression residuals: network map, England only. Red links: morphosyntactic distance is greater than predicted. Blue links: morphosyntactic distance is smaller than predicted. Distance limit: 250 km.

Map C.20 Visualizing regression residuals: network map, Scottish Lowlands only. Red links: morphosyntactic distance is greater than predicted. Blue links: morphosyntactic distance is smaller than predicted. Distance limit: 250 km.

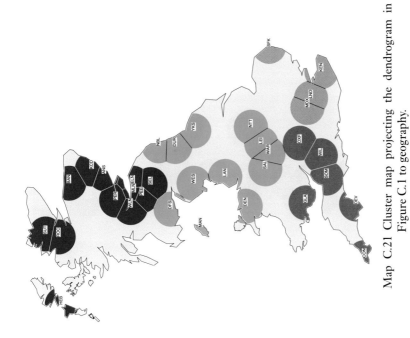

Figure C.1. Dendrogram, as–the–crow–flies distances in Hierarchical Agglomerative Cluster Analysis. Cluster algorithm: WPGMA. Displayed: 4-cluster solution. CPCC: .66.

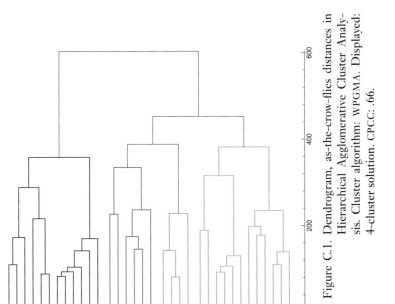

Map C.21 Cluster map projecting the dendrogram in Figure C.1 to geography.

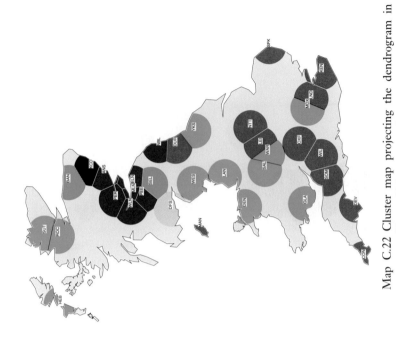

Figure C.2. Dendrogram, morphosyntactic distances in Hierarchical Agglomerative Cluster Analysis. Cluster algorithm: WPGMA. Displayed: 6-cluster solution. CPCC: .66.

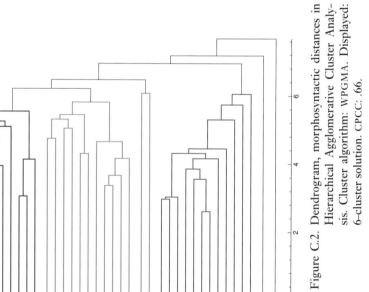

Map C.22 Cluster map projecting the dendrogram in Figure C.2 to geography.

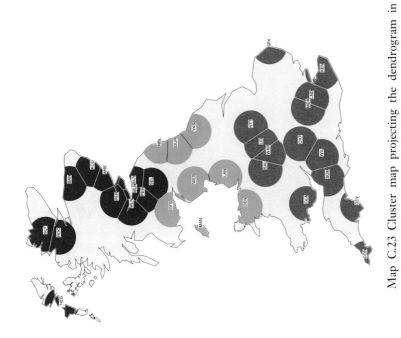

Figure C.3. Dendrogram, as–the–crow–flies distances in Hierarchical Agglomerative Cluster Analysis. Cluster algorithm: Ward's Method. Displayed: 3–cluster solution. CPCC: .69.

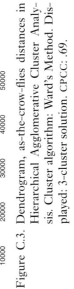

Map C.23 Cluster map projecting the dendrogram in Figure C.3 to geography.

Figure C.4. Dendrogram, morphosyntactic distances in Hierarchical Agglomerative Cluster Analysis. Cluster algorithm: Ward's Method. Displayed: 3–cluster solution. CPCC: .38.

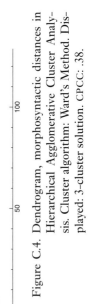

Map C.24 Cluster map projecting the dendrogram in Figure C.4 to geography.

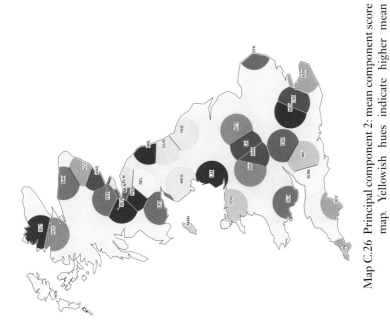

Map C.25 Principal component 1: mean component score map. Yellowish hues indicate higher mean component scores; blueish hues indicate lower mean component scores.

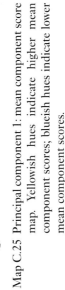

Map C.26 Principal component 2: mean component score map. Yellowish hues indicate higher mean component scores; blueish hues indicate lower mean component scores.

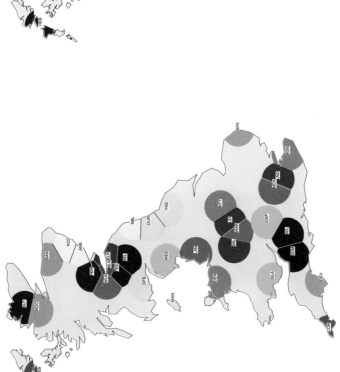

Map C.28 Principal component 4. Mean component score map. Yellowish hues indicate higher mean component scores; blueish hues indicate lower mean component scores.

Map C.27 Principal component 3. Mean component score map. Yellowish hues indicate higher mean component scores; blueish hues indicate lower mean component scores.

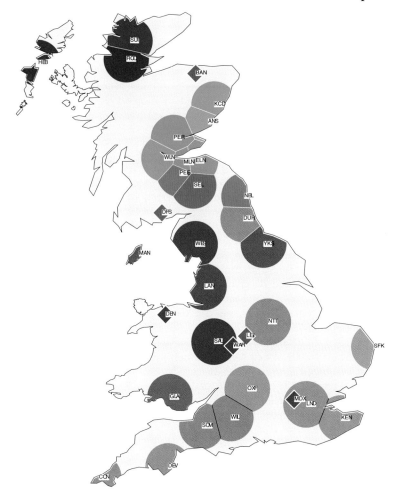

Map C.29. A synopsis map combining the continuum scenario and
the dialect area scenario. Clustering algorithm: Ward's
Method. Shared variance between MDS solution and original distances: $R^2 = 95.9\%$. Outliers discussed in Section
7.1 are mapped as language islands.

# References

Abdi, Hervé. 2007. The Bonferroni and Sidak corrections for multiple comparisons. In Salkind, Neil J. (ed.), *Encyclopedia of Measurement and Statistics*. Thousand Oaks: Sage, pp. 103–107.

Adger, David, and Smith, Jennifer. 2005. Variation and the minimalist program. In Cornips, Leslie, and Corrigan, Karen (eds.), *Syntax and Variation: Reconciling the Biological and the Social*. Amsterdam: Benjamins, pp. 149–178.

Aldenderfer, Mark S., and Blashfield, Roger K. 1984. *Cluster Analysis*. Newbury Park, London, New Delhi: Sage Publications.

Alewijnse, Bart, Nerbonne, John, van der Veen, Lolke, and Manni, Franz. 2007. A computational analysis of Gabon Varieties. In Osenova, Petya, (ed.), *Proceedings of the RANLP Workshop on Computational Phonology*, pp. 3–12.

Anderson, Marti J. 2001. A new method for non-parametric multivariate analysis of variance. *Austral Ecology*, **26**, 32–46.

Anderson, Peter M. 1987. *A Structural Atlas of the English Dialects*. London, New York: Croom Helm.

Anderwald, Lieselotte. 2001. *Was/were*-variation in non-standard British English today. *English World-Wide*, **22**(1), 1–21.

2003a. *Negation in Non-Standard British English: Gaps, Regularizations and Asymmetries*. London, New York: Routledge.

2003b. Non-standard English and typological principles: the case of negation. In Rohdenburg, Günter, and Mondorf, Britta (eds.), *Determinants of Grammatical Variation*. Berlin, New York: Mouton de Gruyter, pp. 507–529.

2005. Negative concord in British English dialects. In Iyeiri, Yoko (ed.), *Aspects of English Negation*. Amsterdam: Benjamins, pp. 113–138.

2009. *The Morphology of English Dialects: Verb-Formation in Non-Standard English*. Cambridge University Press.

Anderwald, Lieselotte, and Szmrecsanyi, Benedikt. 2009. Corpus linguistics and dialectology. In Lüdeling, Anke, and Kytö, Merja (eds.), *Corpus Linguistics: An International Handbook*. Handbücher zur Sprache und Kommunikationswissenschaft/Handbooks of Linguistics and Communication Science. Berlin, New York: Mouton de Gruyter, pp. 1126–1139.

Anderwald, Lieselotte, and Wagner, Susanne. 2007. FRED – The Freiburg English Dialect corpus. In Beal, Joan, Corrigan, Karen, and Moisl, Hermann (eds.), *Creating and Digitizing Language Corpora*, vol. I. London: Palgrave Macmillan, pp. 35–53.

Arppe, Antti, Gilquin, Gaëtanelle, Glynn, Dylan, Hilpert, Martin, and Zeschel, Arne. 2010. Cognitive Corpus Linguistics: five points of debate on current theory and methodology. *Corpora*, **5**(2), 1–27.

Auer, Peter. 2004. Sprache, Grenze, Raum. *Zeitschrift für Sprachwissenschaft*, **23**, 149–179.

Auer, Peter, Baumann, Peter, and Schwarz, Christian. forthcoming. Vertical vs horizontal change in the traditional dialects of southwest Germany: a quantitative approach. *Taal en Tongval*.

Bauer, Roland. 2009. *Dialektometrische Einsichten: Sprachklassifikatorische Oberflächenmuster und Tiefenstrukturen im lombardo-venedischen Dialektraum und in der Rätoromania*. San Martin de Tor: Istitut Ladin Micurà de Rü.

Baugh, Albert C., and Cable, Thomas. 1993. *A History of the English Language*. 4th edn. Englewood Cliffs, NJ: Prentice-Hall.

Beal, Joan. 2004. English dialects in the North of England: morphology and syntax. In Kortmann, Bernd, Schneider, Edgar, Burridge, K., Mesthrie, R., and Upton, C. (eds.), *A Handbook of Varieties of English*, vol. II. Berlin, New York: Mouton de Gruyter, pp. 115–141.

Beal, Joan C., and Corrigan, Karen P. 2006. No, nay, never: negation in Tyneside English. In Iyeiri, Yoko (ed.), *Aspects of English Negation*. Amsterdam: Benjamins, pp. 139–157.

Bergh, Gunnar, and Seppänen, Aimo. 2000. Preposition stranding with *wh*-relatives: a historical survey. *English Language and Linguistics*, **4**(2), 295–316.

Besch, Werner. 1967. *Sprachlandschaften und Sprachausgleich im 15. Jahrhundert: Studien zur Erforschung der spätmittelhochdeutschen Schreibdialekte und zur Entstehung der neuhochdeutschen Schriftsprache*. Munich: Francke.

Biber, Douglas. 1988. *Variation across Speech and Writing*. Cambridge University Press.

Biber, Douglas, Johansson, Stig, Leech, Geoffrey, Conrad, Susan, and Finegan, Edward. 1999. *Longman Grammar of Spoken and Written English*. Harlow: Longman.

Bland, J. Martin, and Altman, Douglas G. 1997. Statistics notes: Cronbach's alpha. *British Medical Journal*, **314**, 572.

Bloomfield, Leonard. 1984 [1933]. *Language*. University of Chicago Press.

Blumenthal, Alice. 2011. Entrenchment in usage-based theories: what corpus data do and do not reveal about the mind. PhD dissertation, University of Freiburg.

Bock, Kathryn. 1986. Syntactic persistence in language production. *Cognitive Psychology*, **18**, 355–387.

Bohnenberger, Karl. 1928. *Über die Ostgrenze des Alemannischen: Tatsächliches und Grundsätzliches. Mit 1 Karte*. [Reprint from *Beiträge zur Geschichte der deutschen Sprache und Literatur*, vol. 52.]. Halle, Saale: Niemeyer.

Bresnan, Joan, and Hay, Jennifer. 2008. Gradient grammar: an effect of animacy on the syntax of *give* in varieties of English. *Lingua*, **118**(2), 245–259.

Bresnan, Joan, Cueni, Anna, Nikitina, Tatiana, and Baayen, Harald. 2007. Predicting the dative alternation. In Boume, Gerlof, Kraemer, Irene, and Zwarts, Zwarts (eds.), *Cognitive Foundations of Interpretation*. Amsterdam: Royal Netherlands Academy of Science, pp. 69–94.

Britain, David. 2002. Diffusion, levelling, simplification and reallocation in past tense BE in the English Fens. *Journal of Sociolinguistics*, 6(1), 16–43.

2007. Grammatical variation in England. In Britain, David (ed.), *Language in the British Isles*. Cambridge University Press, pp. 75–104.

2010. Grammatical variation in the contemporary spoken English of England. In Kirkpatrick, Andy (ed.), *The Routledge Handbook of World Englishes*. London: Routledge, pp. 37–58.

Brown, Keith. 1991. Double modals in Hawick Scots. In Trudgill, Peter, and Chambers, Jack (eds.), *Dialects of English: Studies in Grammatical Variation*. Longman Linguistics Library. London, New York: Longman, pp. 74–103.

Busse, Ulrich. 2002. *Linguistic Variation in the Shakespeare Corpus: Morpho-Syntactic Variability of Second Person Pronouns*. Amsterdam, Philadelphia: Benjamins.

Chafe, Wallace. 1992. The importance of corpus linguistics to understanding the nature of language. In Svartvik, Jan (ed.), *Directions in Corpus Linguistics*. Berlin, New York: Mouton de Gruyter, pp. 79–97.

Chambers, Jack K. 1995. *Sociolinguistic Theory: Linguistic Variation and Its Social Significance*. Oxford: Blackwell.

2004. Dynamic typology and vernacular universals. In Kortmann, Bernd (ed.), *Dialectology Meets Typology*. Berlin, New York: Mouton de Gruyter, pp. 127–145.

Chambers, Jack K., and Trudgill, Peter. 1991. Dialect grammar: data and theory. In Trudgill, Peter, and Chambers, J. K. (eds.), *Dialects of English: Studies in Grammatical Variation*. London, New York: Longman, pp. 291–96.

1998. *Dialectology*. 2nd edn. Cambridge, New York: Cambridge University Press.

Cheshire, Jenny. 1982. *Variation in an English Dialect: A Sociolinguistic Study*. Cambridge University Press.

Cheshire, Jenny, Edwards, Viv, and Whittle, Pamela. 1989. Urban British dialect grammar: the question of dialect levelling. *English WorldWide*, 10, 185–225.

1993. Non-standard English and dialect levelling. In Milroy, Jim, and Milroy, Leslie (eds.), *Real English: The Grammar of English Dialects in the British Isles*. London: Longman, pp. 52–96.

Clark, Urszula. 2004. The English West Midlands: phonology. In Kortmann, Bernd, Schneider, Edgar, Burridge, K., Mesthrie, R., and Upton, C. (eds.), *A Handbook of Varieties of English*, vol. I. Berlin, New York: Mouton de Gruyter, pp. 134–162.

Cliff, A. D., and Ord, J. K. 1973. *Spatial Autocorrelation*. London: Pion.

Costello, Anna B., and Osborne, Jason W. 2005. Best practices in exploratory factor analysis: four recommendations for getting the most from your analysis. *Practical Assessment, Research & Evaluation*, 10(7), 1–9.

Cronbach, Lee J. 1951. Coefficient alpha and the internal structure of tests. *Psychometrika*, 16(3), 297–334.

Dahl, Lisa. 1971. The *s*-genitive with non-personal nouns in modern English journalistic style. *Neuphilologische Mitteilungen*, 72, 140–172.

Danchev, Andrei, and Kytö, Merja. 1994. The construction *be going to* + infinitive in Early Modern English. In Kastovsky, Dieter (ed.), *Studies in Early Modern English*. Berlin: Mouton de Gruyter, pp. 59–77.

Denison, David. 1993. *English Historical Syntax*. Harlow, Essex: Longman.

Downes, William. 1998. *Language and Society*. 2nd edn. Cambridge University Press.

Du Bois, John W., Chafe, Wallace L., Meyer, Charles, and Thompson, Sandra A. 2000. *Santa Barbara Corpus of Spoken American English, Part 1*. Philadelphia: Linguistic Data Consortium.

Duffley, Patrick J. 1994. *Need* and *dare*: the black sheep of the modal family. *Lingua*, **94**(4), 213–243.

Dunn, Michael, Terrill, Angela, Reesink, Ger, Foley, Robert A., and Levinson, Stephen C. 2005. Structural phylogenetics and the reconstruction of ancient language history. *Science*, **309**(5743), 2072–2075.

Dunteman, George H. 1989. *Principal Components Analysis*. Newbury Park, London, New Delhi: Sage Publications.

Edwards, Viv. 1993. The grammar of Southern British English. In Milroy, Jim, and Milroy, Leslie (eds.), *Real English: The Grammar of English Dialects in the British Isles*. London: Longman, pp. 214–238.

Ellis, Alexander John. 1889. *On Early English Pronunciation*, vol. V: *The Existing Phonology Of English Dialects*. London: Trübner & Co.

Embleton, Sheila. 1993. Multidimensional scaling as a dialectometrical technique: outline of a research project. In Köhler, Reinhard, and Rieger, Burghard (eds.), *Contributions to Quantitative Linguistics*. Dordrecht: Kluwer, pp. 267–276.

Fisher, Ronald Aylmer. 1954. *Statistical Methods for Research Workers*. Edinburgh: Oliver and Boyd.

Francis, W. Nelson. 1992. Language corpora B.C. In Svartvik, Jan (ed.), *Directions in Corpus Linguistics: Proceedings of Nobel Symposium 82, Stockholm, 4–8 August 1991*. Berlin, New York: Mouton de Gruyter, pp. 17–32.

Gauchat, Louis. 1903. Gibt es Mundartgrenzen? *Archiv für das Studium der neueren Sprachen und Literaturen*, **11**, 365–403.

Giles, David. 2002. *Advanced Research Methods in Psychology*. Hove, New York: Routledge.

Glaser, Elvira. forthcoming. Area formation in morphosyntax. In Auer, Peter, Hilpert, Martin, Stukenbrock, Anja, and Szmrecsanyi, Benedikt (eds.), *Space in Language and Linguistics: Geographical, Interactional, and Cognitive Perspectives*. Berlin, New York: Walter de Gruyter.

Godfrey, Elizabeth, and Tagliamonte, Sali. 1999. Another piece for the verbal *-s* story: evidence from Devon in southwest England. *Language Variation and Change*, **11**, 87–121.

Goebl, Hans. 1982. *Dialektometrie: Prinzipien und Methoden des Einsatzes der Numerischen Taxonomie im Bereich der Dialektgeographie*. Wien: Österreichische Akademie der Wissenschaften.

　1983. Stammbaum und Welle. *Zeitschrift für Sprachwissenschaft*, **2**, 3–44.

　1984. *Dialektometrische Studien: Anhand italoromanischer, rätroromanischer und galloromanischer Sprachmaterialien aus AIS und ALF*. Tübingen: Niemeyer.

　1993. Probleme und Methoden der Dialektometrie: Geolinguistik in globaler Perspektive. In Viereck, Wolfgang (ed.), *Proceedings of the International Congress of Dialectologists*. Stuttgart: Steiner, pp. 37–81.

　1997a. "Es kracht im Gebälk des CLAE ...". Dialektometrische Beobachtungen zu eigenartigen Polarisierungseffekten in sprachgeographischen Netzen. In Ramisch, Heinrich, and Wynne, Kenneth (eds.), *Language in Space and*

## 194  References

*Time: Studies in Honour of Wolfgang Viereck on the Occasion of his 60th Birthday.* Stuttgart: Steiner, pp. 100–108.

1997b. Some dendrographic classifications of the data of CLAE 1 and CLAE 2. In Viereck, Wolfgang, and Ramisch, Heinrich (eds.), *Computer Developed Linguistic Atlas of England (CLAE)*, vol. II. Tübingen: Max Niemeyer Verlag, pp. 23–32.

2001. Arealtypologie und Dialektologie. In Haspelmath, Martin, König, Ekkehard, Oesterreicher, Wulf, and Raible, Wolfgang (eds.), *Language Typology and Language Universals / La typologie des langues et les universaux linguistiques / Sprachtypologie und sprachliche Universalien: An International Handbook / Manuel international / Ein internationales Handbuch*, vol. II. Berlin, New York: Walter de Gruyter, pp. 1471–1491.

2005. Dialektometrie. In Köhler, Reinhard, Altmann, Gabriel, and Piotrowski, Rajmund G. (eds.), *Quantitative Linguistics / Quantitative Linguistik. An International Handbook / Ein internationales Handbuch.* Berlin, New York: Walter de Gruyter, pp. 498–531.

2006. Recent advances in Salzburg dialectometry. *Literary and Linguistic Computing*, 21(4), 411–435.

2007. A bunch of dialectometric flowers: a brief introduction to dialectometry. In Smit, Ute, Dollinger, Stefan, Hüttner, Julia, Kaltenböck, Gunter, and Lutzky, Ursula (eds.), *Tracing English through time: Explorations in Language Variation.* Wien: Braumüller, pp. 133–172.

2008. Le Laboratoire de dialectométrie de l'Université de Salzbourg. *Zeitschrift für französische Sprache und Literatur*, 118(1), 35–55.

2010. Dialectometry and quantitative mapping. In Lameli, Alfred, Kehrein, Roland, and Rabanus, Stefan (eds.), *Language and Space: An International Handbook of Linguistic Variation*, vol. II: *Language Mapping.* Berlin: De Gruyter Mouton, pp. 433–457.

Goebl, Hans, and Schiltz, Guillaume. 1997. A dialectometrical compilation of CLAE 1 and CLAE 2: isoglosses and dialect integration. In Viereck, Wolfgang, and Ramisch, Heinrich (eds.), *Computer Developed Linguistic Atlas of England (CLAE)*, vol. II. Tübingen: Max Niemeyer Verlag, pp. 13–21.

2006. Neuere Entwicklungen in der europäischen Dialektologie (1950–2000). In Auroux, Sylvain, Koerner, E. F. K., Niederehe, Hans-Josef, and Versteegh, Kees (eds.), *History of the Language Sciences / Geschichte der Sprachwissenschaften / Histoire des sciences du langage: An International Handbook on the Evolution of the Study of Language from the Beginnings to the Present / Manuel international sur l'évolution de l'étude du langage des origines à nos jours / Ein internationales Handbuch zur Entwicklung der Sprachforschung von den Anfängen bis zur Gegenwart.* Berlin, New York: Walter de Gruyter, pp. 2352–2365.

Gooskens, Charlotte. 2005. Traveling time as a predictor of linguistic distance. *Dialectologia et Geolinguistica*, 13, 38–62.

Gooskens, Charlotte, and Heeringa, Wilbert. 2004. Perceptive evaluation of Levenshtein dialect distance measurements using Norwegian dialect data. *Language Variation and Change*, 16(3), 189–207.

Gower, John C. 1966. Some distance properties of latent root and vector methods used in multivariate analysis. *Biometrika*, 53(3/4), 325–338.

Graham-Campbell, James (ed.). 2001. *Vikings and the Danelaw: Select Papers from the Proceedings of the Thirteenth Viking Congress, Nottingham and York, 21–30 August 1997*. Oxford: Oxbow Books.

Greenbaum, Sidney. 1996. *Comparing English Worldwide: The International Corpus of English*. Oxford, New York: Clarendon Press.

Greenberg, Joseph H. 1963. *The Languages of Africa*. Bloomington: Indiana University Press.

Gries, Stefan Th. 2005. Syntactic priming: a corpus-based approach. *Journal of Psycholinguistic Research*, **34**(4), 365–399.

Gries, Stefan Th., and Wulff, Stefanie. 2005. Do foreign language learners also have constructions? Evidence from priming, sorting, and corpora. *Annual Review of Cognitive Linguistics*, **3**, 182–200.

Grieve, Jack. 2009. A Corpus-Based Regional Dialect Survey of Grammatical Variation in Written Standard American English. PhD dissertation, Northern Arizona University.

Gronemeyer, Claire. 1999. On deriving complex polysemy: the grammaticalization of *get*. *English Language and Linguistics*, **3**(1), 1–39.

Gropen, Jess, Pinker, Steven, Hollander, Michelle, Goldberg, Richard, and Wilson, Ronald. 1989. The learnability and acquisition of the dative alternation in English. *Language*, **65**(2), 203–257.

Haag, Karl. 1898. *Die Mundarten des oberen Neckar- und Donaulandes (Schwäbisch-alemannisches Grenzgebiet: Baarmundarten)*. Reutlingen: Hutzler.

Haimerl, Edgar. 2006. Database design and technical solutions for the management, calculation, and visualization of dialect mass data. *Literary and Linguistic Computing*, **21**(4), 437–444.

Hamer, Andrew. 2007. English on the Isle of Man. In Britain, David (ed.), *Language in the British Isles*. Cambridge University Press, pp. 171–175.

Händler, Harald, and Viereck, Wolfgang. 1997. Selective dialectometry. In Viereck, Wolfgang, and Ramisch, Heinrich (eds.), *Computer Developed Linguistic Atlas of England (CLAE)*, vol. II. Tübingen: Max Niemeyer Verlag, pp. 33–49.

Harnisch, Rüdiger. 2009. Divergence of linguistic varieties in a language space. In Auer, Peter, and Schmidt, Jürgen Erich (eds.), *An International Handbook of Linguistic Variation*, vol. I: *Theories and Methods*. Berlin, New York: Mouton de Gruyter, pp. 275–295.

Harris, John. 1993. The grammar of Irish English. In Milroy, James, and Milroy, Leslie (eds.), *Real English: The Grammar of English Dialects in the British Isles*. London: Longman, pp. 139–186.

Haspelmath, Martin. 2009. Welche Fragen können wir mit herkömmlichen Daten beantworten? *Zeitschrift für Sprachwissenschaft*, **28**(1), 157–162.

Haspelmath, Martin, Dryer, Matthew S., Gil, David, and Comrie, Bernard (eds.). 2005. *The World Atlas of Language Structures*. Oxford University Press.

Heeringa, Wilbert. 2004. Measuring dialect pronunciation differences using Levenshtein distance. PhD dissertation, University of Groningen.

Heeringa, Wilbert, and Nerbonne, John. 2001. Dialect areas and dialect continua. *Language Variation and Change*, **13**(3), 375–400.

Heeringa, Wilbert, Nerbonne, John, Bezooijen, Renée van, and Spruit, Marco René. 2007. Geografie en inwoneraantallen als verklarende factoren voor variatie in het Nederlandse dialectgebied. *Nederlandse Taal- en Letterkunde*, **123**(1), 70–82.

Heeringa, Wilbert, Johnson, Keith, and Gooskens, Charlotte. 2009. Measuring Norwegian dialect distances using acoustic features. *Speech Communication*, 51(2), 167–183.

Heine, Bernd, and Kuteva, Tania. 2005. *Language Contact and Grammatical Change*. Cambridge University Press.

Heinemann, Sabine. 2008. Zum Begriff des sprachlichen Kontinuums. In Heinemann, Sabine, and Videsott, Paul (eds.), *Linguistic Change and (dis-)continuity in the Romania / Sprachwandel und (Dis-)Kontinuität in der Romania*. Berlin, New York: Walter de Gruyter – Max Niemeyer Verlag.

Hernández, Nuria. 2006. *User's Guide to FRED*. URN: urn:nbn:de:bsz: 25-opus-24895, URL: www.freidok.uni-freiburg.de/volltexte/2489/. Freiburg: University of Freiburg.

    2010. Personal pronouns in the dialects of England: a corpus-driven study of grammatical variation in spontaneous speech. PhD dissertation, University of Freiburg.

Herrmann, Tanja. 2003. Relative clauses in dialects of English: a typological approach. PhD dissertation, University of Freiburg.

    2005. Relative clauses in English dialects of the British Isles. In Kortmann, Bernd, Herrmann, Tanja, Pietsch, Lukas, and Wagner, Susanne (eds.), *A Comparative Grammar of British English Dialects: Agreement, Gender, Relative Clauses*. Berlin, New York: Mouton de Gruyter, pp. 21–124.

Hinrichs, Lars, and Szmrecsanyi, Benedikt. 2007. Recent changes in the function and frequency of standard English genitive constructions: a multivariate analysis of tagged corpora. *English Language and Linguistics*, 11(3), 437–474.

Hinskens, Frans, Kallen, Jeffrey L., and Taeldeman, Johan. 2000. Merging and drifting apart: convergence and divergence of dialects across political borders. *International Journal of the Sociology of Language*, 145(1), 1–28.

Hock, Hans Henrich, and Joseph, Brian D. 2009. *Language History, Language Change, and Language Relationship: An Introduction to Historical and Comparative Linguistics*. 2nd rev. edn. Berlin, New York: Mouton de Gruyter.

Holman, Eric W., Schulze, Christian, Stauffer, Dietrich, and Wichmann, Soren. 2007. On the relation between structural diversity and geographical distance among languages: observations and computer simulations. *Linguistic Typology*, 11(2), 393–421.

Hoppenbrouwers, Cor, and Hoppenbrouwers, Geer. 1988. De featurefrequentiemethode en de classificatie van Nederlandse dialecten. *TABU: Bulletin voor taalwetenschap*, 18(2), 51–92.

    2001. *De indeling van de Nederlandse streektalen: Dialecten van 156 steden en dorpen geklasseerd volgens de FFM*. Assen: Koninklijke Van Gorcum.

Hotelling, Harold. 1933. Analysis of a complex of statistical variables into principal components. *Journal of Educational Psychology*, 24(6), 417–441.

Houtzagers, Peter, Nerbonne, John, and Prokić, Jelena. 2010. Quantitative and traditional classifications of Bulgarian dialects compared. *Scando-Slavica*, 59(2), 29–54.

Hubert, Lawrence, and Arabie, Phipps. 1985. Comparing partitions. *Journal of Classification*, 2, 193–218.

Hughes, Arthur, and Trudgill, Peter. 1996. *English Accents and Dialects: An Introduction to Social and Regional Varieties of English in the British Isles*. 3rd edn. London, New York: Arnold.

Hundt, Marianne. 2004. Animacy, agentivity, and the spread of the progressive in Modern English. *English Language and Linguistics*, 8(1), 47–69.

Huson, Daniel H., and Bryant, David. 2006. Application of phylogenetic networks in evolutionary studies. *Molecular Biology Evolution*, 23(2), 254–267.

Ihalainen, Ossi. 1976. Periphrastic *do* in affirmative sentences in the dialect of East Somerset. *Neuphilologische Mitteilungen*, 77, 608–622.

1994. The dialects of England since 1776. In Burchfield, Robert (ed.), *The Cambridge History of the English Language*, vol. V: *English in Britain and Overseas: Origins and Developments*. Cambridge University Press.

Inoue, Fumio. 1996. Subjective dialect division in Great Britain. *American Speech*, 71(2), 142–161.

Jain, Anil K., Murty, M. Narasimha, and Flynn, Patrick J. 1999. Data clustering: a review. *ACM Computing Surveys*, 31(3), 264–323.

Jankowski, Bridget. 2004. A transatlantic perspective of variation and change in English deontic modality. *Toronto Working Papers in Linguistics*, 23(2), 85–113.

Jespersen, Otto. 1940. *A Modern English Grammar on Historical Principles*, vol. V: *Syntax*. London: Allen & Unwin.

Johansson, Christine, and Geisler, Christer. 1998. Pied piping in spoken English. In Renouf, Antoinette (ed.), *Explorations in Corpus Linguistics*. Amsterdam, Atlanta: Rodopi, pp. 67–82.

Johnston, Paul A. Jr. 2007. Scottish English and Scots. In Britain, David (ed.), *Language in the British Isles*. Cambridge University Press, pp. 105–121.

Johnstone, Barbara. 2009. Language and geographical space. In Auer, Peter, and Schmidt, Jürgen Erich (eds.), *Language and Space. An International Handbook of Linguistic Variation*, vol. I: *Theories and Methods*. Berlin, New York: Mouton de Gruyter, pp. 1–18.

Jones, Megan, and Tagliamonte, Sali. 2004. From Somerset to Samaná: preverbal *did* in the voyage of English. *Language Variation and Change*, 16, 93–126.

Jucker, Andreas. 1993. The genitive versus the *of*-construction in newspaper language. In Jucker, Andreas (ed.), *The Noun Phrase in English. Its Structure and Variability*. Heidelberg: Carl Winter, pp. 121–136.

Kaiser, Henry F. 1958. The Varimax criterion for analytic rotation in factor analysis. *Psychometrika*, 23(3), 187–200.

Kamvar, Sepandar D., Klein, Dan, and Manning, Christopher D. 2002. Interpreting and extending classical agglomerative clustering algorithms using a model-based approach. In *Proceedings of the 19th International Conference on Machine Learning*, pp. 283–290.

Keller, Adelbert von. 1855. Anleitung zur Sammlung des schwäbischen Sprachschatzes. In *Einladungsschrift der Universität Tübingen zum 27. September 1855*. Tübingen: Fues, pp. 5–24.

Kirk, John M. 1985. Linguistic atlases and grammar: the investigation and description of regional variation in English syntax. In Kirk, John M., Sanderson, Stewart, and Widdowson, J. D. A. (eds.), *Studies in Linguistic Geography*. London: Croom Helm, pp. 130–156.

Klemola, Juhani. 1996. Non-standard periphrastic do: a study in variation and change. PhD dissertation, University of Essex.

2006. *Was/were* variation in traditional dialects of England. *Talk given at ICEHL14*, Bergamo, August 21–25.

Kolb, Eduard. 1979. *Atlas of English sounds*. Bern: Francke.

Kolbe, Daniela. 2008. Complement clauses in British Englishes. PhD dissertation, University of Trier.

Kortmann, Bernd. 2004a. *Do* as a tense and aspect marker in varieties of English. In Kortmann, Bernd (ed.), *Dialectology Meets Typology: Dialect Grammar from a Cross-Linguistic Perspective*. Berlin, New York: Mouton de Gruyter, pp. 245–275.

  2004b. Synopsis: morphological and syntactic variation in the British Isles. In Kortmann, Bernd, Schneider, Edgar, Burridge, K., Mesthrie, R., and Upton, C. (eds.), *A Handbook of Varieties of English*, vol. II. Berlin, New York: Mouton de Gruyter, pp. 1089–1103.

  2009. Die Rolle von (Nicht-Standard-)Varietäten in der europäischen (Areal-)Typologie. In Hinrichs, Uwe, Reiter, Norbert, and Tornow, Siegfried (eds.), *Eurolinguistik: Entwicklungen und Perspektiven*. Wiesbaden: Harrassowitz, pp. 165–188.

Kortmann, Bernd, and Szmrecsanyi, Benedikt. 2004. Global synopsis: morphological and syntactic variation in English. In Kortmann, Bernd, Schneider, Edgar, Burridge, K., Mesthrie, R., and Upton, C. (eds.), *A Handbook of Varieties of English*, vol. II. Berlin, New York: Mouton de Gruyter, pp. 1142–1202.

Kortmann, Bernd, and Upton, Clive. 2004. Introduction: varieties of English in the British Isles. In Kortmann, Bernd, Schneider, Edgar, Burridge, K., Mesthrie, R., and Upton, C. (eds.), *A Handbook of Varieties of English*, vol. II. Berlin, New York: Mouton de Gruyter, pp. 25–32.

Kortmann, Bernd, and Wagner, Susanne. 2005. The Freiburg English Dialect Project and Corpus. In Kortmann, Bernd, Herrmann, Tanja, Pietsch, Lukas, and Wagner, Susanne (eds.), *A Comparative Grammar of British English Dialects: Agreement, Gender, Relative Clauses*. Berlin, New York: Mouton de Gruyter, pp. 1–20.

Kremer, Ludger. 1979. *Grenzmundarten und Mundartgrenzen: Untersuchungen zur wortgeographischen Funktion der Staatsgrenze im ostniederländisch-westfälischen Grenzgebiet*. Niederdeutsche Studien. Cologne, Vienna: Böhlau.

Kretzschmar, William A., and Tamasi, Susan. 2002. Distributional foundations for a theory of language change. *World Englishes*, 22(4), 377–401.

Krug, Manfred. 2000. *Emerging English Modals: A Corpus-Based Study of Grammaticalization*. Berlin, New York: Mouton de Gruyter.

Kruskal, Joseph B., and Wish, Myron. 1978. *Multidimensional Scaling*. Newbury Park, London, New Delhi: Sage Publications.

Kytö, Merja, and Romaine, Susan. 1997. Competing forms of adjective comparison in Modern English: what could be *more quicker* and *easier* and *more effective*? In Nevalainen, Terttu, and Kahlas-Tarkka, Leena (eds.), *To Explain the Present: Studies in the Changing English Language in Honour of Matti Rissanen*. Amsterdam: Rodopi, pp. 329–352.

Labov, William. 1966. The linguistic variable as a structural unit. *Washington Linguistics Review*, 3, 4–22.

  1969. Contraction, deletion and inherent variability of the English copula. *Language*, 45, 715–762.

Lalanne, Théodore. 1953. Indice de polyonymie: indice de polyphonie. *Le Français Moderne*, **21**, 263–274.

Lass, Roger. 2004. South African English. In Hickey, Raymond (ed.), *Legacies of Colonial English: Studies in Transported Dialects*. Cambridge University Press, pp. 363–386.

Leech, Geoffrey N., Francis, Brian, and Xu, Xfueng. 1994. The use of computer corpora in the textual demonstrability of gradience in linguistic categories. In Fuchs, Catherine, and Victorri, Bernard (eds.), *Continuity in Linguistic Semantics*. Amsterdam, Philadelphia: Benjamins, pp. 57–76.

Leino, Antti, and Hyvönen, Saara. 2008. Comparison of component models in analysing the distribution of dialectal features. *International Journal of Humanities and Arts Computing*, **2**(1/2), 173–187.

Leinonen, Therese. 2008. Factor analysis of vowel pronunciation in Swedish dialects. *International Journal of Humanities and Arts Computing*, **2**(1/2), 189–204.

Löffler, Heinrich. 2003. *Dialektologie: Eine Einführung*. Tübingen: Narr.

Mair, Christian. 2002. Three changing patterns of verb complementation in Late Modern English: a real-time study based on matching text corpora. *English Language and Linguistics*, **6**(1), 105–131.

   2003. Gerundial complements after *begin* and *start*: grammatical and sociolinguistic factors, and how they work against each other. In Rohdenburg, Günter, and Mondorf, Britta (eds.), *Determinants of Grammatical Variation in English*. Berlin, New York: Mouton de Gruyter, pp. 329–346.

   2004. Corpus Linguistics and grammaticalisation theory: beyond statistics and frequency? In Mair, Christian, and Lindquist, Hans (eds.), *Corpus Approaches to Grammaticalisation in English*. Amsterdam: Benjamins, pp. 121–150.

   2006. *Twentieth-Century English: History, Variation, and Standardization*. Cambridge University Press.

Mantel, Nathan. 1967. The detection of disease clustering and a generalized regression approach. *Cancer Research*, **27**(2), 209–220.

McMahon, April, Heggarty, Paul, McMahon, Robert, and Maguire, Warren. 2007. The sound patterns of Englishes: representing phonetic similarity. *English Language and Linguistics*, **11**(1), 113–142.

Mesthrie, Rajend. 2006. World Englishes and the multilingual history of English. *World Englishes*, **25**(3/4), 381–390.

Meyers, Lawrence S., Gamst, Glenn, and Guarino, A. J. 2006. *Applied Multivariate Research: Design and Interpretation*. Thousand Oaks: Sage Publications.

Millar, Robert McColl. 2007. *Northern and Insular Scots*. Edinburgh University Press.

Miller, Jim. 2004. Scottish English: morphology and syntax. In Kortmann, Bernd, Schneider, Edgar, Burridge, K., Mesthrie, R., and Upton, C. (eds.), *A Handbook of Varieties of English*, vol. II. Berlin, New York: Mouton de Gruyter, pp. 37–72.

Mitchell, Bruce. 1985. *Old English*, vol. I. Oxford: Clarendon Press.

Nelson, Gerald, Wallis, Sean, and Aarts, Bas. 2002. *Exploring Natural Language: Working with the British Component of the International Corpus of English*. Amsterdam, Philadelphia: Benjamins.

Nerbonne, John. 2003. Linguistic variation and computation. In *Proceedings of the 10th Meeting of the European Chapter of the Association for Computational Linguistics, April, 2003*. Association for Computational Linguistics, pp. 3–10.

2006. Identifying linguistic structure in aggregate comparison. *Literary and Linguistic Computing*, 21(4), 463–475.

2009. Data-driven dialectology. *Language and Linguistics Compass*, 3(1), 175–198.

2010. Measuring the diffusion of linguistic change. *Philosophical Transactions of the Royal Society B: Biological Sciences*, 365, 3821–3828.

Forthcoming a. How much does geography influence language variation? In Auer, Peter, Hilpert, Martin, Stukenbrock, Anja, and Szmrecsanyi, Benedikt (eds.), *Space in Language and Linguistics: Geographical, Interactional, and Cognitive Perspectives*. Berlin, New York: Walter de Gruyter.

Forthcoming b. Mapping aggregate variation. In Rabanus, Stephan, Kehrein, Ronald, and Lameli, Alfred (eds.), *Mapping Language*. Berlin: Mouton de Gruyter.

Forthcoming c. Various variation aggregates in the LAMSAS South. In Davis, Catherine, and Picone, Michael (eds.), *Language Variety in the South III*. Tuscaloosa: University of Alabama Press.

Nerbonne, John, and Heeringa, Wilbert. 1997. Measuring dialect distance phonetically. In Coleman, John (ed.), *Workshop on Computational Phonology, Special Interest Group of the Association for Computational Linguistics*, pp. 11–18.

2007. Geographic distributions of linguistic variation reflect dynamics of differentiation. In Featherston, Sam, and Sternefeld, Wolfgang (eds), *Roots: Linguistics in Search of its Evidential Base*. Berlin, New York: Mouton de Gruyter, pp. 267–297.

Nerbonne, John, and Kleiweg, Peter. 2007. Toward a dialectological yardstick. *Journal of Quantitative Linguistics*, 14(2), 148–166.

Nerbonne, John, and Siedle, Christine. 2005. Dialektklassifikation auf der Grundlage aggregierter Aussspracheunterschiede. *Zeitschrift für Dialektologie und Linguistik*, 72(2), 129–147.

Nerbonne, John, Heeringa, Wilbert, van den Hout, Eric, van de Kooi, Peter, Otten, Simone, and van de Vis, Willem. 1996. Phonetic distance between Dutch dialects. In Durieux, Gert, Daelemans, Walter, and Gillis, Steven (eds.), *CLIN VI: Proc. of the Sixth CLIN Meeting*. Antwerp: Centre for Dutch Language and Speech (UIA), pp. 185–202.

Nerbonne, John, Heeringa, Wilbert, and Kleiweg, Peter. 1999. Edit distance and dialect proximity. In Sankoff, David, and Kruskal, Joseph (eds.), *Time Warps, String Edits and Macromolecules: The Theory and Practice of Sequence Comparison*. Stanford: CSLI Press, pp. x–xv.

Nerbonne, John, Kleiweg, Peter, and Manni, Franz. 2008. Projecting dialect differences to geography: bootstrapping clustering vs. clustering with noise. In Preisach, Christine, Schmidt-Thieme, Lars, Burkhardt, Hans, and Decker, Reinhold (eds.), *Data Analysis, Machine Learning, and Applications: Proceedings of the 31st Annual Meeting of the German Classification Society*. Berlin: Springer, pp. 647–654.

Niedzielski, Nancy A., and Preston, Dennis Richard. 1999. *Folk Linguistics*. Berlin, New York: Mouton de Gruyter.

Nishisato, Shizuhiko. 2007. *Multidimensional Nonlinear Descriptive Analysis*. Boca Raton: Chapman & Hall/CRC.

Nunnally, Jum C. 1978. *Psychometric Theory*. New York: McGraw-Hill.

OED. 2008. *Oxford English Dictionary*. Available online at http://dictionary. oed.com/. Oxford University Press.

Orton, Harold, and Dieth, Eugen. 1962. *Survey of English Dialects*. Leeds: E. J. Arnold.

Orton, Harold, and Wright, Nathalia. 1974. *A Word Geography of England*. London, New York: Seminar Press.

Orton, Harold, Sanderson, Stewart, and Widdowson, J. D. A. 1978. *The Linguistic Atlas of England*. London, Atlantic Highlands, NJ: Croom Helm.

Penhallurick, Robert. 1993. Welsh English: a national language? *Dialectologia et Geolinguistica*, **1993**(1), 28–46.

  2004a. Welsh English: morphology and syntax. In Kortmann, Bernd, Schneider, Edgar, Burridge, K., Mesthrie, R., and Upton, C. (eds.), *A Handbook of Varieties of English*, vol. II. Berlin, New York: Mouton de Gruyter, pp. 102–113.

  2004b. Welsh English: phonology. In Kortmann, Bernd, Schneider, Edgar, Burridge, K., Mesthrie, R., and Upton, C. (eds.), *A Handbook of Varieties of English*, vol. I. Berlin, New York: Mouton de Gruyter, pp. 98–112.

  2007. English in Wales. In Britain, David (ed.), *Language in the British Isles*. Cambridge University Press, pp. 152–175.

Penke, Martina, and Rosenbach, Anette. 2004. What counts as evidence in linguistics? An introduction. *Studies in Language*, **28**(3), 480–526.

Pietsch, Lukas. 2005. *Variable Grammars: Verbal Agreement in Northern Dialects of English*. Tübingen: Niemeyer.

Potter, Simeon. 1969. *Changing English*. 2nd rev. edn. London: André Deutsch.

Pound, Luise. 1901. *The Comparison of Adjectives in English in the XV and the XVI Century* (Anglistische Forschungen 7). Heidelberg: Carl Winter.

Preston, Dennis R. 1999. A language attitude approach to the perception of regional variety. In Preston, Dennis R. (ed.), *Handbook of Perceptual Dialectology*, vol. 1. Amsterdam, Philadelphia: Benjamins, pp. 359–373.

Pust, Lieselotte. 1998. "I cannae see it": negation in Scottish English and dialect data from the British National Corpus. *Arbeiten aus Anglistik und Amerikanistik*, **23**, 17–30.

Puttenham, George. 1589. *The arte of English poesie. Contrived into three books: the first of poets and poesie, the second of proportion, the third of ornament*. London: R. Field.

Quirk, Randolph. 1974. *The Linguist and the English Language*. London: Arnold.

R Development Core Team. 2010. *R: A Language and Environment for Statistical Computing* (R Foundation for Statistical Computing). Vienna, Austria. ISBN 3-900051-07-0.

Raab-Fischer, Roswitha. 1995. Löst der Genitiv die *of*-Phrase ab? Eine korpusgestützte Studie zum Sprachwandel im heutigen Englisch. *Zeitschrift für Anglistik und Amerikanistik*, **43**(2), 123–132.

Rand, William M. 1971. Objective criteria for the evaluation of clustering methods. *Journal of the American Statistical Association*, **66**, 846–850.

Rissanen, Matti. 1991. On the history of *that/zero* as object clause links in English. In Aijmer, Karin, and Altenberg, Bengt (eds.), *English Corpus Linguistics: Studies in Honour of Jan Svartvik*. London, New York: Longman, pp. 272–289.

Rosenbach, Anette. 2003. Aspects of iconicity and economy in the choice between the *s*-genitive and the *of*-genitive in English. In Rohdenburg, Günter, and

Mondorf, Britta (eds.), *Determinants Of Grammatical Variation in English*. Berlin, New York: Mouton de Gruyter, pp. 379–412.

Ross, John R. 1986. *Infinite Syntax*. Norwood, NJ: Ablex.

Sammon, John W. 1969. A non-linear mapping for data structure analysis. *IEEE Transactions on Computers*, C 18, 401–409.

Sanderson, Stewart, and Widdowson, J. D. A. 1985. Linguistic geography in England: progress and prospects. In Kirk, John M., Sanderson, Stewart, and Widdowson, J. D. A. (eds.), *Studies in Linguistic Geography: The Dialects of English in Britain and Ireland*. London: Croom Helm, pp. 34–50.

Sapir, Edward. [1921] 2004. *Language: An Introduction to the Study of Speech*. Mineola, New York: Dover.

Schleicher, August. 1863. *Die Darwinsche Theorie und die Sprachwissenschaft: Offenes Sendschreiben an Herrn Dr. Ernst Haeckel, o. Professor der Zoologie und Direktor des zoologischen Museums der Universität Jena*. Weimar: Böhlau.

Schmidt, Johannes. 1872. *Die Verwandtschaftsverhältnisse der indogermanischen Sprachen*. Weimar: Böhlau.

Schrambke, Renate. 2009. Language and space: traditional dialect geography. In Auer, Peter, and Schmidt, Jürgen Erich (eds.), *An International Handbook of Linguistic Variation*, vol. I: *Theories and Methods*. Berlin, New York: Mouton de Gruyter, pp. 87–107.

Schulz, Monika Edith. 2010. Morphosyntactic variation in British English dialects: evidence from possession, obligation and past habituality. PhD dissertation, University of Freiburg.

Séguy, Jean. 1971. La relation entre la distance spatiale et la distance lexicale. *Revue de Linguistique Romane*, 35, 335–357.

Shackleton, Robert G. Jr. 2005. English–American speech relationships: a quantitative approach. *Journal of English Linguistics*, 33(2), 99–160.

2007. Phonetic variation in the traditional English dialects: a computational analysis. *Journal of English Linguistics*, 35(1), 30–102.

2010. Quantitative assessment of English–American speech relationships. PhD dissertation, University of Groningen.

Shorrocks, Graham. 1991. A. J. Ellis as dialectologist: a reassessment. *Historiographia Linguistica*, 18, 321–334.

1992. Relative pronouns and relative clauses in the dialect of Farnworth and district (Greater Manchester County, formerly Lancashire). *Zeitschrift für Dialektologie und Linguistik*, 39, 334–43.

2001. The dialectology of English in the British Isles. In Auroux, Sylvain, Koerner, E. F. K., Niederehe, Hans-Josef, and Versteegh, Kees (eds.), *An International Handbook on the Evolution of the Study of Language from the Beginnings to the Present / Manuel international sur l'évolution de l'étude du langage des origines à nos jours / Ein internationales Handbuch zur Entwicklung der Sprachforschung von den Anfängen bis zur Gegenwart*. Berlin, New York: Walter de Gruyter, pp. 1553–1562.

Sokal, Robert R., and Rohlf, James F. 1962. The comparison of dendrograms by objective methods. *Taxon*, 11, 33–40.

Sokal, Robert R., and Sneath, P. H. A. 1963. *Principles of Numerical Taxonomy*. San Francisco: W. H. Freeman.

Speelman, Dirk, and Geeraerts, Dirk. 2008. The role of concept characteristics in lexical dialectometry. *International Journal of Humanities and Arts Computing*, 2(1/2), 221–242.

Spruit, Marco René. 2005. Classifying Dutch dialects using a syntactic measure: the perceptual Daan and Blok dialect map revisited. *Linguistics in the Netherlands*, 22(1), 179–190.

    2006. Measuring syntactic variation in Dutch dialects. *Literary and Linguistic Computing*, 21(4), 493–506.

Spruit, Marco René, Heeringa, Wilbert, and Nerbonne, John. 2009. Associations among linguistic levels. *Lingua*, 119(11), 1624–1642.

Stenström, Anna-Brita, Andersen, Gisle, and Hasund, Ingrid Kristine. 2002. *Trends in Teenage Talk: Corpus Compilation, Analysis, and Findings*. Amsterdam, Philadelphia: Benjamins.

Stuart-Smith, Jane. 2004. Scottish English: phonology. In Kortmann, Bernd, Schneider, Edgar, Burridge, K., Mesthrie, R., and Upton, C. (eds.), *A Handbook of Varieties of English*, vol. I. Berlin, New York: Mouton de Gruyter, pp. 47–67.

Swan, Michael. 1980. *Practical English Usage*. Oxford University Press.

Szmrecsanyi, Benedikt. 2003. *Be going to* versus *will/shall*: does syntax matter? *Journal of English Linguistics*, 31(4), 295–323.

    2006. *Morphosyntactic Persistence in Spoken English: A Corpus Study at the Intersection of Variationist Sociolinguistics, Psycholinguistics, and Discourse Analysis*. Berlin, New York: Mouton de Gruyter.

    2008. Corpus-based dialectometry: aggregate morphosyntactic variability in British English dialects. *International Journal of Humanities and Arts Computing*, 2(1/2), 279–296.

    2009. Typological parameters of intralingual variability: grammatical analyticity versus syntheticity in varieties of English. *Language Variation and Change*, 21(3), 319–353.

    2010. *The morphosyntax of BrE dialects in a corpus-based dialectometrical perspective: feature extraction, coding protocols, projections to geography, summary statistics*. URN: urn:nbn:de:bsz:25-opus-73209, URL: www.freidok.uni-freiburg.de/volltexte/7320/. Freiburg: University of Freiburg.

    2011. Corpus-based dialectometry: a methodological sketch. *Corpora*, 6(1), 45–76.

    Forthcoming. Geography is overrated. In Hansen, Sandra, Schwarz, Christian, Stoeckle, Philipp, and Streck, Tobias (eds.), *Dialectological and Folk Dialectological Concepts of Space*. Berlin, New York: Walter de Gruyter.

Szmrecsanyi, Benedikt, and Hernández, Nuria. 2007. *Manual of Information to accompany the Freiburg Corpus of English Dialects Sampler ("FRED-S")*. URN: urn:nbn:de:bsz:25-opus-28598, URL: www.freidok.uni-freiburg.de/volltexte/2859/. Freiburg: University of Freiburg.

Szmrecsanyi, Benedikt, and Kortmann, Bernd. 2009. Between simplification and complexification: non-standard varieties of English around the world. In Sampson, Geoffrey, Gil, David, and Trudgill, Peter (eds.), *Language Complexity as an Evolving Variable*. Oxford University Press, pp. 64–79.

Szmrecsanyi, Benedikt, and Wolk, Christoph. 2011. Holistic corpus-based dialec-
    tology. *Brazilian Journal of Applied Linguistics/Revista Brasileira de Linguística
    Aplicada*, 11(2), 561–592.
Tagliamonte, Sali. 1998. *Was/were* variation across the generations: view from the
    city of York. *Language Variation and Change*, 10(2), 153–191.
    2000. The grammaticalization of the present perfect in English: tracks of change
    and continuity in a linguistic enclave. In Fischer, Olga, Rosenbach, Anette,
    and Stein, Dieter (eds.), *Pathways of Change: Grammaticalization in English*.
    Amsterdam, Philadelphia: Benjamins, pp. 329–354.
    2001. *Come/came* variation in English dialects. *American Speech*, 76(1), 42–61.
    2003. "Every place has a different toll": determinants of grammatical variation in a
    cross-variety perspective. In Rohdenburg, Günter, and Mondorf, Britta (eds.),
    *Determinants of Grammatical Variation in English*. Berlin, New York: Mouton
    de Gruyter, pp. 531–554.
    2004. *Have to, gotta, must*: grammaticalisation, variation and specialization in
    English deontic modality. In Mair, Christian, and Lindquist, Hans (eds.),
    *Corpus Approaches to Grammaticalization in English*. Amsterdam, Philadelphia:
    Benjamins, pp. 33–55.
    2009. "There was universals; then there weren't": a comparative sociolinguis-
    tic perspective on "default singulars." In Filppula, Markku, Klemola, Juhani,
    and Paulasto, Heli (eds.), *Vernacular Universals and Language Contacts: Evi-
    dence from Varieties of English and Beyond*. London, New York: Routledge,
    pp. 103–129.
Tagliamonte, Sali, and Lawrence, Helen. 2000. "I used to dance, but I don't dance
    now": the habitual past in English. *Journal of English Linguistics*, 28, 324–353.
Tagliamonte, Sali, and Smith, Jennifer. 2002. "Either it isn't or it's not": NEG/AUX
    contraction in British dialects. *English World Wide*, 23(2), 251–281.
    2005. "No momentary fancy!" The zero "complementizer" in English dialects.
    *English Language and Linguistics*, 9(2), 289–309.
Tagliamonte, Sali, Smith, Jennifer, and Lawrence, Helen. 2005. "No taming the ver-
    nacular!": insights from the relatives in northern Britain. *Language Variation
    and Change*, 17, 75–112.
Thomason, Sarah Grey. 2001. *Language Contact: An Introduction*. Washington, DC:
    Georgetown University Press.
Thomason, Sarah Grey, and Kaufman, Terrence. 1988. *Language Contact, Creoliza-
    tion, and Genetic Linguistics*. Berkeley: University of California Press.
Tieken-Boon van Ostade, Ingrid, Tottie, Gunnel, and van der Wurff, Wim. 1999.
    Introduction. In Tieken-Boon van Ostade, Ingrid, Tottie, Gunnel, and van der
    Wurff, Wim (eds.), *Negation in the History of English*. Berlin, New York:
    Mouton de Gruyter, pp. 1–7.
Torgerson, Warren S. 1958. *Theory and Methods of Scaling*. New York: Wiley.
Tottie, Gunnel. 2002. Non-categorical differences between American and British
    English: some corpus evidence. In Modiano, Marko (ed.), *Studies in Mid-
    Atlantic English*. Gävle: University of Gävle Press, pp. 37–58.
Trudgill, Peter. 1974. Linguistic change and diffusion: description and explanation
    in sociolinguistic dialect geography. *Language in Society*, 3(2), 215–246.
    1978. *Sociolinguistic Patterns in British English*. London: Arnold.
    1990. *The Dialects of England*. Cambridge, Mass.: Blackwell.

1999. Standard English: what it isn't. In Bex, Tony, and Watts, Richard J. (eds.), *Standard English: The widening debate*. London: Routledge.

2001. Contact and simplification: historical baggage and directionality in linguistic change. *Linguistic Typology*, 5(2/3), 371–374.

2004a. *Dialects*. Language workbooks. London, New York: Routledge.

2004b. The impact of language contact and social structure on linguistic structure: Focus on the dialects of Modern Greek. In Kortmann, Bernd (ed.), *Dialectology Meets Typology: Dialect Grammar from a Cross-Linguistic Perspective*. Berlin, New York: Mouton de Gruyter, pp. 434–451.

2008. English Dialect "default singulars", *was* vs. *were*, Verner's Law, and Germanic dialects. *Journal of English Linguistics*, 36(4), 341–353.

Viereck, Wolfgang. 1985. Linguistic atlases and dialectometry: the survey of English dialects. In Kirk, John M., Sanderson, Stewart, and Widdowson, J. D. A. (eds.), *Studies in linguistic geography: The dialects of English in Britain and Ireland*. London: Croom Helm, pp. 94–112.

1986a. Dialectal speech areas in England: Orton's lexical evidence. In Kastovsky, Dieter, and Szwedek, Aleksander (eds.), *Linguistics across Historical and Geographical Boundaries*. Berlin, New York: Mouton de Gruyter, pp. 725–740.

1986b. Dialectal speech areas in England: Orton's phonetic and grammatical evidence. *Journal of English Linguistics*, 19, 240–257.

1988. The data of the 'Survey of English Dialects' computerized: problems and applications. In Kytö, Merja, Ihalainen, Ossi, and Rissanen, Matti (eds.), *Corpus Linguistics, Hard and Soft*. Amsterdam: Rodopi, pp. 267–278.

1997. The areal analysis of dialectal features: the gravity centre method as applied to SED morphosyntactic data. *Studia Anglica Posnaniensia: An International Review of English Studies*, 31, 305–316.

Viereck, Wolfgang, Ramisch, Heinrich, Händler, Harald, Hoffmann, Petra, and Putschke, Wolfgang. 1991. *The Computer Developed Linguistic Atlas of England*. Tübingen: Niemeyer.

Voronoi, Georgy. 1907. Nouvelles applications des paramètres continus à la théorie des formes quadratiques. *Journal für die Reine und Angewandte Mathematik*, 133, 97–178.

Wagner, Susanne. 2004. "Gendered" pronouns in English dialects: a typological perspective. In Kortmann, Bernd (ed.), *Dialectology Meets Typology: Dialect Grammar from a Cross-Linguistic Perspective*. Berlin, New York: Mouton de Gruyter, pp. 479–496.

Wakelin, Martyn Francis. 1972. *English Dialects: An Introduction*. London: Athlone Press.

Wälchli, Bernhard. 2009. Data reduction typology and the bimodal distribution bias. *Linguistic Typology*, 13(1), 77–94.

Wales, Katie. 2006. *Northern English: A Cultural and Social History*. Cambridge University Press.

Ward, Joe H. Jr. 1963. Hierarchical grouping to optimize an objective function. *Journal of the American Statistical Association*, 58, 236–244.

Warner, Anthony. 1982. *Complementation in Middle English and the Methodology of Historical Syntax: A Study of the Wyclifite Sermons*. London: Croom Helm.

Wenker, Georg. 1886. Über das Sprachatlasunternehmen. In *Verhandlungen der 38. Versammlung deutscher Philologen und Schulmänner in Gießen vom 30. September bis 3. Oktober 1885.* Leipzig: Teubner, pp. 187–194.

Wieling, Martijn, Heeringa, Wilbert, and Nerbonne, John. 2007. An aggregate analysis of pronunciation in the Goeman-Taeldeman-van Reenen-Project data. *Taal en Tongval*, **59**(1), 84–116.

Winford, Donald. 2003. *An Introduction to Contact Linguistics.* Malden, Mass.: Blackwell.

Wolfram, Walt. 1976. Towards a description of *a*-prefixing in Appalachian English. *American Speech*, **51**(1/2), 45–56.

Wolfram, Walt, and Schilling-Estes, Natalie. 1998. *American English: Dialects and Variation.* Malden, Mass.: Blackwell.

# Index